Mary Austin's Southwest

MARY AUSTIN'S SOUTHWEST

An Anthology of Her Literary Criticism

EDITED BY

Chelsea Blackbird and Barney Nelson

THE UNIVERSITY
OF UTAH PRESS
Salt Lake City

09 08 07 06 05   5 4 3 2 1

 The Defiance House Man colophon is a registered trademark
of the University of Utah Press. It is based upon a four-foot-tall,
Ancient Puebloan pictograph (late PIII) near Glen Canyon, Utah.

Library of Congress Cataloging-in-Publication Data

Austin, Mary Hunter, 1868-1934.
  Mary Austin's Southwest : an anthology of her literary criticism /
edited by Chelsea Blackbird and Barney Nelson.
      p. cm.
  Includes bibliographical references and index.
  ISBN 0-87480-820-0 (pbk. : alk. paper)
 1. American literature—Southwestern States—History and criticism.
2. Southwestern States—Intellectual life. 3. Southwestern States—
In literature. I. Blackbird, Chelsea, 1974- II. Nelson, Barney, 1947-
III. Title.
  PS277.A98 2005
  810.9'979—dc22   2004026694

Interior printed on recycled paper with 50% post-consumer waste.

For Brian and Roy

Contents

Acknowledgments

Any book is always an accumulation of favors, other people's expertise, and tremendous amounts of support. We are indebted to the Sul Ross State University Research Enhancement Program for two grants that gave us the financial support to begin and then finish this project. Members of The Association for the Study of Literature and Environment and the Western Literature Association, especially Dr. Cheryll Glotfelty, provided much-needed inspiration and support.

We wish to thank The Archives of the Big Bend, librarians at the Bryan Wildenthal Memorial Library, and Johnny Cisneros in the Media Center at Sul Ross State University for their patience, expertise, and assistance. Amazingly, our small university has acquired an extensive holding of Mary Austin materials. We also thank Sue Hodson, Mary Austin curator at the Huntington Library in San Marino, California, Donald Burge at the Center for Southwest Research at the University of New Mexico in Albuquerque, and employees of the Fray Angélico Chávez History Library at the Palace of the Governors in Santa Fe. Graduate students in Barney Nelson's course on Southwestern literature and the late Dr. Abelardo Baeza also assisted with research. During the search for permissions and copyright holders, we became indebted to hundreds of people. For help with Spanish translations and corrections, we appreciate Dr. Jésus Tafoya. Donna Green, Tiffany Fowlkes, and Kathy Chirinos assisted with clerical work.

Finally, we wish to thank our families. We thank Chelsea's husband, Brian, parents, Denny and Trish Thomlinson, parents-in-law, Roy and Barbara Blackbird, and friends Christi Dalecky and Allison Witt for their love and support. We thank Barney's daughter and son-in-law, Carla and Chris Spencer, and grandchildren, Riley and Jorey, for their patience in doing without many grandma duties. We thank Barney's brother, Richard E. DeGear, and her friend J. J. Tucker for much-needed distractions and support. We thank our friend Tara Edwards and our adopted "family," the employees (especially Kat, Shera, Elaine, Melissa) of the Reata Restaurant in Alpine, where we spent many agonizing evenings poring over manuscripts and wine.

PART I

The Chisera's Fire:
General Introduction

Valuing perspectives and expressions from our nation's mixed heritage seems an obvious fundamental function of art in a democracy. Although writers with diverse backgrounds have always been free to produce literature reflecting this mix of cultures, ethnicities, and religions, an appreciative audience for such literature has not always existed. Today, however, multicultural writers enjoy a growing circle of readers, and many deserve recognition for nurturing this progress. Mary Austin (1868–1934), in particular, should be regarded as a significant trailblazer for literary diversity. However, many of her groundbreaking ideas on place-based influences, narrative techniques, and dramatic development have been overshadowed by the controversies surrounding her life or hidden by reactions to her often abrasive and egocentric personality.

As a young woman Austin homesteaded, along with her mother and brother after the death of her father and sister, on the east side of the California Sierra when that country was first being settled by Anglos. Austin's life was a series of personal disappointments. Often in poor health, she was first a frustrated and sometimes homeless wife, then mother of a retarded child, and then divorced—years before any of these situations were understood or accepted by society. She was also a rebel who cultivated friendships with Indians, Hispanics, and Basques, not because she thought of herself as a "good" person or condescendingly wanted to "help" them—but because she genuinely thought they created fresh and important art, knew more, and led more interesting lives than the Anglo ladies she was supposed to associate with. Picking and choosing among Indian religious customs and often adopting them as her own, she sometimes got into serious trouble with her Christian neighbors for teaching Indian songs and ceremonies to children.

Although active in respected writers' groups in Carmel, Greenwich Village, and Santa Fe, she was far from perfect. The modern reader must squeeze past her often pompous and self-aggrandizing language, past the times when she elevates her own opinion to gospel, and past the times when she herself attempts to impress the academics or New York critics whom she often denigrated. Sometimes she contradicts herself. Sometimes she's overly defensive. Sometimes she's simply wrong or blinded by various cultural and racial prejudices she thought she had overcome. She was also accused of grandstanding, and some of these accusations are quite true. She often did her writing in a tree house or Indian wickiup and dressed in long, flowing Grecian gowns, in lace shawls and large Spanish-style hair combs, or in buckskins and beads as an Indian princess. Some critics called her an "Indian wanna-be"[1]; others said she was "embarrassing" or "ridiculous."[2] Calling herself a prophet, she was perhaps a little too mystical and a little too brave about interpreting subjects of which she had only superficial knowledge. Sometimes a romanticized "Noble Savage" view of native people marred her vision.[3] Both her critics and her admirers were often "fairly unevenly divided as to whether in truth she was to be reckoned as a self-deluded crank or an authentic genius."[4] She liked to be called a sibyl or a *chisera* (medicine woman), while her critics called her "God's mother-in-law."[5]

According to the editors of *Twentieth-Century Literary Criticism*, "Critics often discuss Austin's work in an autobiographical context that accentuates the correspondence between her life and her writings. In particular, critics emphasize her personal development, the unhappy circumstances of her life, her views on various social issues, and her spiritual precepts."[6] Even feminist critics have often concentrated their efforts on analyzing or defending Austin's personality and lifestyle rather than illuminating her work. As Don D. Walker has pointed out, "Western literary criticism has for a long time been dominated by the historian's way of judgment."[7] We think this focus has done Austin a sad disservice and have therefore tried to concentrate on her contributions to Southwestern literary criticism rather than review her interesting history once again. For those readers unfamiliar with her life, we refer them to Austin's autobiography *Earth Horizon* (1932) and three fine biographies: *I-Mary: A Biography of Mary Austin* (1983) by Augusta

Fink, *Mary Austin: Song of a Maverick* (1989) by Esther F. Lanigan, and *Wind's Trail: The Early Life of Mary Austin* (1990) by Peggy Pond Church.

Critics have also done an excellent job of contextualizing Austin into the political and literary history of her day. Some of the best contemporary scholarship in this category can be found in the introductions, forewords, and afterwords of recent reissues of her work, as well as in two book-length scholarly investigations: *Dancing Ghosts: Native American and Christian Syncretism in Mary Austin's Work* by Mark T. Hoyer (1998) and *The Wild and the Domestic: Animal Representation, Ecocriticism, and Western American Literature* by Barney Nelson (2000). In addition, Melody Graulich's and Elizabeth Klimasmith's recent collection of Austin scholarship, *Exploring Lost Borders: Critical Essays on Mary Austin* (1999), places Austin's work in numerous modern contexts: ecocriticism, feminist criticism, Native American studies, consumer studies, postcolonial studies, working-class studies, composition studies, literary autobiographical criticism, and new historicism. Their collection exemplifies Austin's controversial complexity and continuous relevancy. Graulich's excellent introduction explains the difficulty of positioning Austin's work within the "matrix" of cultural and political movements of either her own day or today. As Graulich explains, Austin "resists categorization" and modern readers are still discovering "how to read her."[8]

When Austin began writing in the late 1890s, Americans considered Europe the literary center of the universe. American scholars usually measured American writers by their resemblance to British writers, and European standards typically dictated critical review and trends. American writers, audiences, and critics accepted the British as their literary superiors and models because, as a relatively young country, America lacked the confidence to develop a literary personality of its own. Austin ranted about this "colonial dependency," defended all types of non-canonical works, and constantly berated New York critics for their European, especially British, and urban biases, which caused them to ignore the indigenous roots and multi-ethnic heritage of American literature. Contemporary Indian poet Joy Harjo echoes Austin's views when she says, "The literature of the aboriginal people of North America defines America. It is not exotic."[9]

Eight years before Virginia Woolf's famous essays "A Room of One's Own" (1928) and "Women and Fiction" (1929) were published, Austin had already complained that women had been silenced by the European and East Coast literary critics, whom she considered to be a "wall of men, a filtered, almost sound-proof wall of male intelligence, male reporters, critics, managers, advertisers...men editors, men publishers, men reviewers."[10] Yet even our best feminist historians, like Annette Kolodny, cite Woolf as the "first" to champion women writers because she "grappled most obviously with the ways in which male writers and male subject matter had already preempted the language of literature."[11] Austin would probably simply have pointed out that Woolf was English. If Austin, unlike Woolf, ever felt intimidated by these male critics, her scathing published comments don't sound like it: "One suspects that the New Yorker is only admitted to the making of an exhibitional ass of himself by having his essay published in a London journal because it flatters the English concept of our being still a colonial dependency."[12] This statement appeared in print sixty years before postcolonialism became a field of literary study.

Although Woolf is considered the "first" modern writer to champion the power of the female pen, from one to thirteen years earlier Austin had already published essays with such titles as "The Protected Sex" (1915), "How I Learned to Read and Write" (1921), "American Women and the Intellectual Life" (1921), "Woman as Audience" (1922), "Sex in American Literature" (1923), "Greatness in Women" (1923), "Making the Most of Your Genius I, II, & III" (1923–24), "The Need for a New Social Concept" (1924), "Woman Looks at the World" (1924), "The Sense of Humor in Women" (1924), and "Woman Alone" (1927). Woolf also suggested that women should write something other than novels, but by the time her words appeared, Austin had already published over thirty books and over 250 articles that spanned such genres as novel, short story, essay, poetry, drama, literary criticism, history, autobiography, ethnography, nature writing, and intellectual prose. Typically, Austin's groundbreaking ideas were overshadowed by a European writer.

Austin is difficult to categorize. Unlike other women writers of her day, including Gertrude Atherton, Willa Cather,[13] Edith Wharton, and Kate Chopin, Austin was "preoccupied with matters of class, race, and gender."[14] Many modern critics consider Austin to have been an active feminist,[15] even though in her own autobiography, *Earth Horizon*, she says "talking on Suffrage bored me."[16] Her biographers have also noted that although she never remarried, Austin "preferred the society of men and depended on men for her deepest companionship,"[17] and that she "preferred to identify intellectually with men."[18] We have found that throughout her life she felt men had been as unfairly stereotyped as women—especially rural western men like pocket hunters, sheepherders, hermits, and members of the non-white races, and so she defended both sexes.

Admiring Regional Culture

Fundamental to understanding Austin's seemingly contradictory personality and philosophies is recognizing her belief that the environment held a stronger influence over people and cultures than any other force. She believed environment would eventually mold genders, races, classes, and religions into a new regional culture. She also believed place-based mixes of cultures could be a model for American nationalism and therefore logically for American literature, saying, "If Nationality means anything—and in our case it couldn't mean race—it must mean the unconscious response of a people to their natural environment."[19] Why wouldn't we then, she argues, look to regional influences as a foundation for our culture and arts?

In the Southwest, she found that three groups of people—Indian, Spanish, and Anglo—had lived in the place long enough for it to have shaped them, and that "it has in no case failed to do so."[20] She believed the Southwest had blended languages, races, and religions, creating unique versions of Catholicism, nature worship, ceremonies, and visions, and that this blending caused a form of hybrid vigor that would eventually develop into the world's next great culture.[21] Lois Rudnick, however, says Austin's prediction was "wrong." Although Rudnick calls it a "healthy idea," she says Austin failed to understand that what she "hoped to teach the Anglo world was too rooted in Native American and Hispanic cultures to be 'borrowed' by an increasingly urban, industrial civilization that showed little of the ethos of either group." Rudnick also argues that Austin failed to understand the patronizing attitude she inspired since it was usually the Anglos who determined "what was 'authentic' and 'traditional,'"[22] contributing to what Melody Graulich calls "cultural manifest destiny."[23]

Instead of people imposing their customs on a new land, Austin believed the land itself contained a quiet power that would eventually dictate the way people must live and work. Living in the arid Southwest gave Austin a deep appreciation for connecting and responding to the desert terrain. She believed that every detail of the culture—from how to distribute water to how to celebrate religion—sprang directly from the environment. This land-based lifestyle is what Austin considered inspirational to literature and found worthy of study. Vera Norwood explains that Austin's "vision has little to do with the European tradition of aggression against the land and its people, but depends heavily on the opposite view of wilderness as home."[24] Admiring people rooted in places they had occupied for thousands of years, Austin did not pity Indian people nor sympathize with them, and she did not think of the pueblo tribes as defeated or displaced. Treaties between the pueblos and Spain, and later the United States, were never, she emphasizes, treaties of peace between conquered and conquerors. The pueblos, Austin says, "had always been small independent nations."[25] Maybe the Southwest should not even be considered a former European colony. The Spanish settled it only sparsely beginning in the seventeenth century, and the English-speaking settlers did not arrive until almost time for statehood. Parts of California and northern New Mexico may have been governed by Spain long enough to be called colonies, but most of the Southwest remained ungoverned, and some might say it still is.

Although we would argue that Austin never considered either California or New Mexico "wilderness," she greatly admired the cultures that those arid lands had inspired and thought that their mix of independence, democracy, and a type of socialism, which seemed to be based on irrigation, might be worth emulating.[26] In a speech before the National Popular Government League, defending the pueblo tribes' irrigation rights, Austin says,

> When the Spanish Explorers penetrated what is now the Southwestern part of the United States, they found the inhabitants living in towns of terraced houses, with an orderly, republican form of government, and a well-developed aesthetic culture.

They cultivated the ground, practiced irrigation by methods we have scarcely improved upon, and maintained a trade in cotton, turquoises, woven cloth and salt, which they exchanged with the Plains tribes for dried buffalo meat and skins. Not only did they function successfully in all departments of civilized living, but in some respects such as in their devices for distributing the benefits of their culture to all their citizens and for securing justice and equity, they surpassed the Spaniards themselves, as the Conquistadors were not unwilling to admit.[27]

She also admired Indian systems of land allocation and management, marriage and divorce, raising and educating children, international relations, and determination of justice. She admired their "potlatch" tradition of giving away wealth but knew that in order to give it away one must acquire it. Perhaps she explains her attitude toward economics best in a review of James Barrie's fiction. Discussing his references to poverty, she explains that there is

> ...not one note of bitterness about it. It struck me keenly just now, when all the fiction written by young men in America is full of resentment of not having had as much as everybody else.... Nearly all the people Barrie writes about are poor, but I do not recall a single one who was disagreeable about it.[28]

She also writes in notes for a planned book on the Spanish Colonial arts, which was never completed, that

> There is in Spanish New Mexican Art a tender and gay devoutness such as we attach to the idea of Saint Francis preaching to the birds...a feeling for poverty not as Holy, but certainly not as sordid or discreditable—a capacity for doing without things for living in certain inner realities, the life of the imagination.[29]

Although perhaps romanticizing poverty to some degree, she seems to get at the sense of pride and dignity often observed among Southwestern people for being able "without the possession of things to make the gesture of riches—with a humble life to make the gesture of nobility."[30] Based on these Southwestern models, she did not believe that poverty was necessarily bad and affluence good, nor that equal distribution of wealth was always good, but simply observed with wry humor that the average U.S. citizen seemed to think the rest of the world wants and needs our economic system.[31]

Trying to understand the Southwestern cultures at a deep personal level, Austin recognized not only her own gender's identification with the *Acequia Madre*, or Mother Ditch, but its symbolic importance to the young men of the pueblo who congregated during a full moon to sing to it for luck in love.[32] In 1903 she said, "Every Indian woman is an artist,"[33] at a time when such household items as baskets, pottery, and weavings were simply practical and made from readily available materials. Her interests also went beyond those of a collector. When she wrote about Indian baskets, she prefaced and deepened her observations by talking with Indian basket makers, gathering willows with them, learning when and how to split the fibers and keep them pliable, and contemplating how to plan and execute designs with significant meaning.

Eventually her interests expanded to include textiles, metals, architecture, and food. She and Santa Fe artist Frank Applegate founded the Society for the Revival of Spanish Colonial Arts about 1923. As they collected artifacts, photographs, and furniture and architecture designs, their efforts not only preserved the Sanctuario at Chimayo, the altar and *reredos* from the old church at Llano near Taos, and countless artifacts, but also encouraged and helped support the often aging and poverty-stricken artists themselves.[34] The Art League of New Mexico and the New Mexico Folklore Society were founded about a year apart. In 1931 the two organizations co-sponsored their first exhibit on the Spanish Colonial Arts, and Austin was the featured speaker for the event.

As an organizer of the Indian Arts Fund, Austin preserved and encouraged pueblo artists and art, as well as the Old Santa Fe Association, guiding the growth and development of the city in as genuine a way as possible. Lanigan describes Austin's aversion to the Chautauqua movement, which "sought to present stimulating public speakers who would hold forth on matters of general interest and religious uplift." Although Austin attended some Chautauqua events with her family as a young girl in Illinois, Lanigan explains that in Santa Fe she "spearheaded a movement to prevent a women's organization from establishing a summer Chautauqua, which she believed would jeopardize the environment of the elite artists' colony there."[35] In "The Town that Doesn't Want a Chautauqua,"[36] Austin explains her objections to using artists as puppets for chambers of commerce. She never wavered in her strong belief that real cultures springing from the land would prove to be of more value to both local communities and tourists than anything created solely for tourism. Much of today's genuine cultural preservation in Santa Fe and northern New Mexico is directly related to the influence and efforts of Austin and her friends. Although Vera Norwood argues that "Austin could not foresee the days when the neon representation of the thunderbird would light up the skies more dramatically than its natural occurrence,"[37] Austin often worried that perhaps she had been too successful. Just before her death, in a letter to a friend, she said, "It begins to look as though having spent the last twenty-five years largely explaining the Indian to the American public, I am going to have to spend another twenty-five in defending him from the too great enthusiasm which the public has now conceived for him."[38]

In 1933 Austin received an Honorary Doctor of Letters degree from the University of New Mexico for her "extraordinary mind" and as "an authority on the Southwest."[39] In addition, she served on countless committees that spanned such diverse topics as political relations with Latin America, school curriculum change, or equitable division of the Colorado River's irrigation waters between California, Arizona, and Mexico. Her friends included both U.S. presidents and residents of the Indian pueblos, like Mabel and Tony Luhan.[40] Both figuratively and literally, she has become a part of the Southwest. Her ashes are entombed among granite boulders on Picacho Peak on the edge of the Sangre de Cristo Mountains.

Although there were many facets of early Southwest culture with which Austin was fascinated, perhaps her most significant contribution was the uncovering and revelation of its literary history. Austin seemed to recognize the worth of the Southwest's literary roots before those roots became fashionable, and she insisted that long-time inhabitants of the Southwest were artists, storytellers, poets, and dramatists almost instinctively. She was one of the first to connect the music and poetry in the Spanish language to the Southwest landscape. She collected and analyzed over one thousand old manuscripts of Spanish horseback dramas, romances, *corridos, cantos, décimas, leyendas, coplas*, proverbs, serial legends, riddles, and nursery rhymes, often translating them. Rather than as a "melting pot" designed to "improve" various ethnicities by granting them United States citizenship, Austin imagined the Southwest as more of a "salsa pot" that raised the heat and the creative impulses of the inhabitants. However, like Austin's critics who have concentrated on her life instead of her work, we believe that many Southwestern literary critics have been sidetracked by the politics between the races rather than illuminating the rich literature that these conflicts and compromises have produced.

Illuminating Regional Writing

Most critics agree that Austin produced her best work in the Southwest. Several of her essay collections highlight Southwestern occupations and the environment: *The Land of Little Rain* (1903), *The Flock* (1906), *Lost Borders* (1909), *California: the Land of the Sun* (1914), and *The Land of Journeys' Ending* (1924). Three collections of short stories focused on Southwestern subjects: *The Basket Woman: A Book of Fanciful Tales for Children* (1904), *One Smoke Stories* (1934), and *The Mother of Felipe and Other Early Stories* (1950). In *The American Rhythm* (1923), she explained her ideas on Indian poetry. In addition, her novels like *Isidro* (1905), *The Ford* (1917), and *Starry Adventure* (1931); novellas like *Cactus Thorn* (1988); plays like *Fire* (1912) and *The Arrow-Maker* (1915), and a book of poetry for children, *The Children Sing in the Far West* (1928), all have Southwestern settings and themes. In 1930 she wrote the text for a limited-edition book, *Taos Pueblo*, which featured the black-and-white photographs of an unknown but promising young photographer named Ansel Adams. Her influence on both his thinking and career was extraordinary.[41]

We also argue that Austin produced her best literary criticism in the Southwest. In 1932, she wrote an influential essay, entitled "Regionalism in American Fiction," in which she explains the power of place on writing.[42] B. A. Botkin, reviewing a scholarly star-studded "New Mexico Round Table on Regionalism" in 1933, says the words of Mary Austin "were echoed in one form or another by almost every speaker on the program."[43] Although the concept of regionalism had been bouncing around in literary circles for several years, and authors like Austin, Jewett, Harriet Beecher Stowe, Rose Terry Cooke, and Mary Wilkins Freeman had been labeled "regional writers,"[44] most critics considered regional writing substandard, and Austin sometimes agreed. Many authors who wrote about regions where they did not live, had never lived, or did not live deeply, often failed to capture the essence of either the people or the place. Austin uses the example of Eastern authors writing Westerns: "The trouble with too many Western books is that they are written by Easterners, and if not that, they are written for Easterners, which is a great deal worse."[45] She found that more often than not, the result was usually a story told through a romanticized lens and was not at all representative of either people or place.

Attempting to set guidelines for what regional literature should look like, Austin insisted that a work should be *of* the region, not just *about* it. She made careful distinctions between "local color" and good regional work,[46] distinguishing between exotic trappings and deep roots: "It is a nice point to determine just when a feathered stick, a headdress, or a girdle is properly an item of poetic realization, and when it is to be relegated to the department of stage setting."[47] Austin explains that "the unassailable hall mark of regionalism in literature" is that the story "could not have happened anywhere else."[48] She says, "the region must enter constructively into the story, as another character, as the instigator of plot."[49] If a writer writes in such a way that the story reads the same way with or without the regional aspects, then regional influence has not been achieved. She divided regional influence into four major causatives: land, work, food, and shelter. Responses to these controlling life influences made culture. She was interested in how landscape and environment had shaped not only indigenous and vernacular occupations, methods of preserving and cooking local foods, and environment-based architecture, but also literature. "In the long run," she says with conviction, "the land wins."[50]

Regional writing is sometimes considered closer to folklore than literature. Although Austin was active in the development of American "folklore," she did not consider oral storytelling a substandard form of literature but rather a foundation for regional writing. As Paula Gunn Allen explains,

> Western scholars have labeled the whole body of these litera-
> tures folklore.... But the great mythic and ceremonial cycles
> of the American Indian peoples are neither primitive, in any
> meaningful sense of the word, nor necessarily the province of
> the folk; much of the literature, in fact, is known only to the
> educated, specialized persons who are privy to the philosophi-
> cal, mystical, and literary wealth of the tribe.[51]

However, not all critics agree with this view. In his introduction to
American Indian Literature: An Anthology, Alan R. Velie says, "One
characteristic of traditional Indian literature that sets it apart from mainstream American literature—including that written by Indians—is that
it was an organic part of everyday life, not something to be enjoyed by
an intellectual elite."[52] We think Austin would try to argue that in a
democracy, there should be no ethnocentric elitism, and yet she would
agree with Allen that within a region, only certain individuals would
take the art of storytelling to its highest form.

As literary theorist Edward Said has pointed out, the aesthetics and
prejudices taught in our universities place pressure on authors from
"other" cultures to adopt the favored and taught style in order to be
valued.[53] Modern university-educated Indian scholars explain struggles
with these prejudices. For instance, reviewing the difficulties of collecting Indian women's writings, Gloria Bird, in the introduction to
*Reinventing the Enemy's Language: Contemporary Native Women's
Writings of North America,* says,

> In reading the manuscript submissions, I had to learn to read
> differently, or to unlearn the critical aspect of reading that I
> have been taught in creative-writing workshops and in univer-
> sity literary courses. Basically, I had to confront my own inter-
> nalized views on what constituted literature and recognize the
> learned preference of written over oral literatures in academia.
> I had to acknowledge the oral nature of the submissions and
> value the literal testimony of the women's voices that came
> through their writing.[54]

Bird acknowledges the contributions of educated Indian writers, but
warns that other Indian voices are often rejected when "we judge their

worth through conventional Euro-American standards of what constitutes good literature." Moreover, she adds that

> As women writers, we should note how native women's "voice" has been shaped by the people who have control over the narrative production, and have functioned as editors. Often, the voice of tribal, land-based women writers with ties to community, history, and language has been marginalized and silenced by those who control what is published. Native writers have not been well served by this process.[55]

Bird's ideas seem to echo both Austin's and Said's and help explain the complicated issues involved when trying to classify or rank regional and multicultural literatures.

Although Austin herself sometimes called indigenous literature "primitive," her definition would be more along the lines of classic or minimalist or subtle rather than undeveloped or substandard. She did not think of "primitive" Southwestern people as childlike but as ancient and wise. She compared their literature to classic work like opera and ballet, epic Greek poetry, Japanese Nō drama and haiku. She explains,

> There are other things to be learned here: questions about the beginning of art and literature which European scholars are spending their lives and thousands of dollars annually to discover by combing over the remains of Greek and other ancient Mediterranean cultures, delving in ruins, deciphering inscriptions, piecing together the rotten fragments of old manuscripts. But here in the Pueblos lie the answers to any one of a dozen mysteries European scholars I know would cheerfully give an eye to learn, questions about the origins of rhythm, of poetic accent, of the development of the epic and drama.... I have time only to suggest the cultural and artistic values of the Pueblos. There is a whole new school of American design springing up, based on their textiles and pottery. There is a whole new note in our national music.... We are absorbing these things into our national life because they are expressions of the influence of the American environment on people who have lived longest with it and loved it deeply. Every nation of Europe that has produced a great, distinctive national art, has

done so by absorbing its own aboriginal aesthetic life, precisely
as our own writers and musicians and artists hope to do if we
do not deprive them utterly of the opportunity.... This is the
one great contribution which America can make to world
scholarship which no other nation in the world can ever
touch.⁵⁶

Austin was most interested in authentic genres that had been created
by people who had lived deeply in the Southwest long enough to have
been influenced by it.

However, "authenticity" is contested ground in today's poststructural dialogue. Nathaniel Lewis, in *Unsettling the Literary West: Authenticity and Authorship*, explains that "Authenticity is a code that establishes boundaries that can be mapped and patrolled: this is inside, that
is outside; this is authentic, that is inauthentic." He finds this code
unsupportable, and is instead

interested, first, in how the insider claim of nativeness creates an
outsider status in non-native scholarship and writing, a perspective that reinforces Indian authenticity; and second, how even
within Native American literary circles there exists fierce contests over authenticity, contests that frequently call into question the role of postmodern theory and representation.

He also points out that today's "most gifted" Native American writers,
some of them mixed-blood, have "for two generations ranged widely
through the white academies, from Dartmouth and Cambridge to
Stanford and Seattle; they are not what our ancestors knew as tribal
people." He says questions of authenticity arise even between these
Indian writers and center on "questions of identity (who's an Indian?),
experience (on or off the reservation?), education (tribal or Euroamer-
ican?), and representation (accurate or misleading?)." Because this is a
"touchy subject," Lewis supports claims to "authorial responsibility"
rather than "authenticity."⁵⁷ However, binary thinking (insider/out-
sider, separatism) has never been considered "authentic" pueblo philosophy, as Leslie Marmon Silko has pointed out. Contemporary Chi-
cana critic Tey Diana Rebolledo presents still another perspective,
listing "blending or blurring of various literary forms," empowering
female storytellers, and using a "collective voice" as "narrative strate-

gies of resistance." She explains that the personal "I" binds together various perspectives, but the "emphasis remains on the multiplicity of voices." This allows the storytellers to subvert the "'official' text; the text the dominant culture is to receive."[58]

Where would Austin stand in this modern discussion? As a theorist, she was always most interested in the places where boundaries blurred: between language and music, between religions, between races, classes, and genders. So we would argue that her "lost borders" writing style was closer to poststructural than may appear at first glance. The "truth" for Austin always emerged somewhere between the spaces created in the storytelling tradition. Although A. Carl Bredahl Jr. was the first critic to name Austin's unique style of collecting sketches or stories "divided narrative,"[59] no one has explained and illustrated it better than Mark Schlenz in his introduction to a reissue of Austin's 1904 collection of children's stories, *The Basket Woman*.[60] Schlenz defines divided narrative as a "strategic organizational arrangement of tales [that] creates a powerful framing narrative in which the effect of the whole far transcends the sum of the individual pieces." He says this "requires reading across the gaps between stories" and results in "a connective thematic comprehension from the accumulated inferences in the sequence of tales." Schlenz explains that although both Faulkner and Hemingway scholars have usually credited Sherwood Anderson with development of the divided narrative form in *Winesburg Ohio* (1919), actually it first appeared in regional women's writing: Sara Orne Jewett's *The Country of Pointed Firs* (1896) and Austin's *The Land of Little Rain* (1903). In *The Land of Little Rain*, each chapter conjures a different place: the waterhole, the saloon, the campoody, Shoshone land, the irrigation system, the adobe village. Austin would argue that those who search in only one of these places will never find the "authentic" Southwest, but that an accumulation of familiarity with all of these places will develop a "hunch" about it that transcends any single point of view. She went on to develop the divided narrative further in *The Basket Woman* (1904), *The Flock* (1906), *The Trail Book* (1918), *The Land of Journeys' Ending* (1924), and others. Austin may have been influenced by Jewett[61] or perhaps both writers simply adopted the traditional rural multi-voiced storyteller's form at a time when the power of that form was being felt.[62]

Often right and ahead of her time, Austin sometimes intimidated or embarrassed both her friends and enemies. Very little has been mentioned about her contributions to literary theory or criticism, perhaps because she was sometimes wrong. However, according to Lewis Mumford, "Austin's errors…have a certain fertility and vigor that a great many truths lack; and if every particular point in her thesis should turn out to be wrong, her work should still be an interesting contribution to criticism."[63] In this collection we hope to help the reader recognize Austin as the early theorist she was and get past her daunting veneer to the valuable insights she provided into Southwestern literature. How many seeds did she plant regarding appreciation for regional Indian and Hispanic literary forms that others have since expanded and received credit for? How much art did she inspire? For how many careers has she supplied the wind behind the sails? How many more can she inspire if we read her words again? We hope this collection will encourage new explorations into Austin's rich commentary on regional and multicultural literary work. We do not offer this collection in substitution for, nor as an improvement upon, work being done by modern Indian or Hispanic critics, but as a collection that may trigger old memories or new observations and aid them in their work.

In addition, we hope this collection provides scholars with tools with which to illuminate and appreciate cultural and multicultural literature; to develop a critical lens with which to study gaps, omissions, and silences; and to contextualize Austin in Southwest cultural, political, historical, literary, and economic movements. We hope it generates development of regional theories that can stand up to the disintegrating effects of poststructuralism with room for place, culture, and authenticity. We hope it encourages critical treatments that will trace the influences of older forms of American drama, poetry, and prose on contemporary work. We hope it promotes interdisciplinary scholarship. And, finally, we hope this collection especially inspires Indian and Hispanic scholars who may be able to use Austin's ideas to support their own or as stimulation to argue against her.

In Austin's honor, we have chosen a "divided narrative" organization for this volume. Austin herself said, "If you find holes in my book that you could drive a car through, do not be too sure they were not left there for that express purpose."[64] Like Austin, we prefer to trust the magic and power of communal storytelling over formal or scholarly structure. We have grouped her essays into three major genres—prose, poetry, and drama—but we have discovered, as will the reader, that these divisions blur and blend. In order to place more emphasis on the rich mix of ideas rather than hint toward any linear development based on history or conquest, we have also intentionally mixed the chronology and ethnicities because her ideas about Native American body rhythms, for instance, apply as well to cowboy poetry or *rimas infantiles.* We have made minor corrections in her spelling and grammar but have left her unique (and sometimes confusing) phrasing intact. We have located the traditional scholars' introductory summaries and headnotes in the back of the book in an annotated bibliography, where we believe it will be less intrusive and perhaps more accessible.

The annotated bibliography will help scholars target their own interest areas, as we have included brief descriptions of all the articles related to Southwest literature that we found. We think of Austin's work on Southwest literature as "one-smoke theories," similar to the one-smoke stories she admired. Her theories are short, come from her own experience, often bite, and accumulate into something not quite concrete. Yet "between them, the ingoing and outgoing sense of the universe pulses and spirals with the ascending smoke," as she says about one-smoke stories.[65] During our selection process we attempted not only to choose the material that we felt best expresses Austin's "one-smoke theories," but also to give the reader a broad sampling of her many expressive forms.

We hope this collection will be entertaining as well. As in the literature she studied, it is often difficult to tell where Austin's literary criticism or theory ends and a story begins. She sometimes weaves her own nature writing or personal experiences into the analysis, sometimes imagining that she is sitting around a campfire contemplating ideas as they form in the smoke. So, as we think Austin would prefer, our collection is eclectic. We have included humor, letters, memoir, essay, story, and fantasy. We hope this mixing of Southwestern "flavors" will help the reader "experience" Austin's ideas and thereby develop a deeper appreciation for Southwestern literature.

Notes to *"The Chisera's Fire"*

1. Rayna Green, "The Tribe Called Wannabee," *Folklore* 99 (1988): 43.

2. Peter Wild, *The Opal Desert: Exploration of Fantasy and Reality in the American Southwest* (Austin: University of Texas Press, 1999), 72.

3. Michael Castro, *Interpreting the Indian: Twentieth-Century Poets and the Native American* (Norman: University of Oklahoma Press, 1983), xxi–xxii; Melody Graulich, Afterword to *Earth Horizon: Autobiography*, by Mary Austin (New York: Houghton Mifflin, 1932; Albuquerque: University of New Mexico Press, 1991), 387; Sherry L. Smith, *Reimagining Indians: Native Americans through Anglo Eyes 1880–1940* (New York: Oxford University Press, 2000), 15.

4. Elizabeth Shepley Sergeant, "Mary Austin: A Portrait," *Saturday Review of Literature*, September 8, 1934, in the Fray Angélico Chávez History Library, MSS 31, "Mary Austin Letters, 1931–1933," Box 3, Folder 3, 2.

5. Edward Wagenknecht, "Voices of the New Century," in his *Cavalcade of the American Novel: From the Birth of the Nation to the Middle of the Twentieth Century* (New York: Holt, Rinehart and Winston, 1952), 231.

6. "Mary (Hunter) Austin, 1868–1934," *Twentieth-Century Literary Criticism*, vol. 25 (Detroit: Gale, 1988), 16.

7. Don D. Walker, "Can the Western Tell What Happens?" in *Interpretive Approaches to Western American Literature,* eds. Daniel Alkofer et al. (Pocatello: Idaho State University Press, 1972), 35.

8. Melody Graulich, Introduction to *Exploring Lost Borders: Critical Essays on Mary Austin,* eds. Melody Graulich and Elizabeth Klimasmith (Reno: University of Nevada Press, 1999), xii.

9. Joy Harjo and Gloria Bird, *Reinventing the Enemy's Language: Contemporary Native Women's Writings of North America* (New York: Norton, 1997), 31.

10. Mary Austin, *No. 26 Jayne Street* (Boston: Houghton Mifflin Co., 1920), 6.

11. Annette Kolodny, "Dancing Through the Minefield: Some Observations on the Theory, Practice, and Politics of Feminist Literary Criticism," in *The New Feminist Criticism*, ed. Elaine Showalter (New York: Pantheon Books, 1985), 155.

12. Mary Austin, "New York: Dictator of American Criticism," *Nation* 3 (1920): 29.

13. Esther F. Lanigan, *Mary Austin: Song of a Maverick* (New Haven: Yale University Press, 1989; Tucson: University of Arizona Press, 1997), 127–28.

Lanigan believes Austin and Cather shared "similar views about the craft of writing and the theory of fiction. Both treated region as integral to their fictions, not merely convenient and attractive scenery." But she does admit that Austin "found the older writer guilty of betraying the Southwest in her sympathetic portrayal of Bishop Lamy (in *Death Comes for the Archbishop*), the cleric who thought New Mexico backward."

14. Ibid., 3.

15. Marjorie Pryse, ed., Introduction to *Stories from the Country of Lost Borders* (New Brunswick: Rutgers University Press, 1987), vii–xxxviii. For instance, Pryse's introduction situates Austin within the group of regional women writers and active feminists of her day.

16. Mary Austin, *Earth Horizon: Autobiography* with an afterword by Melody Graulich (New York: Houghton Mifflin, 1932; Albuquerque: University of New Mexico Press, 1991), 327.

17. Sergeant, 4.

18. Lanigan, 3.

19. Mary Austin, "Where We Get Tammany Hall and Carnegie Libraries," *World Outlook* (January 1918), Fray Angélico Chávez History Library, MSS 31, "Mary Austin Letters, 1931–1933," Box 2, Folder 2, 5.

20. Mary Austin, "Sources of Poetic Influence in the Southwest," *Poetry* 43 (December 1933): 163.

21. Mary Austin, *The Land of Journeys' Ending* (New York: Century, 1924), 442.

22. Lois Rudnick, "Re-Naming the Land: Anglo Expatriate Women in the Southwest," in *The Desert is No Lady: Southwestern Landscapes in Women's Writing and Art*, eds. Vera Norwood and Janice Monk (New Haven: Yale University Press, 1987), 25.

23. Graulich, Introduction to *Exploring*, xx.

24. Vera Norwood, "The Photogapher and the Naturalist," *Journal of American Culture* 5.2 (1982): 6.

25. Mary Austin, "Speech of Mary Austin before the National Popular Government League on the Burson Bill," Washington, DC, January 17, 1923, in Center for Southwest Research MSS 611, "Augusta Fink Papers, 1887–1989," Box 2, Folder 37, 2.

26. Austin's novel *The Ford* (1917), as explained by John Walton in a recent reissue's Introduction (Berkeley: University of California Press, 1997), develops this idea as "urban colonialism." He says, "The Owens Valley–Los Angeles controversy, a rural-urban struggle of epic dimensions that began at this time, has persevered throughout the century, resulting in a monumental

aqueduct supplying 80% of Los Angeles' water, legendary grass roots rebellion, precedent-making environmental action, and Southern California urban sprawl as we now know it," xii.

27. Austin, Burson Bill Speech, 1.

28. Mary Austin, "The Writer Who Never Grew Up," *The Ladies' Home Journal* (December 1921): 7ff.

29. Mary Austin, Center for Southwest Research, MSS 97, "Frank G. Applegate Papers, 1886–2000," Box 1, Folder 39.

30. Ibid.

31. Mary Austin, "Mexico for Mexicans," *World Outlook* (December 1915): 6.

32. Mary Austin, *Taos Pueblo* (Boston: New York Graphic Society, Facsimile Edition, 1927): 9th page (no page numbers).

33. Mary Austin, *The Land of Little Rain* (Boston: Houghton, Mifflin and Company, 1903), 63.

34. Mary Austin, "Frank Applegate," *New Mexico Quarterly Review* (August 1932): 213–17.

35. Lanigan, 17.

36. Mary Austin, "The Town that Doesn't Want a Chautauqua," *The New Republic* 47 (July 7, 1926): 157–59.

37. Norwood, 6.

38. Mary Austin, Center for Southwest Research, MSS 589, "Richard Lowitt Papers on Bronson M. Cutting, 1989–1993," Box 3, Folder 13.

39. "Doctorate Conferred on Two Noted Women," *Albuquerque Tribune*, June 5, 1933, Fray Angélico Chávez History Library, MSS 31, "Mary Austin Letters, 1931–1933," Box 3, Folder 3.

40. Austin, *Earth Horizon*, 354. Lanigan, 129. Also, Lanigan goes into great detail about the relationship between Mabel Dodge and Austin, before Dodge married Tony Luhan. Austin engaged in many social discussions with notable people at Dodge's Fifth Avenue apartment in New York City, which included topics like feminism and psychology. For further information about the "Anglo Expatriates" and Austin's relationship with Alice Corbin Henderson and Luhan, see Lois Rudnick's *Utopian Vistas: The Mable Dodge Luhan House and the American Counter Culture* (Albuquerque: University of New Mexico Press, 1996).

41. Stineman has noted Austin's "photographic technique" and her "attention to light." Esther Lanigan Stineman, *Mary Austin: Song of a Maverick* (New Haven: Yale University Press, 1989), 183, 185. In his autobiography, Adams explains his relationship with and admiration for Austin. Ansel

Adams, *Ansel Adams: An Autobiography* (Boston, Little, Brown, 1985), 89–90. An interesting book could be produced comparing many of Austin's descriptions with Adams's photographs of the same places, including those collected in a 1950 edition of *The Land of Little Rain* for which Adams provided illustrations.

42. Mary Austin, "Regionalism in American Fiction," *English Journal* 21 (February 1932): 97–107.

43. B. A. Botkin, "New Mexico Round Table on Regionalism," *New Mexico Quarterly* (August 1933): 157.

44. Pryse, xv.

45. Mary Austin, "The Magazine West," The Mary (Hunter) Austin Collection at the Huntington Library, AU 331:1.

46. Pryse, xix.

47. Mary Austin, *The American Rhythm* (New York: Harcourt, 1923), 48.

48. Mary Austin, Introduction to *Native Tales of New Mexico* by Frank Applegate, 4th page (no page numbers), Center for Southwest Research, MSS 97 "Frank G. Applegate Papers, 1886–2000," Box 5.

49. Austin, "Regionalism in American Fiction," 97, 104–5.

50. Mary Austin, "Regional Culture in the Southwest," *Southwest Review* 14 (1929): 474.

51. Paula Gunn Allen, "The Sacred Hoop: A Contemporary Perspective," in *The Ecocriticism Reader: Landmarks in Literary Ecology*, eds. Cheryll Glotfelty and Harold Fromm (Athens: University of Georgia Press, 1996), 241.

52. Alan R. Velie, Introduction to *American Indian Literature: An Anthology* (Norman: University of Oklahoma Press, 1991), 7.

53. Edward Said, Introduction to *Orientalism* (New York: Vintage, 1979), 1–28.

54. Harjo and Bird, 28.

55. Ibid., 22.

56. Austin, Burson Bill Speech, 12–15.

57. Nathaniel Lewis, *Unsettling the Literary West: Authenticity and Authorship* (Lincoln: University of Nebraska Press, 2003), 202–19.

58. Tey Diana Rebolledo, Introduction to *We Fed Them Cactus* by Fabiola Cabeza de Baca, 1954, second edition (Albuquerque: University of New Mexico Press, 1994), xiii–xxxii, xx–xxi.

59. A. Carl Bredahl Jr., *New Ground: Western American Narrative and the Literary Canon* (Chapel Hill: University of North Carolina Press, 1989), 49.

60. Mark Schlenz, Introduction to *The Basket Woman* (New York: Houghton Mifflin, 1904; Reno: University of Nevada Press, 1999), ix–x.

61. For a good argument that Austin was influenced by Jewett, see Pryse's Introduction to *Stories from the Country of Lost Borders.*

62. Bird explains organizing *Reinventing the Enemy's Language: Contemporary Native Women's Writings of North America* in words that mirror a "divided narrative" style: "In retrospect, this experience wasn't just about reading manuscripts, but creating a narrative. Each piece has gone into the creation of a narrative that is also part of an even larger narrative," 29.

63. Lewis Mumford, "*The American Rhythm*," *The New Republic* 35.443 (1923): 23.

64. Austin, *The Land of Journeys' Ending*, ix.

65. Mary Austin, Introduction to *One Smoke Stories* (Boston and New York: Houghton Mifflin Company, 1934), xii.

PART II

The Great Regional Ceremony: Introduction to Prose

In her study of Southwest literature, Mary Austin discovered a particularly significant Indian ritual important to her own writing. She tells the story of a young Navajo man, stolen from his tribe, who, upon escape and return to his people, "found that his own tribe no longer smelled good to him"—meaning that his sense of appreciation for his tribe had disappeared in his absence.[1] According to Austin, a spiritual elder guided the young man through a ritual in order to restore his "normal condition." Mark Hoyer explains the use of rituals, saying, "Rituals can be defensive (curing), offensive (enacting a vision foretold in prophetic dreams), or both. In any event, it is by means of ritual that the healer realigns or reorients the individual or community along the prevailing lines of power."[2]

The Navajo ritual that Austin describes consists of a nine-day ceremony designed to help alienated tribal members rediscover feelings of nostalgia, appreciation, and acceptance of their fellow tribal members' "smell."[3] This ceremony was especially symbolic for Austin because it represented what she tried to achieve in her writing as she blended voices from the mixture of cultures, religions, languages, and economic views to capture "the smell" of the Southwest. Many of the groups Austin felt should be heard had been alienated from mainstream society; therefore, she took it upon herself to bring their stories to the public. By giving a voice to each, she hoped to enhance a sense of community among the diverse classes and cultures within the region. She believed that if people could get a true sense of each other, this deeper understanding would lead to tolerance, respect, and even affection.

In order to achieve an understanding among conflicting cultures, Austin commonly relied on storytelling. By listening respectively to each other's stories, she believed people could make meaningful connections.

One group she felt were master storytellers worthy of public understanding but often ostracized because of their "smell" was sheepherders. In one of her critically acclaimed works, *The Flock* (1906), Austin gives sheepherders the opportunity to air their "smell" through their own stories. Although her friendships and interviews with them rendered her an expert on the subject, she did not attempt to present herself as one. In the opening chapter of *The Flock*, Austin credits the sheepherders as authors. She says, "I suppose of all the people who are concerned with the making of a true book, the one who puts it to the pen has the least to do with it. This is the book of Jimmy Rosemeyre and José Jesús Lopez, of little Pete…of Noriega, of Sanger and the Manxman and Narcisse Duplin, and many others who, wittingly or unwittingly, have contributed to the performances set down in it."[4] Austin's narrative persona in *The Flock* is journalistic, presenting herself as a simple reporter asking questions, listening to shepherds' stories around campfires, and retelling those stories through a collective multi-voiced style that respectfully gives the shepherds themselves the voice of authority. By providing this forum, Austin hoped to create a direct connection between storyteller and reader, allowing the sheepherders to interact with the audience by telling their stories not only in their own voices and words, but also in context.

Although she is often accused of appropriating,[5] Austin rarely failed to recognize or credit a source, even refusing to take credit for some of what she called "re-expression" of Indian poetry that *The Century* offered to print if she would admit authorship.[6] Acting as both storyteller and critic, she addresses her feelings about story creation, ownership, and plagiarism in "Speaking of Bears," which chronicles the abuses of one trapper's stories.[7] To a degree, Austin agreed that a story traditionally "always belonged to the man who could use it best, as would be proved by reference to the well-known William Shakespeare."[8] But she also knew that storytellers of the Southwest did not necessarily recognize the literary quality of their stories. She collected stories from shepherds, basket makers, and trappers. Perhaps without Austin's brave first steps, the recognition of this work as "literature" might not have happened at all.

Early ethnologists and writers have been accused of "appropriating" or "stealing" Indian culture and material, but, according to

Michael Castro, without their early efforts and recordings much of this rich and sophisticated literary expression would have been lost during the years when the Bureau of Indian Affairs, boarding schools, missionaries, literary snobs, and racists attempted to stamp them out. Although some were possibly only furthering their own careers, others, like Natalie Curtis in *The Indians' Book* (1907) and George W. Cronyn in *Path on the Rainbow* (1918) made genuine contributions toward preserving Indian literary culture and pride.[9] Even contemporary Indian writers still struggle with the same issue, as Flathead author Debra Earling explains: "I write in the hope that I will give voice to those who have never had an opportunity to tell their stories. I write to give voice to myself."[10] Ultimately, Austin gave a voice to disenfranchised people who would not be "discovered" by academia or even their neighbors for several decades.

Austin also knew that something would be lost in the transition from oral to written form,[11] but she hoped to preserve more of the authenticity of the stories by including the accompanying situations, gestures, and expressions. Many Southwestern storytellers passed on their stories orally rather than on paper, and she felt that oral storytelling skills had been honed to perfection by peer pressure, watching the facial expression of their listeners, or circumstances. Austin explains that "By making the story too intimately the possession of the teller, something of the possessiveness of the hearer is lost, and it is indispensable to the primitive teller that the story should stand to the hearer in place of an experience, which is the primary reason it should be told at all."[12]

Austin found that much character is revealed in the way a person tells a story. By recreating the original situation, she allows the reader to draw conclusions based on the teller's own words and actions. For example, in *The Flock*, Echenique tells a campfire story about a bear attacking his sheep and gets momentarily sidetracked by engaging in a technical discussion regarding the best way to outrun bears. Eventually Echenique returns to his original story, recalling how the bear chased him and how he whistled to his dogs to stay close. Right in the middle of this account, just when the listeners would be on edge, he stands up and leaves to tend to his flock, which he has noticed has begun to stir. The story is left unfinished and Austin, using a journalistic voice, simply reports, "Not until they meet again by chance, in the summer mead-ows, will each and several hear the end of the bear story."[13] Unsatisfied, a reader might prefer that Austin finish the story, surmising that she must have heard the full account at some point. Remaining faithful to the situation and the teller, however, she does not finish it and thus allows the reader insight into Echenique's character, most notably his dedication to his work, without having to interfere.

Austin studied storytelling for its effect on both reader and listener. She learned that an audience reacts not only to the story itself, but also to the way in which it is told. Voice, expression, and gesture are all an integral part of a story and the genuine experience of hearing it. This is further illustrated in the story of Sanger and his sheepdog. Sanger begins by telling Austin, whom he refers to as Madame-who-writes-the-book, "I must tell you a story of that misbegotten devil of a he goat."[14] He then instructs his dog to fetch the goat, presumably to let Austin see it for herself. The dog quickly and easily cuts the specified goat from the band of sheep, but Sanger never tells his story. Of this strange fact Austin says, "You will have to ask again before you get your story for it is not [the goat] the shepherd has in mind."[15] Like many shepherds, Sanger is filled with pride in his intelligent dog and sets up the story situation in order to show him off, allowing the audience to witness the dog in action. Readers will be able to "see for themselves" and feel more respect through Sanger's storytelling technique than they would if he bragged about the dog outright.

Another storytelling element Austin learned over the years was the idea of tight, concise narrative. In *The American Rhythm*, Austin cred-its the Indians with teaching her, as Melody Graulich calls it, to "prune."[16] A much "pruned" story occurs when Austin asks one sheep-herder how he came by his "splendid lynx skin." With little detail, he says, "Eh, it was below Olancha about moonrise that he sprung on the fattest of my lambs. I gave him a crack with my staff, and the dogs did the rest."[17] Austin follows the simple story with the comment "You will hardly get a more prolix account from any herder." Again, much can be inferred from the sheepherder's lack of elaboration. This would be a perfect opportunity to exaggerate his own heroics, but instead, he downplays his role and avoids casting himself as a hero. He prefers to focus attention on his sheepdogs, much like Sanger in the earlier story.

Realizing that the stories' situations obviously affected her own respect toward both sheepherders and their dogs, Austin tries to recreate a similar experience for the reader. Austin's experiences with dogs and stories eventually led her to claim that dogs could understand shepherd and hunter stories and respond with either shame or pride, depending on their part in the story. Of possible interest to modern ecocritics is Austin's statement in "The Folk Story in America" that perhaps her "most important contribution to the storyteller's art" was the fact that stories could cross language boundaries between species. From the beginning of her career, she promoted the decentralizing of power and leveling of hierarchies, although those ideas would not become popular in literary circles for several decades. As a literary theorist Austin was years ahead of poststructural thinking. She argued against the idea of ranking literature into good, better, and best or into children, folk, and scholarly. And in the case of working and hunting dogs, she even argued against the assumption that storytelling belonged solely to the human race. She believed good stories could affect audiences regardless of gender, race, class, or species.

Along with pruning and valuing the way oral stories were told, Austin also learned to value the gaps when she discovered that "No Indian ever says all his thought. Always there is some petal left unfurled."[18] In *The Flock*, a few of the sheepherders leave some "petals unfurled" in their stories. A sheepherder named Pete recounts for Austin how he was able to gain access to a particularly lush meadow, fed by natural springs. Other shepherds trailed at his heels and pushed closer to the coveted meadow every day, so Pete wrote a letter to the owner of the land asking for exclusive access. He waited and waited but did not receive a reply. Meanwhile, the competition was closing in. Cleverly, he wrote a fake response letter from the owner granting him access to the grass and water. He had one of his men present it to him when he returned from working as if it had just arrived from the post office. The competing shepherd could not read so had to assume that Pete was granted access to the land. When Austin asked Pete if the real letter ever arrived, he acted grossly offended and replied with mock indignation, "That you should ask me!"[19] Austin responds, "I am not sure if I am the more convinced by the reproachful waggings of his head or the deep, delighted twinkle of his eye." The audience can sense his playfulness by the way he responds to Austin. It is what Pete does not say, the petal unfurled, that "reveals" his story. The reader "sees" his shrewd competitive nature and ability to provide the best pastures for his sheep. We can't say for sure whether or not he steps over the boundaries of honesty because of the gap he leaves in the story.

For most Southwesterners storytelling was more than entertainment. It was typically used to teach lessons, inspire situations, correct stereotypes, promote camaraderie, reveal character, or shape culture. As a student of Native American storytelling, Austin discovered that the "short, short story is the true Indian genre."[20] These stories were shared when their tellers could steal a moment from work, tribal obligations, or other commitments that demanded their time. Although these short ceremonial storytelling sessions originated within the Native American community, Austin found the same principles applied to other Southwest storytellers. According to Graulich, "Along with stagecoach drivers, sheepherders, and a host of other western tale tellers, the Indians taught Austin the importance of the narrator in any story and the arts of irony and ambiguity," also inspiring her to experiment with narrative style as a "result of her lifelong concern with point of view."[21] From them all, Austin learned the importance of offering an audience an experience through story without superfluous explanation and fanfare. This is the essence of the "One Smoke Story," which can be told in the time it takes to smoke one corn-husk cigarette.

We begin with the prose section because these articles illustrate Austin's general ideas about the Southwest's literary individuality: the people, the mix of languages and religion, and regionalism. Here she lays the groundwork for her argument that not only should America look to its indigenous and environmental roots as source and inspiration for its own literary wealth, but that the Southwest should also stand on its own hind legs and not depend on the East Coast or the universities for direction. She encouraged literary representation of the region, with the principle behind the Navajo Mountain Chant ceremony obviously influencing her desire to help the reader rediscover feelings of nostalgia, appreciation, and acceptance of the Southwest's "smell."

We hope that the articles in this section[22] and in the following sections will function as a traditional storytelling session in which stories in a collection work off one another and together to create a larger whole. Interpretation of Austin's ideas should never be considered finished or stagnant, but always pliable and ready for the next reader to add a personal interpretation or for someone in the audience to correct the direction of thought. Our collection is not seamless, not a novel or a story cycle, not a collection of scholarly essays, but something different. We hope it will create something like the magic that Austin witnessed as storytellers traded stories around a campfire, around the kitchen table, or on a smoke break. So, as the smoke begins to rise, we hope you will come to recognize and appreciate the "smell" of Southwestern literature.

Notes to Prose Introduction

1. Mary Austin, "Primitive Stage Setting," *Theatre Arts Monthly* (January 1928): 54.

2. Mark T. Hoyer, *Dancing Ghosts: Native American and Christian Syncretism in Mary Austin's Work* (Reno: University of Nevada Press, 1998), 133.

3. Mary Austin, "Cults of the Pueblos," *Century Magazine* (November 1924–April 1925): 29.

4. Mary Austin, *The Flock*, 1906 (Reno: University of Nevada Press, 2001), 11.

5. Noreen Groover Lape, for instance, claims that Austin would "pose as a transethnic, willingly appropriating native cultural expression" ("There was a part for her in the Indian Life"), in *Breaking Boundaries: New Perspectives on Women's Regional Writing*, eds. Sherrie A. Innes and Diana Royer (Iowa City: University of Iowa Press, 1997), 127.

6. Thomas W. Ford, "*The American Rhythm*: Mary Austin's Poetic Principle," *Western American Literature* 5.1 (Spring 1970): 10–11.

7. In this story Austin mixes story and criticism. As Hoyer explains in *Dancing Ghosts* (xx), "Storytelling in Native American cultures combines theory and practice, and it can serve the function of criticism. The storyteller is at once artist and 'literary' (or cultural) critic."

8. Mary Austin, "Speaking of Bears," *One Smoke Stories* (Boston and New York: Houghton Mifflin Company, 1934), 119.

9. Michael Castro, *Interpreting the Indian: Twentieth-Century Poets and the Native American* (Norman: University of Oklahoma Press, 1983), 9, 17.

10. Joy Harjo and Gloria Bird, *Reinventing the Enemy's Language: Contemporary Native Women's Writings of North America* (New York: Norton, 1997), 454. Hoyer (90) also notes that both Austin and Mourning Dove "seek to give a voice to the voiceless."

11. In describing Austin's "A Case of Conscience" Hoyer (87) says she "ends the story with a hint that there is more to all the stories, originally oral and now retold in her book, suggests the gap between oral and written even as it seeks to narrow that gap, thereby calling further attention to her decision to sometimes withhold information."

12. Mary Austin, "The Folk Story in America," *The South Atlantic Quarterly* 33 (January 1934): 17.

13. Mary Austin, *The Flock*, 45.

14. Ibid., 152.

15. Ibid., 153.

16. Melody Graulich, Introduction to *Western Trails: A Collection of Short Stories by Mary Austin*, ed. Melody Graulich (Reno: University of Nevada Press, 1987), 21.

17. Austin, *The Flock*, 176.

18. Mary Austin, *The American Rhythm* (New York: Harcourt, 1923), 61.

19. Austin, *The Flock*, 163.

20. Austin, "The Folk Story in America," 19.

21. Melody Graulich, Afterword to *Earth Horizon: Autobiography*, by Mary Austin (New York: Houghton Mifflin, 1932; Albuquerque: University of New Mexico Press, 1991), 385.

22. Four essays in this section appear in Ruben Ellis's *Beyond Borders: The Selected Essays of Mary Austin* (Carbondale: Southern Illinois University Press, 1996), which he calls the "first collection of her non-fiction journalism": "New York: Dictator of American Criticism," "The American Form of the Novel," "Regionalism in American Fiction," and "One Smoke Stories." His rich introduction describes the various magazines Austin wrote for and their target audiences.

1

One Smoke Stories

1934

The corn-husk cigarettes, which for ceremonial purposes are still used south of Green River and west of the Rio Grande, last only a little while. Since they are made chiefly of the biting native *tabac*, this is perhaps not to be regretted. You select your husk from the heap and gather your pinch of the weed from the dark bowl as it passes the ancient ceremonial road from east to north by west to south, and, holding the dry roll delicately between your lips, endeavor to dispatch the salutatory puffs to the six, or, if you happen to be among the Navajo, the four, world quarters. Try as you may, you will probably never master the unobtrusive art, though I have seen white men whose standing in the country is that of 'old-timers,' allowing the smoke to escape from their lips in the appointed directions, but in such a manner that they are able, if you accuse one of them of it, to deny it successfully.

Thus, after a day of preparation for the unending seasonal rituals that keep the Indian snug in his environment—sib to it, in the old sense of communicable, answering back again—around the embers sit the meditative Elders. Now and again holding the crisp cylinder between thumb and fingertip, unlighted, one begins, always gravely, and holding on for the space of one smoke, tales, each one as deft, as finished in itself as a ceremonial cigarette. Or, if not a tale, then a clean round out of the speaker's experience, such as in our kind of society might turn up a sonnet or an etching. And between them, the ingoing and outgoing sense of the universe pulses and spirals with the ascending smoke.

The essence of all such stories is that they should be located somewhere in the inner sense of the audience, unencumbered by what in our more discursive method is known as background.

Your true desert-dweller travels light. He makes even of his experience a handy package with the finished neatness that distinguishes his artifacts. How else could they be passed intact from tribe to tribe, from generation to generation? Just before the end, like the rattle that warns that the story is about to strike, comes the fang of the experience, most often in the shape of a wise saying. Then the speaker resumes the soul-consoling smoke, while another takes up the dropped stitch of narrative and weaves it into the pattern of the talk.

This is not to say that the Amerind does not have other types of tellings—hero cycles, epics of tribal adventure, and serial legends that must be tied with the proper formula when in the lapse of time the telling comes to a natural pause. But the one-smoke story is especially designed to be the medium for the communication of experience, and the form is so admirably contrived for oral telling that all anecdote in the Indian country tends to fall into that shape, which accounts for my including in this collection tales of other peoples than Indians.

Folk experience admits many tellable items which, in a world of pretentious sophistication like ours, are inhibited. It admits the friendly dead, the talking animal whose wisdom is profounder than ours because his mysteriousness is nearer to the Great Mystery. It admits the Surpassing Beings whom we blunderingly designate as Gods—the Sacred Trues who are themselves the instigators of experience. Some of the tales most esteemed by the audiences that originally heard them are unintelligible to our so much more objective minds. They dip too deeply, pass beyond our ken into that region mastery over which man reigned as the purchase price of intelligence. Others—and these are often wittiest—are inhibited by our proprieties. Not that I was ever told anything unsuitable for a woman to hear, but between their suitabilities and ours is all the distance we have traveled to know that the joke the Trues played upon man when they tied procreation to responsibility is not a joke to women. But lest you should imagine that the untellables are of a sliminess that characterizes our own untellables, I have included in 'Stewed Beans' a story of the Stone Age such as has ceased to be current among us. For the rest, where tribal women slap their thighs with gusts of laughter, I remain faithful to the taboos of my own tribe.

As for the manner of telling, I hope I shall be found adhering closely to the original method, but if occasionally I am discovered adding to the austere relation such further perception of the scene as is necessary to have the fang of the story strike home, I shall hope it is not too much. In the words of the sacred formula:

I give you to smoke.

2

Speaking of Bears

1925

A ny good bear story is bound to have as many layers as a quamash root. Take that one which you know in the form in which Seaforth's publishers announced it as our most charming nature saga, "The Bears of Quamash." I came across the germinating core of that some fifteen years before the Most Distinguished Citizen quarreled with Seaforth about it, in one of those tall old San Francisco houses, just beyond the devouring line of the great fire in 1906. It was then the home of a man whom it pleased people who knew him best to call the Historian. I had never known him in any other character than that and my good friend, with the light making a halo round the polished dome of his historian's head as he looked up from his labors to minister an occasional sop to my endless curiosity about the Old West. On one of these occasions he showed me a thick, fine-printed volume, the first from his hand, and the only traceable copy left after a fire had destroyed the first edition and the original plates a few days after publication.

It was the story of one Samuel Adams, a mild-mannered, blue-eyed trapper of the scaldic[1] temperament who had made a business of supplying European zoos and circuses with cougars and bears for twenty years before gold was first washed out of the Ventura sands. On one of the occasions when Adams had come down with his captive train to the mission town of San Francisco, which he found mysteriously grown to a world port, my friend had discovered him, and constituted himself the historian of Adams's adventures. "It was the most fun I ever had," sighed the historian. "Such fresh and unlettered and authentic material. It was like playing amanuensis to Robinson Crusoe just off the Island— but you can't get publishers interested in these things nowadays—they want their material *fictionized*!" He brought the word out with an accent that checked a proposal on my lips that I do something like that with it myself if the stuff was really as good as he thought it was. That was the last of the matter for fifteen years.

In the meantime Seaforth succeeded in making the adventures of the hunted sound as absorbing as the lives of the hunters, as produced in his masterpiece "The Bears of Quamash." The tale was so much and so favorably talked about that it attracted the attention of the Most Distinguished Citizen, who had also specialized in bears and took exception to some of Seaforth's statements.

It is the penalty of the Most Distinguished that whatever they say is immediately taken up and elaborated by people without any distinction whatever; in this case with the result that to Seaforth's full-blown reputation there were attached the weasel words of "nature faking."[2]

I had happened, once or twice, to cross Seaforth's trail while he was engaged in his sincere and almost anxious search for authenticity of background, and I knew enough of the man to be certain he would be immeasurably hurt by the charge of fakery. At the same time I was puzzled at his failure to make a more effective defense and, in particular, to insist on the authenticity of the main incidents of the Quamash story, for it was part of his method never to invent incident, but only the machinery by which his story was articulated. He was a man of such transparent honesty as made it certain he would never set down anything which he did not believe to be true. At the same time his simplicity laid him open to the possibility of believing things that had been told him as true, on no other evidence than his own prepossession toward honesty.

All this was so freshly in my mind the next time I crossed trails with him—quite unexpectedly at Summerfield, where I had gone to be present at the annual parting of the flocks—that I could hardly have avoided speaking of it.

Seaforth was to lecture that night at the Woman's Club, whose undying censure I had earned by smuggling him away from their afternoon reception to Noriega's shearing, where the inspiriting smell of dust and wool mixed with creosote and native claret had proved more potent than the half-fermented wine of praise. We were still slightly under that enchantment when we found ourselves happily islanded, after the lecture was over, on the roof of the Summerfield Hotel, deserted by everybody but one pale reproachful waiter.

There was a bright, low moon standing off to the west over Tremblor, and a low round moon of the clock-tower glinting at us from between the acanthus trees. Now and then a warm billow of air reached us from the superheated earth, heavy with the scent of the spring gardens and the crude oil with which the desert sand had been firmed into streets. We talked and talked; and there was no other noise than the tinkling of the ice in the tall glasses and the far off call of a coyote from the hills, keeping the tale of the new-shorn flocks.

Seaforth told me all about his discussion with the Distinguished Citizen, whose estimate of the intelligence of wild things was trimmed to his practice of successfully hunting them. Besides the fact that I would rather hear a bear story from a man who has loved bears than from one who has merely killed them, I was on Seaforth's side. His methods were precisely the same as any novelist pursues in search of the human story, skillfully compounded of observation and intuition, and in comparison with the amount of human nature faking which goes on in the monthly magazines—! At all events, I was sufficiently on his side for him to be willing to tell me circumstantially how he came to write "The Bears of Quamash."

He had always wanted to write a bear story. For years he had absorbed veracious information about bears, from books and from everybody he met, and his own honesty was of such an engaging sort that it would have been a mean soul, indeed, who could tell him anything unworthy to be believed. I judged, however, that he had met one or two such souls. He had, he told me himself, met Al Kellerman.

Kellerman was the pinwheel of the Kurtz News Syndicate, perpetually going round in a whirl of journalistic coruscations with the effect of giving off light which never really lighted anything. He had been a young man of parts, and Kurtz had made him so absolutely to his purpose that when I tell you that Kellerman admired Kurtz and Kurtz was entirely satisfied with Al, I have said the best, and the worst, of both of them. It was Kellerman who had been sent, in the absence of any more compelling headline material, to find the cub grizzly, Muckamuck, which was later presented to the city park in the interest of natural history and increased circulation. All this had occurred several years before Seaforth rose to prominence as the writer of nature sagas, and it was the sight of old Muckamuck wheeling his ton or so of grizzly haunch to and fro behind the bars of his pit at the zoo that had fired my friend with the desire to write the life-history of a grizzly. He had the really bright idea of making it the life of Muckamuck, because a personal instance is always so much more appealing, and it sells better, which is a lawful consideration.

It was natural, under these circumstances, that the incidents of the cub's capture in Seaforth's story should bear some resemblance to the facts as set forth by Kellerman in the letters which he had sent to Kurtz' *Messenger* from time to time during the whole six weeks of his expedition. Seaforth made allowance for the exigencies of newspaper reporting, but he said he felt that, on the whole, Kellerman must have stuck pretty closely to the facts, because of the similarity of the incidents of Kellerman's story to things he had read in a book of unimpeachable veracity.

Below us in the street a team of Basque handball players who had just beaten the visiting professional French team from Los Alamos passed on their triumphant processional from shrine to shrine of the *genius loci.* That is to say, they were making the round of the local bars, gloriously claret drunk, singing an ancient herder's ditty, all the implications of which led us so far afield, and so much deeper into the intimacy of the open, that it ended with Seaforth stripping off another layer, and the sorest, of his story of the story. The waiter, having replenished our glasses, was asleep with his head on a table, and the moon rode well into the middle heaven.

Seaforth finished the manuscript of "The Bears of Quamash" after six weeks' camping in Quamash Meadows to make sure of his background. Then to attest the honesty of his intention, he went home by way of Los Alamos, where he had learned that Kellerman was to be found, wiring ahead for the journalist to meet him. His idea was to read Kellerman his story and to get Kellerman's own notion of just what gracious acknowledgment of indebtedness for the incident of the capture should accompany its publication. The dinner was at the Angelus, one of those repasts which the Easterner knows so well how to pluck from our too profligate board: abalone broth, sand crabs, Seco squabs, avocados, and that bright crimson native wine which goes around the Horn in barrels and comes back to us at double the price under Italian labels.

Between the courses there were delicate Mexican cigarettes wrapped in cornhusk, and installments of the story. One hopes the newspaper man appreciated his privilege. At any rate, he expressed a genial approval; said it was a good story, and that the stuff always belonged to the man who could use it best, as would be proved by reference to the well-known William Shakespeare; and that for himself, he preferred to have no personal mention dim the bright luster of Seaforth's achievement. Then he went home, wrote what he could remember of Seaforth's story, and published it over his own name in next Sunday's supplement of the Los Alamos *Times*.

Seaforth, who went East on the midnight flyer, did not see the *Times*, of course; not until after his own story had appeared. Not, indeed, until the Most Distinguished Citizen had reviewed it.

Then some seventy of his friends and enemies sent him clippings of Kellerman's version of his own version of Kellerman's original story. Fortunately Seaforth had covered himself by mailing a copy of his manuscript to his publishers a week before his meeting with Kellerman; but you see his position with the public.

If Kellerman's original account of the capture of Muckamuck were true, he had as much right as had Seaforth to republish it as the basis of a fiction story. Since Kellerman's account had been used by Seaforth without acknowledgment, there was no way of getting understood, by a large and rather careless audience of readers, just where the journalist had violated any code by using Seaforth's material in his turn. The author who attempts to instruct his public in suchlike fine distinctions of professionalism would much better put in the time writing another story.

I think that from the first, with my sympathies all on Seaforth's side, I had a glimmer of the lie of that trail through Kellerman's mind. Even Kurtz Syndicate men are not wholly without what passes for a professional deadline,[3] which I could, in this case, imagine to be marked only by the conviction in Kellerman's mind that Seaforth's story was a matter of familiar kind with his. I had spent two months in the region in which Kellerman was supposed to have captured Muckamuck as a cub, and I suspected him of yarning throughout. Nothing of this came to the surface of our talk, however, as Seaforth and I got down to the street at last and drifted along its hot emptiness toward the drugstore—

where, amid stationery and sachet powder, a few books were sold—to find a copy of "The Bears of Quamash" which Seaforth could autograph for me.

The next day he went north to finish his lecture tour, and I put in at the gap between Tremblor and Tejon where I had business about sheep. Then I lent my copy to Jerke Johnson who was riding fence on the San Emigdio.

Jerke handed it back in a day or two with the verdict that it was "mighty interstin' readin'!"

"But true, Jerke? Does it sound true?"

Jerke was of the opinion that a lot of things were probably true that didn't in the least sound so. "Sort of reminds me," he dropped, "of the pieces Al Kellerman used to write for his paper when he was a-ketchin' that bear for Kurtz."

"Jerke! Were you in on *that*?!" He had been, I knew, at the center of all sorts of enviable occasions, but this was the first I had heard of Muckamuck. Under much persuasion the story dribbled as negligently as cigarette smoke from Jerke Johnson's lips.

Kellerman, it seemed, after two weeks of unsuccessful beating in the San Gabriel, had attached to himself a bear-tracker of repute, one Doc Shaffer, who had guided him to the 3A Ranch at which Jerke was provisionally employed as a bronco buster. It was a slack time at the 3A and "the boys" took to Kellerman "like," as Jerke figured it, "he was pie and donuts." No bear appeared. But "signs," which in this case took the form of footprints round the spring and in the soft earth along the shallows of Salt Creek, were plentiful. In the intervals of fruitlessly following them, the journalist sat in at the ranch games and prepared his due installments of copy.

"After he had seen our poker play," Jerke admitted, "which sure was pretty, we wa'n't near so anxious for bear as we had been in the first place."

After that Kellerman's daily practice was to go out with Doc Shaffer and have a look at a snapshot of the newest tracks, to set a "coupla Mexes" to trail them, and, after getting off his allotment of hairbreadth escapes and death struggles with bear, to devote the rest of the day to the real business of draw poker.

"After he'd been there a week," Jerke at last gave the tale its way with him, "we wasn't carin' if he didn't find no bear that season. It was plum lonesome at Salt Crick, and the Kurtz checks which he paid his poker losses with was as good as money.

"We done our best by him," said Jerke, "holdin' down on the liquor and pumpin' up his hopes of bear every time the *Messenger* began to get restive.

"Everything was mighty pleasant and sociable for a matter of three weeks or so, and then Kellerman began to get letters from the office intimatin' that Kurtz wasn't near so anxious for bear as he had been. Kellerman would be plum discouraged over these here missives, and allow he'd ought to move over to Castac where he'd hear the bear wasn't so shy and persnickety. But it looked like the Salt Crick bears was keeping tab on his hopes and prospects, for no sooner would he give Shaffer notice to pack the outfit than there would be a regular breakin'-out of bears' tracks around the water-holes and acrost the mud flats where the crick ran when there was any. Then Kellerman would get out and rustle up another bunch of exciting incidents for the *Messenger*. Finally, just about the time Kellerman was gettin' the run of our poker play, come a letter saying:

"'Kurtz doesn't want any bear. Better come Home.'

"We left off goin' for the mail after that for most a week, seein' how it discouraged Kellerman, until Jessup, the cattle boss, had to go over to the station to see about some steers he was shippin', and come back with a telegram which scattered our hopes promiscuous.

"'No more checks will be honored. Come home.'

"That kind of got Kellerman where he lived, for it seems this was the first time he'd ever been sent for a thing without gettin' it. They was a Castac man settin' in with us on the game and had got sort of familiar with the situation. Says he, sort of lookin' down his nose like: 'They is a coupla Mexicans back in the mountains here, got a sure enough charm for bear.'

"'Oh, I say, this is serious.' says Kellerman, and we all looks reproachful at the Castac man, thinkin' it was pretty poor play at this juncture. But our foreman had met this here Castac guy before.

"'You mean them two Greasers over to Whisky Flat?' says he.

"'The same,' says Castac.

"'And you think they could get a bear for Mr. Kellerman?'

"'If they was paid for it.'

"The foreman looked at Kellerman and then at the telegram."

"'Your credit's good until you get this?' he inquires.

"'If it's a sure-enough bear it's good in any case,' says Kellerman, beginnin' to draw breath.

"The foreman puts the telegram back in the envelope and seals it up. 'You left for Whisky Flat this morning,' he says, 'and I ain't a-goin' to deliver this till you come back, which will be in three days. I've noticed,' says he, 'if you give anything three days, it generally comes around right.'

"Well, that was sure-fire prophecy, for along in the third day back they come, Kellerman and Doc Shaffer, a two-year-old grizzly at the end of a hair-rope, and a story of how they captured him that sounded like this one of your friend's only more excitin'.

"It was readin' your friend's book set me rememberin'. They took him to the station, crated, in our chuck-wagon, which they had borrowed express. Only it don't seem no ways natural for a half-grown grizzly to eat out of your hand and answer to the name of Pedro, which is Mexican for Pete, in three days and a half. Howsomever, Doc Shaffer said it was the effect of the charm, and drinks and checks was flowin' free and plenty again, which was the main consideration."

"But you don't mean to say—" I expostulated.

"It was a charm all right," said Jerke, "but it didn't work steady. Long about three weeks after Kellerman had gone back to the city and we was gettin' over missin' him, the two Mexicans came over to Salt Crick on the rampage, lettin' out that it was a pet bear they'd raised from a cub and sold to Kellerman for three hundred dollars, half down and half when he got back to the city, and the half wasn't forthcomin'.

"They got our foreman to take it up for them, but nothin' ever come of it.

"I don't know exactly what was the rights of it—Mexicans mostly lies, in my notion[4]—but Doc Shaffer stood in with them. He was to have had ten percent on the profits for puttin' them on to Kellerman, and mourned copious for what he didn't get. It was while his grief was a-workin' on him that he sort of dropped that them tracks which kept Kellerman in this part of the country was made by him with malice and pretense, as the lawyers puts it. The same bein' a bear's foot which he had cut out of redwood bark, which is shaggy-like, and gets up before daylight to plant around in the damp earth where it would do the most good. Which goes to show," Jerke concluded, "that this here nature fakin' you read about ain't altogether a lit'rary game."

"But Kellerman's reports, the capture, the hairbreadth escapes—," I protested.

"Oh, *them*! He got them out of a book, aided and abetted by us boys, to the extent of our ability, an honest to goodness book, 'Adventures of Samuel Adams, Bear Trapper.' Djever hear of it?"

I had. Also I was to hear of it again in the most unexpected manner. Just then I was occupied with making up my mind whether or not to write the whole story to Seaforth as I had heard it.

I was still debating a year later when I put in at the house of my friend the Historian, to find him still pushing his thin hand, which age had refined, over endless pages of minute notes that only under the glass revealed their marvelous clear roundness. Never sure that I had got his attention, I gave him the count of my year's wanderings, and, strung between Noriega's shearing and certain verifications of early Spanish map-making, the crossing of my trail with Seaforth's.

The name aroused him. The historic method, he insisted, was debased by such intransigent uses—nature faking. Plainly he was on the side of the Most Distinguished Citizen.

"Still, I don't know but I owe them something—." The domed historian's head with the spreading aureole of hair and beard turned from me as he rummaged the shelves behind. "Among them they've talked my book to the surface again—it is to be republished with illustrations. After more than fifty years." He laid the thick brown volume before me. "'Adventures of Samuel Capen Adams,' the best bear book in America, if I did write it—."

The best, as I know it, the incomparable book of bears. The Historian turned it over in his beautiful old hands. "Perhaps I do owe something to the nature fak—fictionists. Fifty years! Maybe in a hundred somebody will take an interest in my history. After all, no genuine book is ever really lost—We may take this as evidence, mayn't we?"

"Never lost." I agreed with him. But what I should like to know—in the general distribution of credits, what share falls to Kurtz and Kellerman?

Notes to "Speaking of Bears"

1. Austin often misspelled the word she wanted to use, so it is interesting to wonder here if she means scald (as in hot) or skald (as in poetic), as either temperament might cause a person to choose the solitary trapper's life.

2. For an excellent explanation of "nature faking" see Ralph H. Lutts, *The Nature Fakers* (Golden, CO: Fulcrum, 1990).

3. Austin does not mean time here, she means boundary that if crossed is justification for death, as in this sentence from *The Land of Little Rain*: "The boundary of the Paiute country was a dead-line to Shoshones" (34).

4. Although some of the language in this story could be interpreted as racist, Austin's subtle storyteller's style disguises one truth—in this story, the *only* people who even might be telling the truth are the Mexicans and the narrator.

3

The Folk Story in America

1934

Now that I can look back on the whole scale of my story interests, I can see that I had always liked the folk story better than any other, the sort of story I heard my own ancients telling, the sort I learned very early to draw up out of incident and anecdote going on about me, and learned to run down in footnote and reminder among my elders. But the sort of story that was prevalent at the time, along in the early nineties when I began to be explicitly interested in the story as a literary medium, was very different from that in which other young people were then interested. I had slipped into the limitation of Washington Irving, when he said 'I consider the story merely a frame on which I stretch my materials. It is the play of thought and sentiment and language, the weaving of characters, lightly yet expressively, delineated, the familiar and faithful delineation of scenes of common life....' But the popular story of that period was not in the least like that. What editors of that day wanted was 'reading matter, next to which' advertisements could expediently be placed, of which the salient ingredient was what went by the name of local color. The more highly colored the better, and you might take as much space as you wanted for elucidating that color and spread it on as thickly as you liked.

But my own notion was that color was something you ought to find already on the reader's hands. What I wanted was a background completely existent, such as you find taken for granted in fairy tales, or in that single example of the short short story in its perfection, the story of the Prophet and the Woman Taken in Adultery. You weren't, in that story, held up on the question of what constitutes adultery, or the common behavior of prophets. The people were simply there with a given pattern of reactions, and the story happened. But the mode of the hour was that authors went to no end of trouble to account for and describe, until the whole atmosphere was so completely drenched with local color that you couldn't get into the story any way but by getting yourself thoroughly sloshed about in it.

There was an excuse for that, perhaps, in the circumstance that the fashion of life in any particular locality in the United States varied to a degree that induced variations in behavior, which had to be fully explained before the track of the story could be securely plotted amid them. But what I wanted was a certain solidity and alikeness of the underpinning of all stories, which you could take in a measure for granted, the way you could the universality of motive and behavior in a story like Cinderella. You didn't, for instance, have to explain the proud Sisters, nor the existence of Fairy Godmothers, and the ease with which pumpkins turned into coaches. But the world of the short story in my young day was so completely at variance with itself that you had to do an immense amount of constructing and explaining to make it come out right with the story incident. I suppose it was the perplexity I was in over this condition that made me notice at once, when I was brought in contact with trained hunting dogs, as I have explained in another place, that they were able to take an interest in stories about their own adventures. They could listen with pride or chagrin to their own stories as told by their owners; and very shortly after, I came in touch with sheep dogs and their attendant herders, and discovered that the dogs not only recognized familiar tales of their own adventures, but could, when the adventure was a lively one, relive it joyfully, and even get the drift of an unfamiliar tale told about some other sheep-herder's dog. The advantage of sheep dogs was, of course, that they were bred for the kind of intelligence that made communication possible between them and their masters, that it went on every day and all day, instead of being reserved for the infrequent occasion of the hunt, and that the vocabulary between dog and master was greatly extended by gesture, which expressed the story in terms of activity. A well trained sheep dog gathered the flock, set it in motion, turned it, stopped it, bedded it, kept count, collected stragglers, and took offensive measures against the enemy of the flock. Thus the dog learned the proper place in the flock of between two and three hundred individual sheep, learned to know when any of them were missing, and how, and in what direction to round them up.

It is probably not realized by the generality that every flock carries one black sheep, or a goat, to every fifty or so of flock members, and that these are placed so regularly in the flock that for more than a handful of flock members to be missing brings the black markers so much closer together that the loss is immediately noticeable. And with all that knowledge, it was possible to tell such dogs a story involving them in a characteristic flock incident. It was in discovering how a flock is patterned by its behavior possibilities that I came to a realization of how a story is made by adding behavior, unit to unit, so that an intelligent dog can enjoy remembered units of activity. And a little later when I came to the story telling habits of Indians, among whom tales are often told quite competently in sign talk, I began to understand that the whole story business consists in the creation of assorted patterns of selected single behaviors.

When I speak of Indian stories as patterns, I mean realistic stories, not myths, which are patterns of thought and ideation plotted on the constitution of life as it is understood among Indians. All Indians have both kinds; stories of the movement of invisible forces at work on the stuff of life, and stories of how life itself gets accomplished. Myth stories are patterned by the Indian's notion of how the invisible life forces are supposed to work, and realistic tales relate what takes place among the visible activities of behavior.

By the Paiutes, among whom I was initiated into the real stories, they were called One Smoke stories, being chiefly the sort of tales that get told around the fire in the intervals between ceremonial rituals, while the company relaxes itself with the little cornhusk cigarets filled with native tabac. One tells while the rest smoke, and then the next one in the circle leaves off smoking and tells another, short and explicit and packed with reality.

By such means I came up through the animal experience to the man nature and the genuine stuff of realistic fiction. To the worker in this field who has lacked my opportunities to study the business of story telling as it goes on between men and animals, it may sound surprising to say that among animal stories I found all the essentials of plot well developed, so that I shouldn't hesitate to tell in your presence a sheep story to sheep dogs who might be complete strangers to me, and guarantee their interested participation in it. One can see auto-storytelling going on among young animals of all the hunting kind, the story around which is plotted the complete activity of tracking out the movements of the prey, the creeping up of the hunter, the pounce, the attack and victory, and the rehearsal of the many times repeated process of successful hunting. Once I even saw a fox who had missed his spring at a rabbit go back and try it over again as if to satisfy his own question as to why he missed. I have often seen young animals rehearsing in advance the tribal complex in which the whole bag of hunting tricks is practiced, and I have seen a hunting mother slap her young for clumsiness in the try-out.

So one gets back to the fundamental of tale telling in the normal incidents of life practice as rehearsal, immensely important to successful life adventure. I can tell a story to wise sheep dogs which has as many as four elements: the flock, considered as an entity, the fraction of the flock which has strayed or been frightened off, the herder, who sets the story plot in motion, and the flock enemy, usually a coyote or a wolf. Later, when I put my knowledge to use in teaching in the Normal School at Los Angeles the art of Oral Story telling, I learned that it is very difficult to tell a story orally to human young which has more than four characters in it, and if there are more than that number, they have to be sorted under one title, as the three proud sisters of Cinderella, or the unassorted group of bystanders in the story of the Prophet and the Woman Taken in Adultery. With hunting dogs, however, I never managed to get more than three elements to a story, the master, the dog, and quarry. By the time I came to Indians, I had learned not only to expect no more than four active elements in a story, or if other elements entered, they were to be grouped under a title which made of them an entity, our tribe, the enemy, my clan, the other animals.

There is a trick which Indians are fond of employing when an incident has been particularly enjoyed, of repeating it, even to the exact words, with simply another character of the same group, another Indian or animal or object, as when in the Paiute story, Tavwots set out to catch the Sun in his snare, he asks and receives help from practically all the trees in the Paiute country, asking them individually, one after another, in the same words and getting the same answer. It is incredible the number of repetitions of that sort a given story will stand, when the primary incident is sufficiently interesting. In general, the number of them can be tied up with the repetitions allowed to other units of design in other arts, the number of times a musical phrase can be employed in the same tune, the repetitions of an item of design in a pottery pattern, of a movement in a dance. Usually, there is a disposition to make such repetitions follow the use of sacred numbers, four or six, according as the quarters of the Horizon are divided or the sacred colors listed. But these are mere literary flourishes, or embellishments, that give sanctity to narratives that have a more or less esoteric character. They are not used in realistic tales of the characteristic One Smoke type.

II

I had already acquired a certain knowledge of Indian tales before the years in which the incidents related began to take place, and I had a realizing dissatisfaction with the current American form of Indian legends, made over as most of them were, on the plan of the existing European folk tale. Whole volumes of Indian stories, as published formerly, have the disability that they have been remade and distorted out of their original form, to bring them into European resemblances, so that they lose all freshness and variety.

I was always, I think, aware of the underlying oriental trend of Indian myth and legend, owed to its Mongolian strain, but now that I was brought into direct contact with the Amerind myth on its native soil, I became aware of distinctions of method and style that even people who undertake to deal with them professionally fail to make. First of these is the differentiation given to every myth by its esoteric or exoteric uses, the values it has as sacred enlightenment, and its values as story merely. These values are almost always accompanied by the distinctions we give ourselves to the mere relation of Bible stories as entertainment, and their values as sacred instruction, which are, on the whole, distinctions of literary style, so that through following it the Amerind tales get into our literature as poetry or prose. And, in most cases, the literary quality which they lose as prose narrative is further depreciated by an attempt to remake them on European models. A few years ago a collection of Indian myths issued from one of our leading universities which failed completely to make this distinction between esoteric, or ceremonial, use of the legend in question, and the exoteric version.

It wasn't all at once, by merely saying the words, that I arrived at these distinctions myself. What I had finally to discover was that the economy of style which characterized the two modes of telling was no mere trick of words, but the essential item of the teller's grip on the quality of life out of which the story issued. If one were to tell Indian tales, or sheepherder's, or cowboy's, or bear hunter's—any sort of distinctively folk stories—they must be the sort of tales such people told each other with complete adjustments of the mode of life and the environment involved. The environment had absolutely to disappear into the story, with nothing left over. The story itself would have to be completely resolved, every item so satisfyingly disposed of that no question remained to be asked, nor explanation offered. Occasionally an explanatory phrase is offered, where a story is related from one tribal group to another, but in the main the tale carries all its implications as necessary strokes of the telling. Nor did I ever come, with all my inquiry into folk methods, upon the trick ending. With all due respect to Mr. Henry, in whose work the quality of folkness abounds, the trick ending is no true story teller's device. The nearest one arrives at a technical trick, in Amerind story, is that odd little stir of the tale, the pointing up of its intent, just before the end, like the warning rattle that advises one that the story is about to strike. When one listens to an Indian telling a story to other Indians, this is always shrewdly discernible, so that if you do not get it, you may be sure that the teller is taking account of your alien quality as a listener, or that what he tells figures in his own mind as a sketch, the shadow of a story not yet completely resolved.

III

Of minor technicalities, besides the skill with which the story is completely swallowed in the environment, there are two or three that cannot be omitted. One of these is the sparing use of names, which are seldom employed except where it is important to the story to do so. One tells a story of a man and his friend, "a woman that he likes," "that Sioux," any device whereby the actor is made to disappear into the background. When the teller is a character in the tale, he is kept in a state of nearly complete detachment. Of all the impulses that lead to story telling among aboriginals, exhibitionism figures least frequently. In telling, the mood of the incident is struck almost immediately, within the first two or three sentences, and it is always the mood of the story and not of the teller. No mistake that we make in the retelling of a first person story is further from the aboriginal method than to begin with the attitude of the teller to the tale, and gradually ease him into its complications. With the aboriginal, before the story is offered to an audience, its umbilical cord has always been cut.

What annoyed me excessively in my first volume of short stories was the insistence of the publishers that they should be each introduced by explanatory comment growing out of their occasions. Among aboriginals this sort of thing is never done. By making the story too intimately the possession of the teller, something of the possessiveness of the hearer is lost, and it is indispensable to the primitive teller that the story should stand to the hearer in place of an experience, which is the primary reason why it should be told at all.

I have used the term "realistic," the thing that happens, to describe the sort of story that gets called Folk Tale as distinguished from the Myth, in which things, figurative and imaginative, are made to do duty for realities not physically apprehended. But one has to remember that, for the primitive, many things get credit for actually happening which really occur in that borderland between things that have a palpable existence, and other things which have only a psychic reality; dreaming true, talking animals, mountains that walk, dead that return, and Gods that appear and hold converse. All of these things have a kind of believable reality to the Indian, on a plane from which he draws the note of mystery in dealing with them. One finds the same thing in Negro tales.... The point about the occurrence of these matters in Indian mythology is that where they occur without interference of another, allegedly higher culture, they are found in forms that go distinctly by the title literary, with beauty and dignity of language and ritual of phrasing. It is probable that this is the case everywhere where the language is native and uncorrupted. Certainly we realize that condition in the ancient languages of the world, precisely as it is known to be the case in the older Indian tongues, like the Zuni, and the Delaware, and the most developed languages of Old Mexico, so that we face the loss of explicit literatures, worthily so called, in every advanced tribe, dying out with its cultural decay, hymns, tribal epics, origin myths, histories, noble and persuasive moralities, all clothed with that quality of form which we agree in calling literary.

One of the items that may keep us permanently from securing these treasures of primitive literature, being cast away in the neglect of our tribal cultures, is, of course, the sacred characters they keep within the tribe, which makes them incommunicable. There is, for instance, at Taos Pueblo, still recited annually the tribal epic which takes two men each two hours to recite consecutively, of which not one line has yet been communicated to White attention. Presumably, there is a separate version of the epic for each of the remaining language groups of the New Mexico Pueblos, which, if we judge by the one which the skill of Frank Hamilton Cushing preserved to us from Zuni, is of superior literary quality, fully on a par with the scriptures of the ancient Jews, on which we so much depend for our own origins. And it is unlikely that we will ever get anything of them except the broken fragments that come down to us in their exoteric form as folk tales, disjointed, prosified, and shorn of their esoteric significance.

I do not mean to say that here in the Southwest the whole color and pattern of this rich folk literature is lost. Perhaps we are catching it in time to keep the original color and flavor of that portion of it which has shed its extra sacred quality, as it is actually told to Indian children. The loss of religious sanctions for these things has the advantage that it releases the material for literary treatment by younger members of the tribe. This new movement of appraisal which has begun at Duke University should prove helpful, and the presence in New Mexico of many writers intelligently aware of what there is to save or lose. Much of it has already passed by the process of osmosis, in contact around the camp fires of the desert. Something of the Indian method has been taken over by the Spanish speaking population, just as something of the legendary lore of Saints has been taken up from the Spanish by the Indians, something of the terseness and figurative quality has gone from the Indian to the cowboy and prospector. Will Rogers has served to slither the dry alertness of Indian humor into the American occasion. I recall with interested amusement that it was *The Mercury*, the smartest, forwardest of American magazines, that began first to publish my One Smoke Stories, and that other magazines were not too long in following with the Short, Short Story which is the true Indian genre.

One of the factors which works unconsciously in the mind to hasten the use of the native American folk tale, is the felt need of generically American expressiveness, figures, illustrations for the native quality of our national life which shall have an intrinsically American significance, things seen or remembered which take only native color, give back only a truly American resonance, something more valid than the faded hues of European myth. We have ceased to be even homesick for the European relevance; we are disposed to find in The Canoe That the Partridge Made, or The Man Who Walked with the Trues, the complete figure of comparison, the pattern coming out of our own primitiveness for our immediate emergency. All in all, there is a freshness about the native encounter which can be best matched, without more truly native adventure, with the land, the animal, the explicitly American instance. We are aware of being, at last, no longer merely past European nor prospective citizens; we are the Folk, the present American reality, disposed to realize on our immense and colorful inheritance of Folkness.

4

Supernaturals in Fiction

1920

The mind of man is a very curious place. It is a place in which it appears entirely logical to turn the professional ghost raiser, at a dollar a ghost, over to the police, and the same evening pay two dollars to see the Ghost of Hamlet's Father walk, by way of uplift. It is a place in which one may be nourished on tales of Talking Heads and Magic Carpets, and look with deep suspicion on the time- and space-exceeding marvels of modern invention. There never was an age that spent so much intellectual ingenuity as this one in proving that there never were and never could be any sort of beings but men. But among the stories most enjoyed by human kind and longest in circulation, about one character in every five is Supernatural, or one in every five incidents originates in a supernormal contrivance or attribute. Measured against the history of human society, any doubt that the world is crammed full of non-human, unordinary beings, is almost as new as electricity. The farther back you go into good and popular fiction, the fewer humans, the more gods, genii and fairy godmothers, the more elixirs of life and instantaneous transportations.

After an examination of the world's fiction which has been enjoyed long enough to be called classic, one inevitably concludes that if a story is to survive more than four or five generations, a liberal proportion of its elements must be non-natural.

Begin, for example, with Cinderella, beloved of the world's childhood: There is Ella herself, the proud sisters, who for structural purposes are to be treated as one, the stepmother, and the Prince. And for Supernaturals, there are the Fairy Godmother, the pumpkin coach, the magic transformation—three to four of the humans. Aladdin gives us five qhumans against the Slaves of the Lamp and the Ring and innumerable magic happenings, and this proportion holds throughout that universal favorite *The Arabian Nights Entertainment*. In the story of Joseph, making one element of all eleven brothers, and three of all the dreams since they figured on three occasions, we still have only five to three in favor of the natural. In the Iliad and the Odyssey we have the whole Olympian family so placed in juxtaposition to Trojans and Greeks that their mutual contacts furnish practically the entire machinery of the story.

So the proportion stands until after the collapse of Greek culture, when story making suffered an eclipse for several centuries. It did not rise again until the commonality had provided itself with a complete new set of Supernaturals, saints, angels, the whole Heavenly Host. Within the next five or six centuries the body of European fiction was increased by the addition of the Scandinavian, the Gaelic and British story cycles, each with its appropriate cast of superhuman characters. Apparently there were no important fictional inventions for some twelve or fifteen centuries except where Supernaturals could be found upon which to hang them.

It was the Greeks, however, who gave us the clue to the inevitableness of the not-man elements in every really treasured man story. They had to be there to satisfy man's invincible desire to see the wheels of the universe go round.

That is an academic and wholly unreliable bias which explains the long life of the Joseph and Aladdin and Ulysses tales on the ground that they were literature. It would be far truer to say that they became literature as a result of being liked: for whatever the ethnologists say of the origin of these stories, there is no doubt whatever that they have been popular.

Tales of Troy existed generations before Homer enclosed them in the clear amber of his verse. It is the best stories of any age that get the attention of the best stylists of that age. Few people read the original Mallory nowadays, but any one who will take the trouble to compare that version of the King Arthur legends with a modern Tennysonian rendition, will see the process of decanting a popular story from the "literature" of one age to another visibly going on. The test of a really popular story is the number of times it will survive such rebottling. The point at which these metamorphoses inevitably stop is the point at

which the Supernaturals are turned out of it. Because, as the Greeks discovered, the Supernaturals are necessary to make the story hang
together.

I do not suppose that, at the time Greek literature was at its best,
the Greek authors believed in their Olympians any more than Will
Shakespeare believed in the ghost of Hamlet's father. But the Greeks,
like ourselves, had a hankering to have the Universe explained. They
must know why, as well as how, things happened. And, as knowledge
then stood, without the intervention of the gods the story would not
hang together.

Precisely as we moderns go peering and poking under the dramatic
and spectacular phases of the European war, to put our finger on the
forces that would make it seem less of a delirious nightmare, so the
Greeks and Trojans must have sought for some sort of reasonableness
under the monstrous folly of a ten years' struggle. Clearly, something
bigger than Greeks or Trojans had been at work here. Otherwise there
was no logic or dignity in human living. Why should an Achilles sulk or
Ulysses waste himself at the court of Circe? Happily there were the
Olympians with a known propensity for meddling in human affairs.

Unfortunately for Greece, however, the shoving of responsibility
back upon the gods reached a point just a little beyond the capacity of
the average intelligence to follow. As soon as the gods began to stand
for abstractions, in the mind of the Greek writers, they ceased to be
interesting to Greek audiences.

No sort of literature can go on for very long, produced outside the
popular concept. When there were no more credible Olympians, and
the laws of social evolution had not been offered in their places, there
was nothing left but an unrelated jumble of incident. The end of the
Greek gods was also the end of Greek fiction.

A few centuries later, the rise of Christianity with its collocation of
Blessed Personages gave a new lease of life to the story-telling instinct.
By the introduction of St. Anthony, the Virgin, or, saving their pres-
ence, the Devil, any sort of a story could be rendered logical and sound.
For nearly ten centuries longer the world was a place about equally
inhabited by humans and non-humans, who got on fairly well together.

But with the spread of modern education the number of Supernaturals who could be credibly introduced into adult fiction, shrunk to

the few who still gathered under the wing of Romanism. After the Reformation the Devil himself lost dignity.

Dante and Milton, each in his way did what the Greek Dramatists had done for popular story making, and put an end to the use of the Christian Supernaturals as protagonists in fiction, by taking them out of the region of popular concept. From that time there was nothing left but your honest ghost to loose the springs of human action.

Though he has changed his character, the ghost is still so popular in story that even our remote and sophisticated Henry James could not forbear his own particular *Turn of the Screw*, and I have always believed that if Mr. Ibsen could have named the *deus ex machina* of his masterpiece, The Ghost of Oswald's Father, instead of the Law of Heredity, he would have made a much more popular business of it.

I have omitted the Christs out of their historic location in the cycle of Supernaturals, because, curiously, the Christs seem to have no sequence in time. Always there have been Christ stories, but whether they occur B.C. ten thousand or A.D. one, they differ only in details. All the other Supernaturals shape their behavior to the time in which they appear, but the Saviors of men have one story and one common behavior.

Considered as literary phenomena this is very interesting. All the god and devil stories appear to be efforts to explain the gaps and inconsistencies of human destiny. All the Christ stories are designed to close the gap between the Great God and Man.

We seem to have thought of as many ways of accounting for drouth, disease, sudden wealth and even death as there are tribes of men to think of these things. But in no land have we been able to think of more than one way of being reconciled to the Heart of the Universe. There have been as many Saviors as there have been people to need saving; but there had never been but one Christ plot. The only way we are able to imagine the world being saved is for a man to pay down himself on behalf of a protesting and unappreciative people.

Consider our own supreme achievement in this line, the story of Jesus. Could any fictionist who ever lived have invented anything with so wide an appeal and so long a hold on time? Its humans are so very human and its Supernaturals so far beyond the tarnish of "natural" evidence. We think sometimes that modern psychology has disposed of the "voices" and "visions" that very sparely characterize the story. But who will undertake to set a date at which we shall positively prove that there are no such things as angels, and that men may not return from the dead?

Actually, as a very little inquiry among your neighbors will convince you, the number of people who believe that there are no other sort of personalities than ours within the range of our environment, is small. And when you think of the democratic spiritual significance of the Jesus story, who, even, at the present rapid progress of democracy, can set a term to its sufficiency?

So it appears that, for the most precious things we have our relation to the Infinite and to one another, as these are expressed in story form, we are still tied up to the Supernatural, at any rate for another thousand years or so.

There is something diverting in all this, and something infinitely consoling. It goes to show that at bottom the human mind is absolutely convinced that life is not the haphazard affair it seems. There is an answer to the riddle, a string somewhere that if properly grasped will pull the whole business into order and beauty. The varied company of Supernaturals that have figured in our fiction are but the masks of a reality felt and appreciated but not known. And because these Supernaturals stood for the really vital things in human story, the rise of the modern novel, constructed wholly within the scope of things recognized as "natural," could not occur until we had developed a philosophy of social evolution.

The beginning of the movement to turn the Supernaturals out of fiction was noticeable almost as soon as the Anglo-Saxon strain began to make itself felt in European literature. It showed itself as a disposition to invest the supernatural elements in powers more than in personages. Magic came to take the place left vacant by the gods, the genii and the saints. In place of Hermes and St. Anthony there were Merlin and Morgan le Fay.

We had Faust, who acquired his super-normal powers in exchange for his soul, and Cagliostro who got his from nobody was quite certain where. Later we have Svengali and Sherlock Holmes as the most popular figures of current fiction.

Examine any "six best sellers," and the compelling characteristic of half their heroes, you will find, is the ability to make the unusual happen unaccountably. The explanation of just how it did happen is the obliging author's effort to save our face. It is the marvel which really interests. And if you doubt that the Supernatural has, though disguised, a hold upon our best literature, ask yourself what you will find in modern English fiction which for chances of longevity can be set beside *The Brushwood Boy* and *They.*

The modern problem novel at which every earnest fictionist tries his hand, is the Homeric Epic with its undashed attempt to explain the incidental in man's life by means of the fundamental.

And by just as much as the modern Homer is obliged to refrain from personifying his fundamentals, making laws and abstractions of them instead of Olympians, he restricts his audience to those who are as familiar with laws and abstractions as the ancient Greeks were with their gods.

If you doubt that the non-human elements, which we can no longer call supernatural, but agree on as superusual, are still formative in our written fiction, you may easily discover how large a part they play in the tales we tell informally to one another.

I do not refer to the healthy appetite for horror among the unlettered, with its train of "hants" and Walkers of the Night, but to the sort of incidents that any of your acquaintance might easily tell you out of their own lives, or their friends'. Ask, for example, for what the next ten persons you meet honestly believe to be genuine stories of any of the following:

The "hunch."

The presentiment.

The message from the dead.

The "psychic" communication.

You will probably find that the hunch is more widely believed in than any saint or genii ever was, is much more of a factor in private behavior than any social precept ever succeeded in being.

The hunch is no doubt a universal experience, the core of all the guardian angels, saints and "familiars" known to story. Having outlived all these avatars, it remains in possession of the field.

Remains also the fact that we do not know any better than we did before, what a hunch really is.

A hunch is something that seems to tap you on the shoulder of your sub-conscious being and advise you that a certain line of conduct is the most advantageous for you to take. If it pleases you to call it St. Joseph or the spirit of your dead grandmother there is no proved reason why you shouldn't.

The presentiment probably belongs to the same class of experiences as the hunch. It needs only to be accompanied by a strong faculty for visualization, or for auto-suggested sense perception of any sort, to become "clairvoyance," "audition" or "vision." As such it might take the place of the Voices, Annunciations and Spirit Warnings of the past. But still we do not know how we happen to have presentiments.

It also seems likely, from what we know of psychology at present, that communications from the dead or from living people at a distance, have common psychic elements. Most people have, or think they have, experiences that come under one or the other of these two classes. Although all the great spiritual leaders of the past attributed these experiences to Beings—Jesus spoke of them as Spirits, Joan of Arc believed them to be Saints and Angels, and Luther reports conversations with the Devil—it is not the fashion to do so now except in very limited circles.

What has happened, however, is that as we have discarded one personal hypothesis after another, there is a growing disposition to treat the experiences which gave rise to the ideas of gods and devils as veridical, worthy of serious attention.

The mind of man is, as I have remarked, a curious place. Shadows of all the great inventions, telegraphy, telephony, wireless, airships, submarines, have flitted through its dim regions since the beginning of time. Always they have come in the guise of imagined persons or powers. Hypnotism, auto-suggestion and thought transference figured in fiction long before they put on mortar board and gown.

When you come to think of these things, fiction seems the truest science in the world, the truest knowing. Once men told stories of amulets and magic formulas. Then there was a period when amulets and formulas were despised as childish and incredible. Now we understand that the powers did not reside in the charm but in the user, the power of auto-suggestion. Now educators use both medal and formula as aids to the self-residing power.

In regard to all these experiences are we going through similar phases which give rise to the assumption of beings not ourselves? Shall we come to a realization of these experiences as extensions of ourselves and our own powers far beyond our former limited conceptions of ourselves? Is the hunch not so much the advice of a friendly and communicable outsider, as an accidental use of poorly developed faculty? Do the dead really send us messages, or have we some rudimentary sense by which we become faintly aware of a world filled, as we have always believed it, with other Beings?

Then there are the Christ stories: all the saviors of mankind, Buddha, Prometheus, Quetzalcoatl. Why do we never change the pattern in all these reincarnations? Is it because there is something about the pattern as inevitable as the sum of the other two angles in a right angled triangle? Is it possibly, because there isn't any other pattern whereby men may be saved?

I have been thinking of these things rather frequently since the war, seeing men on all sides seeking for a new expression of reality.

I have asked what a fictionist might have to contribute, and I am struck as never before with the prophetic power of fiction in the realm of things that matter most to people at large. I have seen it point the direction of man's exploration of the material universe, the lands under the rim of the sea, the flying carpet through the air. I do not know any reason why fiction should prove any less the prophet in the realm of spirit. Could we, indeed, have such an appetite for fiction if it were not the first course of the final truth?

It gives at least, a new zest to reading, to think that this might prove to be the case.

5

Folk Literature

1928

It would be interesting to trace the divagations of a word that was originally meant to include all of us, and has come at last to refer only to
those minority groups whose social expression is the measure of their
rootage in a given environment. For by folk in this connection we mean
precisely people whose culture is wholly derived from their reactions to
the scene that encloses them, taking nothing from extra-tribal sources
except as these forcibly constitute themselves factors of that scene. It
was not in the original intention of the Founders that there should be
any such in the Republic. The early American ideal of the homogenous
group, completely penetrated by the Press and polarized by the Public
Schools, under an equality of opportunity which provided for every
individual his due ray from every part of the concave heaven, took no
account of the automatic limitation of receptivity by the completely
accepted background. Yet it is in the capacity for such acceptances, as
final in its fixation of social allegiance as the acceptance of the predestined mate, that the quality of Folk-ness is universally established.

And at the same time that the doctrine which was to free the major
American group from the condition of folkness was being set forth in
phrases that still have a ringing sound, provisions were being made for
the systematic exclusion of two minor fractions from this hypothetical
spherosity guaranteed by the Constitution. Thus from the very initia-
tion of the Democratic experiment, the predetermined limitation of the
social and economic environment of Indians and Negroes was creating
the circumstance once disclaimed by good Americans who, when
inquiry was afoot for the folk-product, cherished by European peoples
as the peculiar sign of their social integration, blandly explained that
"we have no folk literature because we have no folk." We fancied

ourselves then—and still, in many quarters—so completely exposed to all the cultural influence of the world at large as to be completely exempt from the disposition to local rootage. And we believed, perhaps as the inevitable corollary of our general repudiation of intimacy between man and the scene that supports him, that literature was only produced in the neighborhood of Universities, or at least of Lyceums and Chautauquas and other popular substitutes for the same.

Let me not be understood as slighting the sincerity, the industry, the gallantry, with which the major population of these United States gave themselves to achieving that condition of universal receptivity which alone would justify the democratic adventure. Nor was there lacking the missionary effort to induct the Indian and the Negro, without altering their environmental isolation, into the footless culture of first century of the Republic. Fortunately both Indian and Negro proved immune to cultural intimations unrelated to the actuality of their social environment. It is quite possible because folk-ness stood in the American mind for invidious social distinctions such as the Republic was constituted to deny, that our efforts have been so much more concerned with obliterating its evidence than with removing the conditions from which it took its rise.

At any rate, folk activity did go on in song and story and latterly in the plastic arts, untouched by our sedulously cultivated inter-tribal sophistication. It went on among the Negroes chiefly as lyrics—the only contribution of its kind in America which receives and deserves the classification of "spiritual"; it went on among the Indians as the still living fragment of an inestimable, wasted treasure of myth and music, dance, drama, and decorative design. All along the border of economic security, wherever pioneer conditions made of the natural environment a profoundly personal influence, folk literature arose with the lusty speed of American enterprise; among Creoles of the south, cowboys of the west, lumberjacks of the north. Early in the history of the Republic a considerable group of our best middle-class English stock were pushed, in part by the circumscription of their economic environment through slavery, back into the southern mountains where, in the course of three or four generations, out of that readjustment arose one of the most interesting folk literatures of the world. Its interest rests chiefly in the reversion of a language which at the beginning of this isolation had reached a degree of literary sophistication not surpassed in Europe. Here, cut off from contributory French and German influence, poor-white English reverts to an incisive, delicately florated Gothic dialect—Gothic, I mean, in its structural decoration—which, as revealed by Percy MacKaye, has all the "wildness of beauty and strangeness" of a fifteenth century Gothic carved wood interior which has miraculously rooted and grown into the leafage and jointure of a Kentucky and Tennessee woodland. In form the folk literature of the piney woods can be traced to English balladry and anecdote of the Hanoverian dynasties. Where it breaks into dialogue there are touches of splayed Elizabethan rugosity, but its imagery and descriptive phraseology exhibit an immortal freshness, such as seems to have characterized that other great Nordic transmutation in the Hellenic peninsula.

While this fortunately neglected offshoot of the King's English was budding, in the Spanish colonies, by similar process of isolation and adaptation, there stemmed, out of the great age of Lopa de Vega and Cervantes and all that Golden Century of Spain, a local culture, which by the time it was included, more by inadvertence than by actual conquest, within our territory had definitely taken on a folk character. Originally wholly Spanish in their mode of expression, the settlements along the Rio Grande actually received more from the deeply rooted Indian tribes of that region than any other of our European colonies. This was, of course, partly because the Indians of our Southwest had themselves arrived at a higher status of cultural sophistication. In taking over the food crop, the architecture and general economic complex of the Indians, the Spanish colonist gave to their folk-product an objective superiority which it still retains, so that the folk art of New Mexico, where it is still found at its best, is chiefly pictorial and plastic. What is left of its lyrical disposition, as was to be expected, is chiefly lyrical and dramatic.... Drama is scarcely written freshly in Spanish New Mexico anymore, but one still finds *corridos*, poetical narrative and comment on current events, springing spontaneously from people who are not always able to commit them to writing unaided. The folk song flourishes here, under the primitive copyright which makes it an offense to perform any man's song without his consent, and *coplas* as an accompaniment to ballad dancing are still made.

So much is being said of Negro folk-literature, and of Indian, though not always dependably, that it is unnecessary to recapitulate. Indian myth and song have had almost more than due attention, and have suffered much from the prevailing disposition to revamp them according to European models. This practice is especially to be regretted since it robs us of the essential service of Indian literature, which is to delimit from the racial elements the pure influence of the American scene as a constituent of literary form. Yet garbled as it has been, the resemblances of Amerind to American pattern reactions is sufficiently evident. It is more than probable that in the summing up of America's contribution in these two folk achievements of the profound influence of landscape line on literary composition will be the first, as the folk-reversion of English in the Kentucky mountains will probably prove to be the second, in importance.

Almost it begins to look as though that furious obsession of alikeness which has expressed itself in our culture through the medium of the Lyceum, the Chautauqua, and the Outline-Story, has defeated itself by the haze of its own speed to achieve what now is found to be fruiting from secret and neglected roots—literature which shall reveal in its form and flavor the true tang of the American soil. For on closer examination such roots are discovered threading their way to the core of American life from almost any aspect of it which, for any reason, is sufficiently ignored by the religiously undertaken programs of what is called culture. Wherever we have a group reaction to any aspect of our common life, expressed on no other experimental basis than the necessity of mechanical adjustment to it, we have folk attitude, invoking a folk expression. If most of the notions of Capitalists and Capitalism drawn and written in the *New Masses* are not folk lore, then our definition of folk lore needs revising. Here one meets again the swollen figure of the Ogre and the Giants that Jack killed, delimited by the same processes that gave birth to those ancient figures, and the labor hero nobly appareled as Jack Dullard who married the King's daughter....

And this brings us to the problem which has never been satisfactorily solved for the erudite, as to whether folk literature has been in every case produced by folk. Did the British Ballads aforesaid originate in the pot-house and the servants' halls, or in the Great Hall of the Manor, from which they eventually reached, by a normal process of abandonment, the levels of appreciation which have preserved them? One suspects the latter. Did not the ancient skalds and harpers sing and harp before Kings and heroes as well as to the underlings to whom listening was graciously permitted?...The really pertinent question to be asked here is whether, in a Democracy like ours, any other sort of literature is to be expected. For what we seem chiefly to have learned about democracy is that however much it may equalize opportunity, it has little or no effect on the range of individual receptivity.

6

The American Form of the Novel

1922

The novel has always concerned itself with such incidents of the life performance as have been found significant by the age in which they occur. Its scope has been combat when combat was the major occupation for men. When complete stratification had taken place in European society, the story-telling emphasis shifted to the set of circumstances by which the hero was introduced into the social strata in which he was henceforth to function. Thus, where the Greek long story was content to deal with the adventure of arms, the mediaeval romance made a feat of arms the means, subordinate to the event, of the hero's admission into high society, slaying the enemy as a prelude to marrying the king's daughter and sharing the kingdom.

When, however, the goal of man's serious endeavor became, as it did in the last century, some sort of successful escape from social certitude, the scope of the novel was extended to include the whole ground of his struggle and its various objects. Then came America and brought a state of things in which uncertainty multiplied as to what the objective of man's secret and incessant search should be. Except in a limited, personal sense we have never known in the United States just which of us is villain and which hero. In addition to the decay of recognized social categories, our novelists find themselves under the necessity of working out their story patterns on a set of shifting backgrounds no two of which are entirely conformable. I myself, and I suspect my experience to be typical, have had to learn three backgrounds, as distinct, except for the language spoken, as Paris, Gopher Prairie and the Scottish Highlands. While I do not complain to the gods of these things, I maintain that it gives me a disadvantage compared to Mr. Galsworthy, say, who, however rotten he finds the warp of English society to be, still finds it regularly spaced and competent to sustain the design of any story he may elect to weave.

There can be, of course, as many arrangements of the items of individual experience as there are ways in which experience can widely happen. But these are not so many as might be supposed. Varieties of personal adventure are more or less pulled together by the social frame in which they occur. One of the recognized criterions of veracity in a novel is the question, could, or couldn't, the main incident have occurred in that fashion in a given type of society. But such a question can only be asked by people who have acquired the capacity to feel truth in respect to their own environment. It can never be asked by people for whom appreciations of pattern, as it affects the literary expression of experience, have been stereotyped to the warp of relationships which are no longer admitted as social determinants. For every novel that the reviewer elects for critical attention, he discards a dozen others of possibly equal workmanship, for no reason but that they deal with patterns that have ceased to have—or perhaps never did have—constructive relation to the society in which we live. Or, in cases where high veracity and perfection of form compel his admiration, as in The Age of Innocence, he makes his point out of the very failure of validity in the background, itself a fragment of an earlier, outworn social fabric. Below the limit of a possible claim on his attention, every reviewer is also aware of scores of novels, eyeless and amorphic, kept moving on the submerged social levels by the thousands of readers who never come any nearer the surface of the present than perhaps to be occasionally chilled by it.

Aside from the questions of form, is not the difference between novels which compel our attention and those we lightly discard, just this validity of relation between social warp and individual pattern? It is not necessary that the supporting structure of society appear as subject matter, but a certain clear sense of it in the writer's mind.

It is hardly possible yet in America to produce so smooth an overwoven piece as Mr. Wadddington of Wyck, with the technique of one of those detached motifs of Chinese embroidery, in which, though everywhere to be traced, not one thread of the sustaining fabric is visible. Miss Sinclair works under the conviction that the social structure ought never to be treated by the novelist as part of his undertaking, but that, I suspect, is due to her never having worked on the disconcertingly spaced and frequently sleazy background of American society. What we have to look for here is the ability, on the part of the writer, to fix upon the prophetic trend of happenings. Such a novel as Main Street should sustain itself a long time as a record of our discovery of the Community as villain, or, if you feel as some of us do toward its leading lady, as hero.

It is this necessity, forced upon us by recent social developments, of finding new, because as yet undeclared, points of balance in the arrangements of the American elements of story design, that has given rise to the notion that in America the novel need not concern itself with form primarily. But this can hardly be the case if we are to think of novel writing as an art, subject to the condition of survival in time.

The novel, more than any other written thing, is an attempt to persuade, at its best to compel, men to give over for a moment the pursuit of the distant goal, and savor the color, the intensity and solidarity of experience *while it is passing.* It is of no particular moment which one of the currents of experience that loop and whirl and cascade and backwater through the stream of human existence, is selected. It is important however, that it be presented in the idiom, that is to say in the life pattern, of the audience for whom it is intended. What I mean by pattern is the arrangement of story elements in true relation to the social structure by which they are displayed. In this sense form becomes a matter of the span of perceptive consciousness of the selected audience.

This gives, in our inchoate American life, the greatest latitude of incident, but confines the novelist rather strictly to a democratic structure. It deprives him of fixed goals of social or financial or political achievement as terminal points, since none of these things have any permanence in the American scheme of things. The utmost the American novelist can hope for, if he hopes at all to see his work included in the literature of his time, is that it may eventually be found to lie along in the direction of the growing tip of collective consciousness.

Preeminently the novelist's gift is that of access to the collective mind. But there is a curious secret relation between the novelist's point of access and his grasp of form—and by form I mean all that is usually included in style, plus whatever has to do with the sense of something transacting between the book and its reader. Whoever lays hold on the collective mind at the node from which issues the green bough of constructive change, finds himself impelled toward what is later discovered to be the prophetic form. What, after all, is the slow growth of appreciation of a novelist of the first rank, but the simultaneous widening of our social consciousness to a sense of its own direction.

American novelists are often accused of a failure of form. But is this anything more than an admission of failure of access on the part of the critics? Characteristic art form is seldom perfected until the culture of which it is an expression comes to rest. Of all the factors influencing the American novel form, I should expect the necessity, inherent in a democratic society, of conforming more directly, at any given moment, to the *state* of the collective consciousness rather than to its *direction*, to be the determining item. This is what, generally speaking, conditions the indispensable quality of access. Under the democratic condition it can be achieved only by participation. There is no place in the American consciousness for the superior being, standing about with his hands in his pockets "passing remarks."

The democratic novelist must be inside his novel rather than outside in the Victorian fashion of Thackeray or the reforming fashion of Mr. Wells. He may, like Mr. Sherwood Anderson, be so completely inside as to be unclear in his conclusion about the goal, but there he is, Americanly, on his way. The reference of personal conduct to an overhead Judgment which forced the earlier novelist to assume the god in the disposition of his characters, has here given place to a true democratic desire of man to see himself as he is seen by the people with whom he does business. His search is not so much for judgment as revelation, quick, nervous appreciations of place, relationship and solidarity. But in every case the validity of the American form will rest upon that intuitive access to the collective consciousness, which it is the dream, and probably the mission of democracy to achieve.

7

Regionalism in American Fiction

1932

"Regionalism in literature," says Dorothy Canfield in a recent review of what she considers an excellent example of it, "is the answer to the problem of getting any literature at all out of so vast and sprawling country as ours." She might as truthfully have said it of any art and any country which is large enough to cover more than one type of natural environment. Art, considered as the expression of any people as a whole, is the response they make in various mediums to the impact that the totality of their experience makes upon them, and there is no sort of experience that works so constantly and subtly upon man as his regional environment. It orders and determines all the direct, practical ways of his getting up and lying down, of staying and going out, of housing and clothing and food-getting; it arranges by its progressions of seed times and harvest, its rain and wind burning suns, the rhythms of his work and amusements. It is the thing always before his eye, always at his ear, always underfoot. Slowly or sharply it forces upon him behavior patterns such as earliest become the habit of his blood, the unconscious factor of adjustment in all his mechanisms. Of all the responses of his psyche, none pass so soon and surely as these into that field of consciousness from which all invention and creative effort of every sort proceed. Musical experts say that they can trace a racial influence in a composition many generations back, and what is a race but a pattern of response common to a group of people who have lived together under a given environment long enough to take a recognizable pattern?

Everybody has known this a long time. We have known it about classic Greek and ancient Egypt. We know that the distinctions between Scotch and Irish and British literature have not been erased, have scarcely been touched by their long association of all three under one political identity; we know in fact that at last the pattern on Irish regionalism has prevailed over polity, and it is still a problem of the Irish Free State to withstand the separative influences of regionalism on their own green island. We recognize Moorish and Iberian elements in Spanish art, at the same time that we fully realize something distinctive that comes to this mixed people out of the various regional backgrounds within the Spanish peninsula. Knowing all this, it is rather surprising to find critics in the United States speaking of regionalism as something new and unprecedented in a territory so immensely varied as ours. The really astonishing thing would have been to find the American people as a whole resisting the influence of natural environment in favor of the lesser influences of a shared language and a common political arrangement.

Actually this notion, that the American people should differ from all the rest of the world in refusing to be influenced by the particular region called home, is a late by-product of the Civil War and goes with another ill-defined notion that there is a kind of disloyalty in such a differentiation and an implied criticism in one section of all the others from which it is distinguished. It would be easy to trace out the growth of such an idea, helped as it is and augmented in its turn by the general American inability to realize the source of all art as deeper than political posture, arising, as people truly rudely say, in our "guts," the seat of life and breath and heartbeats, of loving and hating and fearing. It is not in the nature of mankind to be all of one pattern in these things any more than it is in the nature of the earth to be all plain, all seashore, or all mountains. Regionalism, since it is of the very nature and constitution of the planet, becomes at last part of the nature and constitution of the men who live on it.

Since already a sense of truth of these things, as applicable to our own country, has worked through to the uncommon consciousness, our real concern is not to argue the case, but to fortify ourselves against the possibility of our missing the way again by failing to discriminate between a genuine regionalism and mistaken presentiments of it. We need to be prompt about it, before somebody discovers that our resistance so far has been largely owed to intellectual laziness which flinches from the task of competently knowing, not one vast, pale figure of America, but several Americas, in many subtle and significant characterizations.

As a matter of fact, our long disappointed expectation of the "great American novel," for which every critic was once obliged to keep an eye out, probably originated in the genuine inability of the various regions to see greatness in novels that dealt with fine and subtle distinctions in respect to some other region. But we have only to transfer this wishful thinking for a single book, or a single author, who would be able to overcome our inextinguishable ignorance of each other, to Europe to become aware of its absurdity. To Europeans our American regional differentiations, all comprised under one language and one government, are very puzzling. That is one reason why they have seized so promptly on *Main Street* and especially on *Babbitt* as just the broad, thin, generalized surface reflection of the American community and American character which the casual observer receives. Babbitt is an American type, the generalized, "footless" type which has arisen out of a rather widespread resistance to regional interests and influences, out of a determined fixation on the most widely shared, instead of the deepest rooted, types of American activity. That Babbitt is exactly that sort of person and that he is unhappy in being it, is probably exactly what Mr. Lewis meant to show. But that millions of Americans rise up to reject him as representing "our part of the country" only goes to show that, deep down and probably unconsciously, all the time that one set of influences has been shaping the shallow Babbitt citizen, another set has been at work to produce half a dozen other regionally discriminated types for whom there is, naturally, no common literary instance.

Perhaps the country does not fully realize that in rejecting Babbitt as our family name, it has declared for the regional types such as the best American fictionists have already furnished us. Probably the American reading public never has understood that its insistence on fiction shallow enough to be common to all regions, so that no special knowledge of other environments than one's own is necessary to appreciation of it, has pulled down the whole level of American fiction. It is more than likely that even the critics, who can be discovered surrendering to the idea of strongly marked regional fiction, have no notion of the work they are cutting out for themselves under the necessity of knowing good regional books when they see them. But there it is, the recognition and the demand. People of the South aren't satisfied to go on forever reading novels about New York and Gopher Prairie, people of the

Pacific Coast want occasionally to read "something more like us." They are willing to be tolerant and even interested in other regions on consideration that they get an occasional fair showing for themselves.

Fortunately, if we go back far enough, we have plenty of regional fiction to furnish a prototype and a criterion of criticism. It is, in fact, the only sort of fiction that will bear reading from generation to generation. Any confirmed novel reader of more than a generation's experience, or any teacher of English, should be able to name a score of them offhand. I begin my own list with *Queechy* as the best novel of rural life in New England ever written. I should begin with one of Herman Melville's, except that I am trying to omit for the moment regionalism which has also a narrow time limit; the environment of the whaler's sea that Melville knew has already been eaten up in time. I would name Hawthorne's *The House of the Seven Gables* rather than *The Scarlet Letter*, the latter being less of the land and more of the temper of Puritanism, more England than New England. To these I would add something of that gifted author of *The Country of the Pointed Firs*, Sarah Orne Jewett. Of Henry James, *Washington Square* most definitely fulfils the regional test of not being possible to have happened elsewhere. Out of New York I would choose *The House of Mirth*; but we have Hergesheimer's *Three Black Pennys* and *Balisand* and James Branch Cabell's least known, and to my thinking, best, *The Rivet in Grandfather's Neck*....

In the Mississippi Valley, one thinks at once of *Tom Sawyer* and *Huckleberry Finn*. Along the Middle Border there are Hamlin Garland's earlier tales, such as *Main Travelled Roads*; and on the edge of the Plains are Ed Howe's neglected masterpiece, *The Story of a Country Town*, and Willa Cather's *My Antonia*. Of the Southwest, unless you will accept the present writer's *Starry Adventure*, there is as yet very little genuinely representative—not that there are not stories of that country which are well worth the reading, and at least one immortal short story, Stephen Crane's *The Bride Comes to Yellow Sky*. Our Southwest, though actually the longest-lived-in section of the country, has not yet achieved its authentic literary expression in English. On the California coast there are a number of entirely characteristic short stories. Chester Bailey Fernald's *The Cat and the Cherub* comes instantly to mind, and at least two of Frank Norris' novels.

This is to name only those titles which occur irresistibly in this connection—fiction which has come up through the land, shaped by the author's own adjustments to it—and leave out many excellent and illuminating works which are colored, not only by the land, but by the essence of a period, a phase of its social development, a racial bias, a time element too short to develop essential characteristics. Such as these are the short stories of George W. Cable, and Grace Medard King of Old Louisiana, Bret Harte's tales of "Forty-Nine," and such delicate but inerasable sketches as F. Hopkinson Smith's *Colonel Carter of Cartersville*. I should think, indeed, that an importantly readable anthology of tales dealing with these local rather than regional shorter phases of American life could be easily gathered; but I am concerned chiefly to establish a criterion of what is first class regional fiction than to name every item that could possibly be included in that category. Lovers of W. D. Howells will wonder why his name does not appear here. If it belongs here, it is largely on account of *Silas Lapham*. Many sections of America could have produced Silas, but the things that happened to him in Howells' story could have happened only in Boston, and in that sense it is a true regional expression, and very likely will be estimated as Howells' best piece, chiefly because it has that deep-rooted motivation which is the essential quality of regionalism. But it has always seemed to me that Howells was the first, and the most eminent, of the American novelists responsible for the thinning out of American fiction by a deliberate choice of the most usual, the most widely distributed of American story incidents, rather than the most intensively experienced....

In all this instancing of archetypes, we must by no means leave out the books for children which belong in this list, and more than any other sort of literature overlap in the lists. We begin chronologically with Cooper's tales, of which half a dozen are absolute types, and then think at once of *Tom Sawyer* and *Huckleberry Finn*. It is only because the Alcott books are less picaresque that we fail to realize them as not the less regional, possible only to a long settled culture, so much longer settled than most American cultures at the time they were written, that much of their charm for the country at large lay in the note of nostalgia for the richer and more spiritual life which they aroused. This writer, who read as they came fresh from the pen of the Boston spinster, knows well how intimately they presented the social and moral aspirations of the still crude Middle West of that time. It is their profound fidelity to what was the general American feeling for the best in family life that makes the Alcott stories still moving and popular. It is the greatest mistake in the world not to recognize that children are affected by these things, being at heart the most confirmed regionalists. What they like as background for a story is an explicit, well mapped strip of country, as intensively lived into as any healthy child lives into his own neighborhood....

If I name nothing modern it is because my acquaintance with modern literature for children is too scanty for me to feel sure of naming the best. When I was young the best of everything appeared in *St. Nicholas*, and the best was always explicitly localized, dealt with particular birds and beasts, trees and growing things, incidents that had their source in the four great causatives: climate, housing, transportation, and employment....

But there is another story-region to which every American child has right of access, all the laws of which have been so violated by well-meaning and ill-formed writers, that it ought to be a penal offense to keep on doing so—I mean the world of American Indian lore. This world begins in the dooryard of every American child; it can be fully entered at the edge of every American town, it can be looked out upon from every train window and crossed by every automobile. But so ignorant of this region are most grown up Americans, that there are but three guides to whom I could unhesitatingly recommend the exploring child to trust: Joel Chandler Harris, James Willard Schultz, and Arthur Parker. There are, of course, individual works, such as Frank Hamilton Cushing's *Zuni Folk Tales*, which are absolute in their transcription of Indian regionalism.

But the trouble with ninety-nine out of every hundred Indian books offered to American children is that their authors fail to know that everything an Indian does or thinks is patterned by the particular parcel of land which is his tribal home. Thus at its very source the processes of regional culture, from which the only sound patriotism springs, are corrupted by the same inchoate jumble of environmental elements which so irritates us when pointed out by distinguished foreigners.

Until within the last twenty years the literary expectation of the United States could be quite simply allocated to New England; New York City; a "misty midregion" known as the Middlewest, as weird as Weir and not any more explicitly mapped; to which append the fringing Old South and the Far West. At the present, the last two have completely receded into the dimension of time past, The Old South has given rise to the New South; the Far West has split into the Southwest, the Northwest, the California Coast, and the Movie West. Cleavages begin to appear in the Middlewest, outlining *The Great Meadow*, the title of the best book about the section just south of Ohio. Farther north lies the Middle Border and Chicago. Within New York City we are aware of the East Side and Harlem which is the capital of the new Negro world, each producing its own interpreters. Even in Indian region there is faint indication of splitting off from the children's Indian country of a meagerly explored adult interest.

To the average citizen, notice of these recent annexations to the literary world comes in the form of a new book which everybody is talking about, dealing with life as it is lived there, as it unmistakably couldn't be lived anywhere else. And immediately the average citizen who, however much he wishes to read what everybody else is reading, secretly hankers to be able to discriminate for himself, begins to cast about for a criterion of what acceptable regionalism in literature should be. For to be able to speak of the credibility of reports of the various countries contained within our country requires a nimble wit and a considerable capacity for traveling in one's mind. How, the reader inquires inwardly, without having lived it myself, shall I feel certain that this book does give in human terms the meaning of that country in which the action of the story takes place? One might answer shortly, by the same means that it has become a proverb in the country where I live that "a wool grower knows a wool buyer." Whoever has lived deeply and experientially into his own environment, is by so much the better prepared to recognize the same experience in another. But there are criteria not to be ignored for recognizing regionalism in literature.

The first of the indispensable conditions is that the region must enter constructively into the story, as another character, as the instigator of plot. A natural scene can never be safely assumed to be the region of the story when it is used merely as a back drop—not that the scenic backdrop cannot be used effectively by way of contrast, or to add a richer harmonization to a story shaped by alien scenes. . . . Willa Cather does it most appealingly in *Death Comes for the Archbishop*. I am often asked if this last is not what I mean by a "regional" book of the Southwest. Not in the least. The hero is a missionary arriving here at an age when the major patterns of his life are already set; a Frenchman by birth, a Catholic by conviction and practice, a priest by vocation, there is little that New Mexico can do for him besides providing him an interesting backdrop against which to play out his missionary part. Miss Cather selects her backgrounds with care, draws them with consummate artistry, in this case perverting the scene from historical accuracy, and omitting—probably, herself, in complete ignorance of it—the tragic implications of its most significant item and so makes it convincing for her audience. I am not saying that this is not a legitimate literary device. That Archbishop Lamy, who was the historic prototype of Miss Cather's leading character, also missed the calamity to Spanish New Mexican culture, of the coming of the French priests, is the one profoundly human touch that so competent a literary artist as Miss Cather should not have overlooked. It makes her story, with all its true seeming, profoundly untrue to the New Mexican event, which removes it from the category of regional literature.

One of the likeliest mistakes the inexperienced reader will make in allocating books to their proper regional source, is to select stories about the region rather than of it. Such a reader would for example class *Uncle Tom's Cabin* as a southern book, when, in fact its approach, its moral and intellectual outlook is New England from the ground up, and so are its most telling characters. The South never saw itself in Harriet Beecher Stowe's light, never looked on slavery as she displayed it. Southerners would not deny the book's regional character, but they are still protesting it after nearly three-quarters of a century that it is not of their region. In the same manner, old Californians, forty years ago, could be heard denying the regional authenticity of *Ramona*. They recognized neither themselves nor their Indians in Helen Hunt Jackson's presentation. The regionally interpretive book must not only be about the country, it must be of it, flower of its stalk and root, in the way that *Huckleberry Finn* is of the great river, taking its movement and rhythm, its structure and intention, or lack of it, from the scene. In the way that Edna Ferber's *Cimarron* isn't of the land but pleasingly and reasonably about it.

With these two indispensable conditions of the environment entering constructively into the story, and the story reflecting in some fashion the essential qualities of the land, it is not easy to put one's finger on representative regional fiction.... Work of this kind comes on slowly. This is the essence of the undertaking, time to live into the land and absorb it; still more time to cure the reading public of its preference for something less than the proverbial bird's-eye view of the American scene, what you might call an automobile eye view; something slithering and blurred, nothing so sharply discriminated that it arrests the speed-numbed mind to understand, characters like garish gas stations picked out with electric lights. The one chance of persuading the young reader to make these distinctions for himself would be to whet his appreciation on the best regional literature of our past so that he may not miss the emerging instance of his own times.

8

Art Influence in the West

1914

Whoever undertakes to discuss art influence brings up sooner or later at the Greeks. I prefer to begin there, and to begin with that one of its sources which is not peculiarly Greek, but eternal: I mean with Greece. Whatever a people may make will resemble the thing that people look on most; so that the first guess as to what is likely to come out of any quarter is a knowledge of the land itself, its keen peaks, round-breasted hills, and bloomy valleys. Greek polity had never so much to do with the surpassingness of Hellenic art as the one thing the Hellenes had nothing whatever to do with—the extraordinary beauty of the land in which they lived.

However much it is possible to derive the varied and intimate art of Italy from Greek influence, it is impossible to ignore the variations that mark just the differences between the topographies—mass, contour and color—of the two peninsulas. In attempting to forecast the probable shapes of art in any quarter in America, it becomes of prime importance to know whether the contours of that region are austere, dramatic, or slow and gracious, and, above all, whether it is colorful. Given to all quarters an equal chance at man, the richest in color will bring the quickest reactions. And of all America the most strikingly colored is the strip lying along the south Pacific coast "nearest to the terrestrial paradise," as the old Spanish romance puts it, "called California."

In the early days, when all the West was full of a belt-loosening, breath-easing sound as men accommodated themselves to its largeness, the color of California was a thing to make one gasp. It affronted the puritan temperament with its too abundant charm; gold it was, and blue and amber, over miles and miles of up-flung foot-hill slopes and indolent mesa. Beyond that it melted, between green and blueness, to peaks of opalescent white. It was a country of which one of the wittiest of its writers said, "You couldn't tell the truth about it without lying," and got into the blood of the Iowans and New-Englanders within a generation. It charged not only their hopes, but their speech; made it rich in figures, full of warmth and amplitude. It had even more obvious and commercial results.

On one of those frequent cross-continent trips growing out of an inability to reconcile a desire to enjoy the charm of the West with the necessity of doing business in New York, I met a buyer of women's garments for a large Los Angeles house. In the course of the acquaintance she explained why it was that my clothes, which seemed quite all right in South Occidental Boulevard, had the effect on Fifth Avenue of being noisily out of place. They were perfectly good clothes and appropriately expensive, they bunched up in the right places or displayed a modish slimpness; but they put me decidedly out of the picture. The distinction was too subtle for me to grasp, but knowing nice distinctions of that kind was the buyer's business. She said it was a question of color; not so much of intensity, but of expert arrangements by which the dress of the Westerner is made to reflect the total effect of bright sun, richtoned landscapes, and a life spent largely in the open air. The buyer expressed it more crudely than that, but she knew to a dollar in buying for Los Angeles how far she could carry the instinctive feeling of human kind for harmony with its environment.

It comes out, this lurking preference of the land for color, in that latest toy of the West, a world exposition. Whether or not they succeed in making it a bigger or a better or more interesting exposition, in one thing the West has satisfied the secret desire of its heart: it has made this exposition the richest dyed, the patterned splendor of all their acres of poppies, of lupines, of amber wheat, of rosy orchard, and of jade-tinted lakes. Beside a sea which runs from lion color to chrysoprase and sapphire blueness, they have laid down a building scheme which is as bright as an Indian blanket. This is the first communal expression of the kind on a scale large enough to take account of. Probably one would have to hark back to the days of Pompeii and the Greco-roman splendor to find its like, and be safe in prophesying from it a more vivid burst of decorative art. That is to say, if there is anything in comparative influences, for the color of California is to the color of Italy as a rose is to its pressed remembrance in a book.

Taking that good look at the West which is the first requisite to knowing what is to come from it, one is struck at once with the extraordinary definition of form in the landscape. The high mountain-edges deserve their specific name, Sierras—toothed, cutting edges. The foothills, even under thick chaparral, never lose their bold outlines; the pines upon the farthest ridges preserve their perfect spires; and the low, round-headed oaks, both the roble and the encina, have all been put into the landscape with the same brush. Farther south and east the buttes, squared to the sky-line, repeat the flat note of the mesas with insistence. One has, however, to turn square about, face to the Old World for a moment, to understand just what this may mean in the final product of the West. One must recall that the glory of Gothic architecture comes from its being a sublimated memory of a forest, its clustered trunks, its crossing boughs, leaf-stained light and rare chiaroscuro, and that the Egyptian expressed the massiveness of natural stony outcrops and the relief of shadowy caves from the glare of the sun. Lands which have strongly accented features from the hands of the World Builder are those which produce the lasting types of architecture, not only by the superior degree to which they stamp themselves upon the memory, but in the demands which they make for special ways of being lived in. Here in the West the suggestion made by the soil and the wild growth has already been accepted by the aboriginal. The castellated mesas have produced the flat-roofed pueblo types of dwelling, which, mixed with the elements happily introduced by the Spanish missionaries, has become one of our most characteristic styles of domestic architecture. But the peculiar gift of the Southwest to a genuine American form is the one which takes its name from the Indian bungalow on which it is remotely based. In fact, it is very little like anything in India, and has much more kinship with the American Indian wickiup both in its form and its adaptation to the exigencies of living. In other words, it is derived from the forms of life native to the land. Go up beyond Pasadena some day when the chaparral is in full leaf, and you will discover that the preferred type of dwelling repeats the characteristics of the encinal, with low, slightly pitched roofs and pillared entrances. You dive into one out of the heat and glare of the day as the rabbit into its tunnel. Southern California runs to encinal and bungalows as naturally as the North runs to sharp, sloping roofs and pointed firs. It is written in the Baedekers that the form of Milan's marble miracle was suggested by the springing stalks of marsh grasses, but it is not said anywhere often enough that if a man with the soul of an architect were brought up in the California Tulares, amid all those miles and miles of thin, graceful reeds, breaking at the top into arching, airy inflorescence, he might easily touch the inspirational sources of Milan. It is all a question of looking four hundred years forward or four hundred years back.

These two, then, must be thought of as affecting the final form of Western art—color and high simplicity of form combined with great intricacy of detail.

It is inevitable that the first response of a people to the shaping hand of beauty would be expressed in that which meets the eye, but there is another factor in life in California likely to have a profound effect on the kinds of qualities of its art product, one which brings us a little nearer to the influence of ancient Greece and Italy: I mean the element of pageantry in life as it is lived there.

Variations in the artistic product of any nation can be scaled very nicely to the degree to which the people live with their land rather than off it. There is much in the difference between Greek and Italian art which can be directly traced to such obvious circumstance as that the Greeks, when they were not conquering, talked philosophy, and the Romans returned to their farms to raise turnips. It is only critics of art, and not artists, who maintain that art and turnips have nothing to do with each other. For the Romans did not only plant turnips and harvest them; they understood that there is a god of turnips, an essential essence of plowed fields and dung-heaps and steaming oxen, which must all be brought into harmony by prayer and sacrifice before turnips could come forth properly to feed and comfort the nation.

Just how it works is not easy to say,—it is in part perhaps a matter of feeding—but the great art-producing peoples have also been great agriculturists, much given to the joyous expression of their relation to the land they live in by green-corn dances, cherry-blossom fetes, and processions to Pomona. Any one familiar with the West must see in the tendency toward rose tournaments, apple fairs, and festivals of Raisina Regina, a return to this instinctive method of dramatizing the working partnership between man and the forces of nature.

No doubt it is in part the effect of topography. Everything, even the daily alternation of night and morning, tends to appear more dramatic in a mountain country; mile-long shadows move as dials across the valleys, cloud masses do not sail an open sky, but wheel and enfilade between the ranges; storms are not obscured in a flat horizon, but are seen to gather and break, and suns come out as in an amphitheatre. When I first knew that country which is watered by the Merced, Tuolumne, Kings, and Kern rivers, a country now producing food enough to support a small kingdom in Europe, it was overrun by little, long-armed Basque and French herders and their wandering flocks. It embraces in Hetch-Hetchy, Yosemite, and Kings River Cañon, the most stupendous scenic panorama of America, but the herders read it as a dog reads the face of its master. I remember how in May and June they would go peering along the edge of the down-pouring rivers for the floating yellow scum, pollen drift from the forests hundreds of miles away on the uplifted flanks of the Sierras. By the date of the first appearance of the floating pollen, and the quantity, they judged whether the summer feed would be full or scanty, and on indications as slight as these they bargained with the dealers who came out from San Francisco for their spring lambs. Intimacies such as these between the land and the people breed poets faster, and much better ones, than do universities.

Undoubtedly, the development of the creative spirit in the West is affected by the sense of sustained vitality in nature. A blossoming almond-orchard is not only a beautiful thing; it is also an inescapable thing; it scents the air for almost as many miles as its delicate, roseate cloud takes the eye along the foot-hill slopes. Swarms of fallen petals drift in the roadways like snow. And the long rows of the low-trimmed muscats, reaching out from vine to vine with advancing summer as though to take hands against the weight of the harvest—how they assault us with the visible process of earth and sun and air made into wine and food for man! At every turn the consciousness of something doing, something vitally connected with the large process of nature and our own means of subsistence, raises the plane of expectation. There *is* something doing every minute in a country of such varied topography, as the procession of harvest follows the season. Orange-picking begins in December and overlaps the pruning of the deciduous orchards. The smoke of the last burning has scarcely passed from the shorn trees of the highest, most northerly valleys when the flowering of almonds and apricots opens the honey harvest. The berry-pickers move in solid phalanxes from the cherry lands of Napa and Santa Clara to the river bottoms, and from that on to the August hop-picking and the raisin-drying, all labor is in flux. It passes up and down the great Twin Valleys in "free companies," working, eating, and as often as not sleeping in the open. During the brief season of the rains it is housed in packing sheds and preserve factories, but for the greater part of the year the human laborer is as much a part of the great outdoor pageant as the woodpecker or the ant.

All this makes for a kind of understanding of nature that is as different from the afternoon-walk kind of nature-loving as marrying a woman and having children by her is different from writing a sonnet to one's mistress's eyebrow. The mastery of rivers and snows and granite mountains and their conversion into crops and light and mechanical power raises the average plane of human activity all through.

It should mean that in California we shall have not necessarily poems written to a redwood and pictures of snow-capped ranges, but that whatever is written and printed should evince breadth and power. The final achievement of the people among whom this takes place ought to be a newer and more consoling expression of man's relation to the invisible, to the trend and purpose of things. In other words, one would expect the art of the West to be strongly religious in its implications. Already one sees indications of this tendency in that most native of institutions, the outdoor theatre. There are enough of these delightful places of entertainment in California to be able to speak of their development as a feature of Western community life, and their evidence as to the trend of community thought is singular and convincing.

One instance of the earliest and most notable of these, the theater of the Bohemian Grove, serves our purpose better for being the best known and most unconscious. The grove, a stately recess in the redwood forest north of the bay, is the summer playground of a group of San Franciscans who are supposed to have distinguished themselves either in the creative arts or in the more personal art of living. Outside of this summer precinct they are preeminently of that strip for whom the whole of American literature is supposed to be keyed down to the compass of a grown-up nursery-tale, the t.b.m.'s who hang around the neck of American drama like the traditional millstone to prevent its soaring to its possible and predestined heights. And every summer these tired businessmen, on an occasion denominated "High Jinks," produce a play which by popular deduction ought to be the concentrated extract of all the Broadway atrocities ever perpetrated in the name of entertainment. Only it isn't. It is usually poetic in form—excellent poetry, too, on more than one occasion—it is symbolic in character, and distinctly religious in tone. That is to say that it tends to choose for its theme some aspect of man's relation to the invisible, inescapable forces of life. A year ago it was the conquest of fear in that dark region of the heart of man which once found its expression in the gargoyles of our most Christian cathedrals, the spawn of cowardice and imagination. And if the conquest of fear isn't an effort in the direction of true religion, what is it? As nearly as can be made out by report, for no woman can know anything of them except by report, the Bohemian performances approach more nearly the Elysian mysteries than any modern occasion. All without conscious imitation and by the simple process of giving the Bohemians exactly what they want. It is true, however, that there are many things one can not even want in the presence of trees that might remember the drouth in the time of King Ahab, when the ravens fed Elijah.

It is not so easy to discern this native tendency behind so stupendously mechanical a thing as a world exposition. You have to see it not as the final expression, but as a pageant of things, the procession around the Sabine farm in honor of the god of the turnips which Lucilius ate; the joyous recognition that there is a god of seed-time and harvest, of bridges and rivers and dams, and that we are on very good terms with him.

Another determining force in shaping the art of a country, which it is impossible to overlook, is the prepossession which the citizens bring to it. The Argonauts of forty-nine brought the spirit of romance, and left us with the joyous disregard of artistry which is the best ground for a new art to spring from. The Franciscan fathers contributed one of our two dominating types of architecture and a style of furniture which gains favor steadily. The Conquistadores bequeathed a little of the romantic manner and a poetizing tendency in names of places. The Japanese and Chinese have done much in their wares to satisfy and foster the Western love of color in decoration....

It has remained for the rejected and downtrodden aboriginal to leave a determining mark. In color, in decoration, and in design the Indian note has struck upward like the thorn through the foot which treads the thorn-bush. It is very noticeable in the Exposition of San Diego; it is shaping by slower and less sensible degrees the forms of verse and drama, it sounds not as an alien strain through the music of the West, but as the plaintive, intimate note of the land itself, the earth cry below the song of the harvest. What one observes at present is a resemblance growing out of something like the aboriginal surrender to the environment rather than any deliberate appropriation of aboriginal motives. Not until this vanishing race attains the full dignity of extinction will its musical themes and decorative units pass into the artistic currency of the West.

But when you reflect that the Greeks began with just these things, great natural beauty, an adventuring, colonizing people such as settled the Sacramento and San Joaquin, and with a legendary and dramatic representation of man's relation to vast invisible forces, it is possible to believe that people beginning there and on a scale so much more magnificent will be justified in any expectation. Any one going west to look for it must find the index of what the art of the West is to be not in the art palace, but in life as it is lived there, in the mastery of modes of living in which the West suggests its as yet unutterable things.

9

Non-English Writings II: Aboriginal

1919

Probably never before has a people risen to need a history of its national literature with so little conscious relation to its own aboriginal literature. Yet if we extend the term America to include the geographical and racial continuity of the continent, unbroken at its discovery, we have here the richest field of unexploited aboriginal literature it is possible to discover anywhere in the world....

Something more than a scholarly interest attaches to this unparalleled opportunity for the study of a single racial genius. To the American it is also a study of what the land he loves and lives in may do to the literature by which the American spirit is expressed. These early Amerinds had been subjected to the American environment for from five to ten thousand years. This had given them time to develop certain characteristic Americanisms. They had become intensely democratic, deeply religious, idealistic, communistic in their control of public utilities, and with a strong bias toward representative government. The problem of the political ring, and the excessive accumulation of private property, had already made its appearance within the territory that is now the United States. And along with these things had developed all the varieties of literary expression natural to that temperament and that state of society—oratory, epigram, lyrics, ritual-drama, folk-tale, and epic.

In any competent account of this aboriginal literature of ours it will be necessary to refer to the points, in Mexico and Peru, where the racial genius that produced it reached its highest expression. But between the St. Lawrence and the Rio Grande the one item which primarily conditioned all literary form was complete democracy of thinking and speaking.

Such education as the aboriginal Americans had was "free" in the sense that there were no special advantages for particular classes. Their scholars were wise in life only; there were no "intellectuals." The language being native, there were no words in it derived from scholastic sources, no words that were not used all the time by all the people. It was not even possible for poet or orator to talk "over the heads" of his audiences. There was a kind of sacred patter used by the initiates of certain mysteries, but the language of literature was the common vehicle of daily life.

This made for a state of things for which we are now vaguely striving in America, in which all the literature will be the possession of all the people, and the distinction between "popular" and real literature will cease to exist. And in aboriginal literature we have interesting examples of how this democracy of content modifies the form of what is written....

If utterance was out of the Indian heart, it could be sung or danced. But all Indian life was so intensely democratic that there was very little to be danced and sung which had not to be danced and sung in common, by the group or the tribe. When literature is danced or chanted in common there must be some common measure, some time-keeper. Among the Indians this was the drum, that "breathing mouth of wood," the hollow log or hoop with a stretched skin. All Amerind literature is of these two classes: it can be drummed to, or it cannot.

Of the literature which came out of the Indian's head, too little has been preserved to us, and that little by ethnologists rather than literary specialists. Translators have been chiefly interested in mythology, in language, in anything except literary form.

Sir William Johnson, the earliest observer of oratory among the Five Nations, that original American center of political corruption and senatorial sabotage, was impressed by the "Attic elegance" of diction and the compelling rhythm of their orators. The necessity for a unanimous vote on all important measures in Indian councils made the man who could weld the assembly with his voice the great man among them. The exercise of a gift for speech-making was not confined to the formal assembly, however. If a man "felt in his heart" that he had anything to say, he went from village to village claiming an audience, preceded by an advance agent who made all the necessary arrangements. There were prophets in those days, religious enthusiasts and reformers as well as politicians, and successful "spellbinders" who did not decline to teach their art to neophytes. Effects were studied. Apt illustrations and figures of speech would be remembered and appropriated by other orators. The flowing and meaningless gestures, so dear to our own early republican orators, did not enter into Indian speech. Descriptive pantomime and mimicry were used with profound effect, as when the Wichita chief, standing before a commission which would have made windy terms with him, stooped, gathered a handful of dust, and tossing it lightly in the air replied: "There are as many ways as that to cheat an Indian." So seriously was the business of speech-making undertaken, that Powhatan is reported to have instantly slain one of his young men who interrupted him. And, so the chronicler relates, the only interruption to the speech was the carrying out of the body.

Examples in translation from the speeches of Logan, Red Jacket, and the Seneca chief who was called Farmer's Brother show traces of that balanced and flowing sentence structure which we associate with the Old Testament prophets. Direct observation of Indian speech-making leads the writer to conclude that the aboriginal orator composed his speech in units, the order and arrangement of which were varied to meet the special audience. This, if true,—and the decline of tribal life has occasioned such a decline in the art of speech-making that this is only an inference,—would relate the art of oratory to drama and cover one of the two or three gaps in the development of stanza form. Oratory had, however, an important function in relating literary composition to the audience, for it was the only art practiced wholly for the purpose of affecting the decisions of the tribe.

Literary allusion, drawn from their folk or hero-tales, is part of the Amerind daily speech. Of an affair which makes a great stir without getting forward the Micmac will say: "It goes like a canoe that the Partridge made." The point of the comparison is in the fable of the Partridge who, observing that a canoe goes faster when the ends are well rounded, conceived the brilliant idea of a canoe which should be rounded on the sides also. The result was a bowl-shaped structure which went round and round without progress.

There was an apt anecdote like that for every occasion, or if there was not, somebody made one on the spot. This quick facility for noting resemblances, and the play of humour, has given us a body of folk-tale and fable not surpassed by any country in the world, folk-tale and fable which would illustrate our common American life with far more point than the things we derive from Europe.

Unfortunately, writers who have undertaken to utilize this material have missed its native quality, and attempted to crowd it into the mould of European fairy-tales, though in fact both the mood and the method of Amerind folk-tales are as distinctively American as the work of Mark Twain. In some respects Mark Twain in his shorter anecdotes, and Edgar Lee Masters in the *Spoon River Anthology*, have come nearer the mark of Amerind humour than any direct translation or interpretation. The one really notable success at transcription of the Amerind mode seems to have been accident, that sort of divine accident that one wishes might happen oftener. It appears that Joel Chandler Harris did not himself know, when he wrote them, that his Br'er Rabbit and Br'er Fox were original Cherokee inventions. In the reports of the Bureau of Ethnology, where you will find their Amerind forebears, the tales have a grim quality, a Spoon River quality, which to our understanding misses the humouresque which they had to the Indian. Coming to Harris as they did through the modified primitiveness of the Negro, their essential frolicsomeness is transmitted with surprisingly few African interpolations. Undoubtedly there were exchanges between Indian and Negro slaves and assimilations took place at all their points of contact....

All our conclusions about aboriginal prose style are more or less conjectural. Because of the necessity of carrying it wholly in mind, sacred matter was committed almost wholly to song and symbolic ritual. Explanation and narration of the story, necessary for the carrying out of these rites, took place only before the novitiates. When the rites themselves were made public, the story on which they were strung was sketchily the common possession. In the kiva or earth-lodge, in whatever sacred privacy they were rehearsed, the story was a solemn narrative, developed by repetition to explicit form. Beginning as informal prose, such a narrative tended to become more and more rhythmic, until it made a matrix within which the lyric and symbolic elements were enclosed. Tribal ceremonies in all stages of this logical development can be found among the American tribes, well on their way to becoming epic and drama....

It is possible that the literary mode of the Amerind epics has been influenced by the native choice of story interest. While all of the longer poems begin with the creation of the world and purport to record the early wanderings of the tribe and its subsequent history, there is a notable lack of the warrior themes that occupy the epics of the old world. The Amerind hero is a culture hero, introducer of agriculture, of irrigation, and of improved house-building.... It is not, however, the significance of Amerind literature to the social life of the people which interests us. That life is rapidly passing away and must presently be known to us only by tradition and history. The permanent worth of song and epic, folk-tale and drama, aside from its intrinsic literary quality, is its revelation of the power of the American landscape to influence form, and the expressiveness of democratic living in native measures. We have seen how easily some of our outstanding writers have grafted their genius to the Amerind stock, producing work that passes at once into the category of literature. And in this there has nothing happened that has not happened already in every country in the world, where the really great literature is found to have developed on some deep rooted aboriginal stock. The earlier, then, we leave off thinking of our own aboriginal literary sources as the product of an alien and conquered people, and begin to think of them as the inevitable outgrowth of the American environment, the more readily shall we come into full use of it: such use as has in other lands produced out of just such material the plays of Shakespeare, the epics of Homer, the operas of Wagner, the fables of Aesop, the hymns of David, the tales of Anderson, and the Arabian Nights.

Perhaps the nearest and best use we can make of it is the mere contemplation of its content and quality, its variety and extent, to rid ourselves of the incubus of European influence and the ever-present obsession of New York. For we cannot take even this cursory view of it without realizing that there is no quarter of our land that has not spoken with distinct and equal voice, none that is not able, without outside influence, to produce in its people an adequate and characteristic literary medium and form.

10

Regional Culture in the Southwest

1929

The question as stated, whether "the Southwestern landscape and tradition..." can develop a distinctive Southwestern culture, presents at the outset one of the most usual misconceptions of the nature of regional cultures, which if persisted in will inevitably delay the evolution of such culture.

A regional culture is the sum, expressed in ways of living and thinking, of the mutual adaptations of a land and a *people*. In the long run, the land wins. If the people does not adapt itself willingly and efficiently, the land destroys it and makes room for another tribe. When a people is aboriginal in any land they mutually nurse each other into a relationship of cooperation which is marked definitely with the characteristics of both. If the people happens not to be of particularly good stock, the culture though distinctive, will not be high. As we have seen in the history of Europe, a people with a distinctive but mediocre culture has often been supplanted by another people of larger capacity.

It is impossible then to say what will happen to the culture of the Southwest except in relation to the quality of the peoples who contribute to it. And not only to their quality, but to their cultural disposition. It is important to know whether a given people tries to understand and develop the country upon which it lives, or thinks of itself as imposing its derived notions of the Good Life upon the land.

Of the mixed Indian and Spanish early inhabitants of our Southwest, we know well that they succeeded in establishing a mode of life that had agreeable and—in the case of the Indians—valuable elements of the Good Life. They lived happily with the land and expressed their life in Things Made that had the quality of imperishability which for want of a better word we call art.

But can we say as much for the White elements which have from time to time added themselves to the population of the Southwest? Certainly not for most of them. Conditions prevailing throughout the United States make it impossible to be very explicit in ascribing cultural capacity to any particular regional group. Americans in general have been much more interested in being "cultured" than in creating cultures. That is to say, they are more interested in possessing the assets of other cultures than in producing anything of their own. For example: to be musically "cultured" in America means to know the history of music and to be able to recognize and assign to their regional and historic places the best examples of it, and to take pleasure in so doing. But to be a part of a musical culture would mean to have produced a kind of music which is not only expressive of life as it is being lived among us, but is at the same time spiritually satisfying. And the only people among us who have done that are the Indians and the Negroes. People who study such things intimately say there are signs that, beginning with these two folk methods of music, we are gradually evolving a mode of musical expression which is recognizably American. Similarly, beginning with the architectural pattern developed among our Indian pueblos, adding steel and adapting it to urban conditions, we are creating an American architecture. In literature we are approaching forms that are natively expressive. By the time we have developed all these things to the point at which they are instinctive, and complement one another in a genetic relation to American life, we will have an American culture.

But we would have all this much more quickly if, instead of attempting the general, we should confine our efforts to the particular, so adapting ourselves regionally that in the place where we live we would achieve a continuous process of living and expressing, neither of which could be mistaken for living and expressing in other localities.

But traveling about our Southwest, one can not avoid the conclusion that such distinction has not yet been generally made. You can own a house in Los Angeles of any imaginable style of architecture except one native to the soil: you can purchase in Dallas beautiful objects from everywhere in the world but Dallas: only in Santa Fe, of our Western cities, can you find things originating and still made in that town. When it comes to ideas, spiritual perceptions, types of social accommodation, I doubt if there is any discoverable difference in the four or five states that make up the Southwest, from any other five states.

What we come back to, in this discussion, is neither the landscape—by which I suppose is meant the whole geographical complex of crops, climate, and native scene—nor the tradition, which is fairly unified. We come back to the cultural disposition of the people, the disposition which would lead them to reject the easy satisfaction of human wants through the mail-order catalogue, and to demand in housings and furnishings, in social accommodation and personal expression, something native both to themselves and to their land.

I believe there is the root of such a disposition and such a demand in the Southwest. It seems to me sufficiently alive to make it worth while to cultivate. But then I have always had a better opinion of the age I live in than, in the general summing up, seems to be justified. When I go about through the homes of the Southwest I am often shocked and discouraged by the feebleness with which a desire for regional adaptation so loudly professed, is privately expressed.

It need not be said, by me at least, that the country itself has everything to offer out of which competent regional cultures are built. The landscape is magnificent, the tradition rich and appealing.

But I see everywhere too much disposition to overlay the tradition with complacencies of the present hour and disregard the subtleties of the scene for imitations of what has been conspicuously praised elsewhere, to feel confident of an immediate rise of cultural response. The business of interpreting the West in wise and suitable ways of living will be studious and long, and only the humble are likely to succeed at it.

PART III

"Teatro de Corrales": Introduction to Drama

Although the modern taste in theater leans toward professional actors performing on an indoor, technically lighted stage with a darkened audience, Austin reminds us that the Greeks, the Japanese, even Shakespeare used open air and sunlight. Because she wanted to embrace the power of place, Mary Austin believed drama was best performed out of doors, where the beauty of the natural surroundings adds an aura not possible indoors. She explains that the early Spanish often roped off a section of the street for a "Teatro de corrales," producing plays on horseback in huge open-air theaters. Where else could plays be performed on horseback except in the expansive llano, mesa, and desert country of the Southwest? With what greater effect could a horseback drama be enacted than during a time when the pueblo people were awed by Spanish horsemanship? Was the conversion of the American Indian to Christianity due to the martyrdom and dedication of early priests or due to their fascination with the horse in these early horseback dramas? Larry Torres, in his recent important anthology preserving six of these early New Mexican folk dramas, says the earliest forms of drama were "performed by the light of a bonfire," often imitating "sounds found in nature," encounters with animals, or ritual hunts.[1]

Austin believed that the best plays were written for or adapted to local players. She builds an especially good case for the importance of local theater in her analysis of the influence of the Delight Makers on tribal society, as they produced social correction through community building and used laughter as a reinstatement of humility.[2] She champions the ability to produce plays on a shoestring with minimal props, using the body as stage through body painting, ornaments, and masks. According to Austin, the space inside a circle of juniper boughs or a bridge over the *acequia madre* could also become stages. She says the

Papago encircles the saguaro-wine drinking place with strings of feathers, the Pueblo will outline a dancing place with blue cornmeal, and rhythms from the Southwestern wind will add emotion. Sometimes it seems she sifted every possible grain of support for her literary one-smoke theories from the sands of time, including recognizing the Navajo sand painting as a sacred stage around which Indian drama was produced. With the arrival of the Spanish and the introduction of sheep and hand weaving into the Navajo culture, she said these sand paintings could be permanently woven into rugs and hung on the hogan wall where their use as backdrop or stage became more apparent. She says early stagecraft is exemplified in a "forerunner of the theatrical 'transformation scene' still so dear to popular taste" when "the yucca is made to appear as growing from the newly planted root to flower and fruit in about the space of an hour."[3]

A genuine believer in the beauty of diversity, Austin found that along the Mexican border, drama had been influenced by both Spanish and Indian sources. For instance, she says the Matachina plays are a blend of the old Spanish ballad dances with traditional Indian dance-dramas. Southwestern drama mixes Christian costuming and props with the corn-mother ceremony, or blends the Spanish religion with Mexican history, as in the Matachina bride character who can represent the Virgin Mary, the Virgin of Guadalupe, or Cortez's Aztec mistress, Malintzin (or "La Malinche"). Costuming includes robes and crosses from the Spanish, as well as colored ribbons and feathers from the Aztec. Music comes from guitars and violins as well as drums and gourd rattles.

In her search for ways to appreciate Southwestern drama, Austin studied many world religions and literatures. She recognized deep similarities between Native American forms and Egyptian gesture, grand opera, African dance, and ballet. Because Greek drama and poetry were considered "classical" in her day, Austin worked hard to convince the New York critics and university professors that Greek sophistication could be found in Indian dance drama.[4] Describing an Indian performance commemorating the coming of the Spanish—which was obviously created after the discovery that Spanish horsemen were not gods—she says "the Indians have worked out, apparently on their own initiative, horses after the fashion in which horses are shown in Chinese

Drama.... The element of exhibitionism so emphasized in Early Spanish horsemanship is amusing and conspicuous, and the lordly manners of the Conquistadors are successfully satirized."[5]

In "American Indian Dance Drama" Austin observes that Hopi drama "bears a technical relation to the Nō plays of Japan." Although she does not elaborate, this may have been one of her most interesting observations. The costuming, masks, and highly stylized body movements of Indian dancers are quite similar to this ancient form of Japanese drama. A Nō production with its bare stages and mere suggestions of place and simple props, like a fan to suggest a weapon or falling snow, are reminiscent of the Indian's preference for "occupying space without filling it."[6] The Indian koshares, or Delight Makers, perform a service similar to that of farcical kyogen breaks in the sometimes five-hour traditional Nō productions. Both are austere, long, understated productions with highly controlled, subtle movement. Rhythm was as important to the elevation of emotion and creation of community within the Nō audience as within the Indian audience. Both contain miming, dancing, and chanting to the accompaniment of drums and flute.

Most of Austin's ideas about the importance of rhythm occur in her descriptions of poetry; however, she emphasizes the blending between the two genres of drama and poetry, reminding readers that the tribal poet "has no term which distinguishes verse from dancing. Nor has he any name for drama."[7] Although most critics consider rhythm a memory aid for easier transmission of stories from generation to generation, Austin argues that the power of rhythm comes mostly from its use as an emotional intensifier. As Paula Gunn Allen explains, "Some critics have said that [repetition] results from the oral nature of American Indian literature, that repetition ensures attention and makes the works easy to remember. If this is a factor at all, however, it is a peripheral one, for nonliterate people have more finely developed memories than do literate people."[8] Austin's theories about the power of rhythm to act as a cohesive force within a dramatic audience have never been taken seriously, yet how many of us felt an unexplainable sense of emotional harmony and community as we seemed to sway with the entire world when the Beatles chanted "Hey, Jude"?

Austin was attuned to the unique varieties of Southwestern drama: the passion play, miracle play, dance-drama, matachina, masking, and reenactment, but perhaps her most important contribution to the investigation into Southwest drama centers around the idea that the drama she was studying was very serious, never intended for entertainment. Even in Western culture, drama began as religious pageant and reenactment of miracles. What is religion after all if not an experience similar to that created by drama: suspension of reality, a heightening of emotion, and catharsis? In the Southwest, she found that the reenactment of the death of Christ by the penitentes was so deeply passionate and realistic that it sometimes resulted in the actual fatal crucifixion of one of its members. The whips on bare backs were real; the blood oozing from knees crawling through rocks was real. So serious was this drama to the practitioners that their reenactment became more sacred to them than the church rituals performed by priests, and was therefore often banned by the church.

Indian drama was equally serious, not staged for entertainment. Austin's explanation of Indian pottery illuminates this concept well. Drama, like pottery design, was less about adornment and more about promoting a successful life among nature and the gods.[9] The purpose of Indian drama was not to plead with or appease their gods, but to command and communicate with them. If holding a mirror up to human behavior and allowing people to see themselves as others see them works to alter human behavior, should it not work on gods as well? If drama has subliminal power over human emotion, then what greater power could be harnessed as a way to influence the universe? Rain dances, corn dances, deer dances all fall under this category in Austin's mind. She says Indian drama was intended to "get things done" rather than entertain. It was not about performing for each other but about working together to "raise the voltage." Drama was staged in order to produce rain, increase the hunter's prey, relieve sickness, or survive battle. Although drama has always been touted as the genre with the most power to affect an audience, Austin recognized the deep religious seriousness in Indian dance drama and ceremony and searched for ways to explain this power.

When she calls Indian drama "primitive," what she means is classic or "better"—before dialogue and stagecraft took the spotlight and replaced gesture, rhythm, place, and all the subtleties she admires. The same is true when she uses the word "simple" to describe the sincerity and passion of the Hispanic dramas of the Southwest. She does not mean "unintelligent," as that word has come to be defined, but rather simple in the Zen sense of austere, balanced, and pruned, or, in her own words, "If simple at all only as the bud is simple within which are packed leaf and stem and flower."[10] Although she describes the "progression" of primitive to modern, she does not equate progress with improvement but seems instead to imply that we have progressed from the subtle and classic to "fidgeting." Austin says gesture is a universal form of sign language that communicates meaning of its own. Gesture in modern "sophistication" she says has "progressed" to become merely a form of emphasis to support words, which to Austin causes it to lose much of its power. She says gestures "have gone as flat as uncorked champagne"[11] and that special effects have gradually replaced the power of place and imagination, and all of the movement, color, and melody "was later occupied by dialogue."[12]

Without the positive spin she gives to "simple" or "primitive," Austin's own dramatic creations have also been described in those terms and have received little appreciative critical attention. One notable exception is Mark T. Hoyer's *Dancing Ghosts: Native American and Christian Syncretism in Mary Austin's Work*. Hoyer explores at length Austin's ability to dramatically interpret her extensive knowledge of Native American and Biblical imagery, symbols, myths, and stories into a cohesive work relatable and recognizable to both cultures. Albert Keiser also gives her a favorable review in his book *The Indian in American Literature*. He calls Austin's play *The Arrow-Maker* "the best Indian drama produced during the last eighty years" and says she has portrayed its many characters "with a fidelity to truth characteristic of the scientific investigator and delineator."[13] The play is about a medicine woman who falls in love with a young arrow-maker and uses her power to make him a leader in the upcoming war. However, he then marries the chief's daughter instead of his benefactor, and the play revolves around the medicine woman's anguish, revenge, and final resolution.

Austin wrote three plays, all with Indian topics. In the Foreword to her drama "Fire," which Hoyer calls her "Indianization of the Christ story,"[14] she says, "One is reminded in attempting to utilize Indian material for the stage, that the form of Greek tragedy with its swift stroke on stroke of destiny and its sustaining chorus, developed from exactly this necessity for carrying on all life's most urgent occasions in the presence of the tribe."[15] All three plays have been treated with controversy by critics, some calling the same play "a smash hit on Broadway"[16] or claiming that it "flopped."[17] It will be for future scholars to determine whether she ever achieved the kind of product she wanted in her own plays or whether our critical tools have not yet progressed to the point where we can appreciate and understand what she has done.

With today's emphasis on interdisciplinary scholarship, perhaps the time is right for serious study of literature that blurs the boundaries of dance, gesture, rhythm, religion, history, and nature. According to Torres,

> New Mexico drama is both archaic and modern at the same time. It does not belong to any ordinary classification in the development of world theatre. It can be both tragic and comic. It can be American or anti-American. It is both social and romantic. It is sacred and profane, realist and surrealist. It has elements of opera and ballet and at the same time, it is filled with elements of zarzuela. It is presentationalist because audiences participate in it. New Mexico theatre has invented and reinvented itself so many times that it seems like a microcosm of the greater world theatre.[18]

The study of Southwestern drama may well be for the purpose, as Austin suggested, of our re-instruction in the fundamentals of theater. We also include in this section her poignant plea for money to preserve Southwestern drama. She warns scholars about cultural losses due to missionary work, acculturation through education, and exploitation of these sincere dramatic forms as mere entertainment or fodder for chambers of commerce.

Since Austin probably found it impossible to talk about drama in education or re-instruction in the fundamentals of theatre without Shakespeare's name coming up, she obviously felt the need to include him in her discussion. But, as typical of her "American" personality, she refuses to worship at his shrine, since he was British. In one of her unpublished manuscripts preserved in the Huntington Library's Mary (Hunter) Austin Collection, she gives Shakespeare a slight nod as a folk-playwright:

> If you have been thinking of a Folk-lorist as one of those inoffensive gentlemen who spend their lives finding out why people pick up pins and what the Cannibal-Islanders did to keep witches out of the house, this statement calls for some explanation. But if you realize that Grimm Brothers, whose fairy tales you enjoyed so much as a child, were Folk-lorists, that the Arabian Nights is one of the best known collections of Folk-lore, and that the Old Testament is much of it in that category, then the inclusion of Shakespeare seems less extraordinary.[19]

She says that a really great play stirs up "something which is in a great many people so that they feel it at the same time" and that the best place Shakespeare found this "something" was in the folk-mind. Austin, of course, finds this folk-mind alive and well in all cultures, especially in a country that is attempting to govern itself "by folk-wisdom rather than by the specialized wisdom of particular classes." She notes that most scholars agree that Shakespeare stole and reshaped his plays from popular and ancient stories, human experiences, proverbs, fables, and fairy lore, and says that "his most charming figures and his best lines were simply 'lifted' from the common speech, transfigured by his genius." She says that the "best evidence of all that the plays were not written by a schoolman like Sir Francis Bacon is that they originate nothing." In summary, she simply includes Shakespeare as the voice of the common man:

> It would appear from this that it is the simplest thing in the world to write a three-hundred-years popular play. You have only to find the greatest common factor of your audience and raise it to the highest power. The secret of doing this is not only the secret of all great literary art, it is the secret of absolute democracy of spirit. That is why it is even more fitting to celebrate Shakespeare in America than in the country which produced him.[20]

The next logical step for Austin was to broaden this Shake-spearean/folkloric base to include all world influences, as well as the untapped voice of the American Indian. The story of King Lear, she says, is for instance "so old and so human that it might easily be one of those 'one-smoke' tales which Indians love to tell while the pipe makes one round of the group about the fire."21

Notes to Drama Introduction

1. Larry Torres, Introduction to *Six Nuevomexicano Folk Dramas for Advent Season*, translated and illustrated by Larry Torres (Albuquerque: University of New Mexico Press, 1999), xi.

2. Mark T. Hoyer, *Dancing Ghosts: Native American and Christian Syncretism in Mary Austin's Work* (Reno: University of Nevada Press, 1998), 126. Hoyer makes an interesting point about white audiences' ability to react to Indian ritual or performance with appropriate humor. He says Austin has had to "excise 'Indian humor,' which is very much a part of such rituals and often carries with it a 'profound mystic quality'... she indicates that [the audience's] 'tribal understanding' is so underdeveloped that they've lost the sense that laughter is a natural and appropriate response in the face of the mysterious." Because they associate sacredness with rituals, it is beyond them to find the use of humor in such instances and so they cannot recognize it as an integral part of the act.

3. Mary Austin, "Non-English Writings II—Aboriginal," *The Cambridge History of Literature*, eds. William Peterfield Trent, John Erskine, Stuart P. Sherman, Carl Van Doren (New York: The Macmillan Co., 1945), 633.

4. Esther F. Lanigan, *Mary Austin: Song of a Maverick* (New Haven: Yale University Press, 1989; Tucson: University of Arizona Press, 1997), 172.

5. Mary Austin, "Folk Plays of the Southwest," *Theatre Arts Monthly* (August 1933): 604.

6. Mary Austin, "Primitive Stage Setting," *Theatre Arts Monthly* (January 1928): 56.

7. Mary Austin, Foreword to "Fire" in *The Play-Book*, published by the Wisconsin Dramatic Society, Vol. II, No. 5, October 1914 (MSS31, Box 2, Folder 4 University of New Mexico Center for Southwest Research), 6.

8. Paula Gunn Allen, "The Sacred Hoop: A Contemporary Perspective," in *The Ecocriticism Reader: Landmarks in Literary Ecology*, eds. Cheryll Glotfelty and Harold Fromm (Athens: University of Georgia Press, 1996), 241.

9. Mary Austin, "Indian Pottery of the Rio Grande," Booklet III B, Enjoy Your Museum Series, ed. Carl Thurston (Pasadena: Esto Publishing Company, n.d.): 2.

10. Mary Austin, *The American Rhythm* (New York: Harcourt, 1923), 28.

11. Mary Austin, "Native Drama in Our Southwest," *The Nation* 124 (1927): 440.

12. Austin, "Primitive Stage Setting," 50.

13. Albert Keiser, *The Indian in American Literature* (New York: Octagon Books, 1970), 97.

14. Mark Hoyer, "Ritual Drama/Dramatic Ritual: Austin's 'Indian Plays,'" *Exploring Lost Borders: Critical Essays on Mary Austin*, eds. Melody Graulich and Elizabeth Klimasmith (Reno: University of Nevada Press, 1999): 59.

15. Austin, Foreword to "Fire," 6.

16. Michael Castro, *Interpreting the Indian: Twentieth-Century Poets and the Native American* (Norman: University of Oklahoma Press, 1983), 13.

17. Sherry L. Smith, *Reimagining Indians: Native Americans through Anglo Eyes 1880–1940* (New York: Oxford, 2000), 175.

18. Torres, xi.

19. Mary (Hunter) Austin Collection. Huntington Library, San Marino, CA, AU 142, 2.

20. Ibid., 11.

21. Ibid., 4.

11

Community Make-Believe

1914

People who find themselves surprised at the sudden development of
public interest in community theaters need to be reminded occasionally that nothing was more likely, since nowhere in the last fifty
years has life been going on more dramatically and on a larger scale
than in America.

The movement toward the expression of community life in drama
and pageantry which has flowered into forms of greater or less promise and permanence, began—from the theatrical point of view—in the
most unlikely quarter. It received its first formative impulse in the
reflective period following on the most dramatic episode of American
life—I mean the series of struggles that culminated in the Civil War.

About the time Booth Tarkington, William Allen White, Clayton
Hamilton, and half a dozen others who are largely responsible for the
renaissance of American literature west of the Alleghenies, were old
enough to be taken to see it as an important item of education, the first
vital American drama made its appearance in a loosely constructed version of a book that stirred community feeling as no "best seller" has
ever succeeded in doing. Following close on the heels of "Uncle Tom's
Cabin" with its pack of "genuine bloodhounds" and its "*two Little
Eva's*," about fifteen years after the war, came a melodrama known as
"The Confederate Spy" or "The Union Spy," according as it was performed north or south of Mason and Dixon's line. On the occasion of
passing that political boundary all the heroes and villains promptly
changed sides.

The play was usually introduced to the community by some actor
manager, who, traveling with a full equipment of scenery and costumes,
played the leading role himself and made up the cast from the local tal-

ent. The supers were always old veterans who delighted in the rehearsal of realistic "business" out of the memory of their own campaigns. Something of the spirit of Oberammergau prevailed in the allotment of the parts among families who had served best or suffered most, and everybody, including the Methodist minister, went to see it. How they loved that play and how revived in it the most spiritualizing experience of their lives only those can know who have learned to see in the conflict of '61, the crisis, *on both sides*, of a tremendous moral passion.

It was this spiritualizing element which constituted the value of "Uncle Tom" and "The Spy" to the young people of the generation who took part in them. It was the first dramatic venture which overcame the old Puritan ban on the stage and made us realize its possibilities as a means of social expression. It came, too, just at the time when the decline of neighborhood activities in the form of the husking-bee and the quilting party had left us casting about for some method of satisfying the spirit of togetherness which played such an important part in the building of the Middle West.

More or less consciously this spirit has played through all the scattered dramatic ventures which have recently localized in half a dozen nonprofessional organizations in New York, in the Open Air Theater in California, and the latest and most promising Little Country Theater movement in the Northwest. It was very definitely in my own mind when, some twenty years after being driven through the cold Illinois winter to see the dramatization of Mrs. Stowe's tremendous story, I began to experiment in community drama at Lone Pine.

The play, "Pygmalion and Galatea," chosen for that attempt, was one which would, I think, have been the very last selected by any one to whom the Passion Play of the Mississippi Valley had not come as a great illumination. It was the only one at hand which provided the indispensable basis of common experience for the audience, which was made up of Mexicans, Indians, miners, and the miscellaneous agricultural population which supports a mining district. That common experience, vested in *Pygmalion* by the playwright, is a very human one, the experience of a man desiring something with all his soul, demanding it of his gods, and being utterly confounded and nearly destroyed by getting it. Since that venture in the little town under the shadow of the highest Sierra, I have seen a great deal of community drama both in

Europe and America, but I have seen nothing which has not confirmed the conclusion drawn from those two early experiments.

It is that the success of any community theater depends on the extent to which it expresses the community experience. Without such a common fund the movement could have no stability, and without the spirit of social activity it could scarcely come into existence; these two are the bowl and the spoon between which the material of a great national drama is shaping.

This is all very exciting to people who are interested in drama as an art, but there is something even more valuable to the community that produces it, and that is the opportunity the neighborhood theater affords for the expression of national character. For drama is always the evidence of something done. In its simplest form it goes back to the village festival, the green corn dance of the Indian pueblo, the husking and house-raising of pioneer neighborhoods. It is a representation of what has been suffered and enjoyed and accomplished not by a gifted individual, but by a number of people working together. It was once, and may easily become again, the most beautiful form of social coordination; it is now almost the only means left us of developing that spirit in the young.

The chief objections to the commercial drama in the small town are that it does not spring from any real need of the community, but from the financial exigencies of some one outside it, and the fact that the community can take no part in it. It arouses emotion in the young without at the same time providing a suitable outlet. The sort of stock company that shows at small towns in general is not an *ex*pression of anything, but an *im*pression and often a bad one. Of course, if the community theater is to follow in the track of the old-fashioned amateur theatricals and be the sole opportunity of a few vainer or more gifted individuals, very little can be hoped for it, but where the principle is that which prevails in the Children's Theater in New York, of assigning the parts with a view to the development of the individual, it becomes a great educational force.

And this is the case whether the end in view is to affect something in the world of art or to provide legitimate entertainment for a community cut off from the stock company circuit. The spirit of working together is the one indispensable item of success. So rapidly has interest spread in the theater as a social instrument, especially in view of the success of the Little Country Theater movement in Dakota, that it seems worth while to set in order the methods, very much alike in all instances, by which success has already been attained.

Once the theater has been settled upon as the best outlet for the social activity of the neighborhood, two general forms of organization are possible, each with results of such utterly different character that it is important, before deciding upon one of them, for the organization to be perfectly certain of its own preferred end.

In the first of these the activity is centered about some playwright or producer of undisputed talent, who works out some individual concept, with the cooperation of an interested group. The other is a more democratic form in which the management is vested in a council or committee, accountable to the majority. The first of these forms was amply illustrated in the Aldborne Village Players, of England, under the direction of Mr. Charles MacEvoy; and the second has a notable example in the Forest Theater at Carmel, California.

But whatever the character of the initial society, it is important that its operation should be simple. Hard and fast constitutions should be avoided, and rules of membership be interpreted lightly. Drama is the most fluctuant of all arts; contraction and expansion of the original impulse must be allowed for and be accepted as natural. The medium should always be sensitive to the local need. Probably the best arrangement is secured by dividing the management into three groups: Dramatic Art, which should include the selection and production of the play; General Management, concerned with publicity and all public or community aspects; and Business Management, having to do with finance and the care of the society's property. The first two should change frequently, but ordinarily it is better to keep the financial arrangements as stable as possible, and it is advisable to have the benefit of accumulated experience in the offices of stage carpenter and electrician.

Provided there is a building at hand in which entertainments may be held, the problem of financing a community venture of this sort is not very serious. There are dozens of plays that may be acceptably produced in any community of from three to five hundred souls, and made to yield a profit. With economy, and by working over the costumes and properties, it is possible in the course of three or four such performances to accumulate a reasonable sum to be invested in stage "sets" or to serve as the nucleus of a building fund. A great many organizations have dispensed altogether with a building, and have succeeded perfectly with some natural amphitheater in the hills, or with some forest glade which makes an incomparable background for almost any play. In this case the most valuable property which the society can acquire is a set of movable benches or folding chairs. I remember that when I was producing Shakespeare in little mining towns, to audiences of two or three hundred, we got along very nicely with benches arranged by laying a board on two soap boxes, and in one town, where we frequently played in a building used as a warehouse, huge piles of wool or sacks of grain served as a gallery in the rear which was regularly occupied by as many Paiute Indians as could raise "two bits" for a seat. The comfort of the audience is, however, an important item in the appreciation of the play, and should be one of the first considerations.

The question of costume and setting is one in which every society is bound to make several mistakes before settling on the happy solution. In the Bohemian Grove midsummer plays, now world-famous, at first painted canvas screens were introduced in order to give an outdoor setting to what is now recognized as the most beautiful natural amphitheater since the times of ancient Greece! But the Bohemians, when they had learned their lesson, learned it so thoroughly that their productions are now the standard of open-air performance. Yet in spite of all this, one of the best known of our outdoor theaters committed itself last year to the infelicity of cheaply painted "indoor sets."

The greater number of plays suitable for community production are what are called "costume plays," that is to say, the dress and accouterments are not modern; but in every case I would advise the making of stage dresses at home rather than hiring them from the professional costumer. It may occasionally be necessary to do the latter in the case of armor or weapons, but the exercise of ingenuity and the study of the period and the key in which the scene is to be played are not the least part of the benefit derived from the local theater. Sometimes a real genius for costumes may lie undiscovered under our very noses.

The dress of the players is a part of the language of the drama, and it is more important that it should make the right suggestion to the audience than that it should be historically accurate. Not infrequently the conventional, wholly uninspired, and mechanically correct creation of the hired costumer intervenes like a foreign phrase between the audience and the meaning of the play. On one occasion, in a certain western town, I found the pupils of the public school giving a performance of selected scenes from "The Merchant of Venice." It was given without costume, and in the court scene, where it was necessary to disguise her sex, the sixteen-year-old *Portia*, never having heard of a judge's gown and being a little shy of trousers, found nothing to do but don a pair of bib overalls and tuck up her hair under a cap. To the audience, who knew no more than the young lady of the traditional dress, this seemed a reasonable proceeding, and not one of them appeared to be put at fault by it. Nevertheless, the enjoyment of any modern audience is heightened by pleasing the eye with harmonies of line and color.

It would seem the natural order of things to begin the conduct of a dramatic venture with the choice of a play, but in fact the selection of the particular play is conditioned by all the things just mentioned, by the nature and location of the stage, by the amount of money that is permitted to be spent, by the extent to which the acting is to be supported by costume and setting. Most of all it is controlled by the character of the audience which is to see it.

The choice of a good acting play is one that can be made only by a person of experience; therefore, the first step is to cut out from the list of possibilities all plays that are not positively known to have had successful professional performances. The list of good acting plays is very large; out of these the cautious manager will do well to discard all so-called "problem" plays, all plays of the future or of the too-immediate present. Drama is an art that more than any other "reaches back"; it dips into the reservoir of common experience, and the deeper it goes the greater the number of the audience who will be touched by it. Historical plays of our own country, of the best known periods of English history, and very sparingly of European history, are safe to choose, but the best of all are those dramas of no specific period which strike upon some common human chord.

Contrary to professional opinion, plays of a religious significance, poetic and symbolic plays prove universally popular on the community stage, and during the last two or three years the demand for them for this purpose has greatly stimulated their publication. This is a real achievement, and will undoubtedly have a wholesome effect on the commercial stage.

The point at which too many dramatic organizations come to grief is after the play is chosen and they face the problem of the acting. The mistake is always to make too much of it; for the community theater never can afford to make a point of so highly technical an art. Important as it is in the development of a national drama, it must be borne constantly in mind that acting is a subsidiary art, it cannot exist by itself, and it has little relation to the purpose of the community.

Good enunciation, intelligence, and an instinct for social coordination, for *working together*, are far more important considerations in casting the parts than any degree of "talent for acting" likely to develop in the small community. Just as soon as concessions begin to be made to any such talent, the tendency runs very quickly toward the choice of plays for their theatrical rather than for their spiritual and dramatic possibilities. Instead of self-expression we have self-exploitation. The possessors of the supposed talent insist on all the good parts, and the advantage of participation as a whole is lost to the community.

The play, if it is to yield the greatest benefit, must never be regarded as a performance; it must be taken as an experience, an opportunity to run our thoughts in other and nobler molds. It is a fine thing for one whose life provides no occasion for heroic acts to attempt them upon the stage; it is good for a clodhopper occasionally to be a king, and the fact that Miss So-and-So plays the heroines very nicely is an excellent reason for not allowing her to do it continuously. Great art is secured only by complete subordination to a spiritual idea. This is the explanation of the success of Oberammergau, and of the fact that the most notable unprofessional performances in America have been religious or at least inspirational in character.

The most interesting of these is John MacGroarty's pageant play at San Gabriel. Mr. MacGroarty had no previous experience as a playwright, and gives no evidence of becoming one; his work smashes all but the two indispensable rules of dramatic composition; it was performed by a cast largely amateur, in a location not very convenient to traffic, and yet has enjoyed a run that would make the fortune of a Broadway playhouse. He was fortunate in having for his subject that phase of California's past most dear to her people—the founding of the Missions; but the real drawing power of the play was the religious spirit in which it was conceived and carried out. For these are the two indispensable rules: community of interest between audience and play, and sincerity in execution.

There is another point which illustrates the difference of result as indicated in the choice of one or the other of the two forms of organization. Mr. MacGroarty's was the only mind concerned with the production of the Mission Play.

This is the primary difference in the two modes of organization: individual direction tends to produce forms of art more permanent and of wider appeal than those which result from community management. Community-managed theaters in most cases are managed too much. There is too much manipulation in the interest of things which have nothing to do with drama—not necessarily selfish interests or personal vanities. With the best intentions in the world, fatal concessions are made to the desire to have things proceed smoothly, to conciliate this or that interest or to conform to some ideal of organization without respect to the end to be sought. In the name of "tact" the indispensable condition of sincerity is lost sight of, and in a mistaken notion of the value of amateur acting, elements are retained which might better be discarded. But where any considerable number of a community can get together, and without taking any account of talent, but with a common idea and the determination to keep every part of the performance subordinate to that idea, results of extraordinary artistic power can be obtained.

This is what happened in the Nativity play at Pomfret, Connecticut, where the world-myth was presented by plow hands and village maids, with the utmost simplicity and with an entire absence of theatricality; and yet with a spiritualizing power that was felt not alone by the audience but by those to whom the mere rumor of the performances reached.

This is a difficult thing to achieve, but it is in just this possibility of social coordination that the greatest service of the community theater is rendered. To be able to take one's place as the unegoistic unit of a design without ever losing the sense of the play as a whole, is an excellent training for citizenship, and youth should be encouraged to try for it. And if our young people aren't in some appreciable way better members of the community for such participation, why should there be any such thing as a community theater?

12

Gesture in Primitive Drama

1927

Drama which is properly to be called primitive separates itself from the drama of sophistication along the line at which words take precedence of all the other mediums through which the dramatic idea is communicated. For, in the beginning of dramatic expression, man made free use of posture, dance, gesture,—that is to say, motion of the extremities as distinguished from movements of the torso,—vocalization, melody, ritualized mimicry, color, costume, pantomime; in about that order of evolution. Along this evolutionary curve, words began to appear, rising from crest to crest of emotion impossible to be fully completed in action, or bridging the hollows of time and space between such emotional rises. Even after drama had reached the high perfection of Greek tragedy we find this special use of words, syncopating time and space, persisting in the Greek Chorus along with rhythmic motion, the primitive matrix from which dramatic action proceeded; while from the emotional crests sprang dialogue.

But if one could watch—as you can if you know where to look for it—drama in the stage just approaching its literary permutation, there can be found, supplementing and extending the scant word content, a gesture language much more closely related to ideation and basic action than the completely vocalized speech of modern play acting. For this primitive gesture *is* speech, older, more nearly universal as a medium of communication, than any living language. Gesture, as it can be studied at the *Comédie Française* at its highest modern pitch, has become something less than speech, the exquisitely placed finials and flourishes of words, the rubric of the actor's personal contribution. But your true primitive knows nothing of gesture as idiosyncrasy. He never fidgets; he has no need of gesture to discharge the suppressed by-product of intellectuation; never expresses himself, but only his thought, and that by intention and for purposes of communication. The fidgets and flourishes of our modern necessity are the half remembered tag ends of the sign language once universally prevailing among mankind.

Not only in the unconscious hand motions by which our own speech is underscored and emotionally inflected, in Greek vase paintings, on Egyptian tombs, in the bas-reliefs of Assyrian temples, but still actively in use in intertribal gatherings of American Indians, is the evidence of this fundamental pre-speech medium, executed with grace, dignity and style. It is upon this foundation of sign language that the gesture of all primitive drama is based, and from it all our modern gesture is derived. The raised right hand, palm outward, canted toward the protagonist, or vibrated once or twice in that direction, by which silence or attention is modernly secured, is the Indian sign for "stop" or "wait." Our wagged forefinger of admonition is the equivalent of the Indian right index moved forward emphatically from the corner of the mouth, "This that I tell is the truth." The rubbing together of lightly clasped palms is a world-wide word of self congratulation. The modern survival of direct sign language can be best noted in the characteristic gestures of Jews, as precisely the gestures likeliest to have been retained by a strongly marked race, dispersed among and subjected to persecution by aliens: hands clasped and rubbed together "I congratulate myself on your interest"; hands out, palms up and inclined toward the protagonist, "I crave your mercy"; hands thrown out sideways after touching the breast, "I show you my heart" (sincerity); hands raised to head level, palms slanted up, "I submit to your judgment." These gestures, which are in use today among Indians, in exactly the same significance can be seen on the reliefs celebrating the triumphs of Sennacherib, and in the statues of the Christian saints adorning the Vatican. So too surviving the ancient "thumbs down" of Roman combat among Sicilians is the same as the sign word, used by Indians for kill,—right hand closed, thumb outside, pressed close as in grasping a knife, jerked, thumb edge down, sharply. But among Indians the thumb is kept straight, the motion is severe but dignified, while the Sicilian projects his thumb slightly and jerks viciously, to emphasise his temperamental version of "Give him the knife." Without having arrived at a general understanding of the rationale of communicative gesture, and temperamental and local modifications of emotional content and emphasis, it is impossible to evaluate the subtle transitions from word gesture to pantomime as these occur in primitive drama.

In a general way a sign word may be said to be an abstraction of the content of the idea to be expressed, and bears about the same relation to pantomime that primitive African sculpture bears to living form. Pantomime is always representative. Generalizations must, however, never be taken too seriously. In so far as I am acquainted with primitive drama, which is only so far as I have been able to observe it among American Indians, dramatic abstraction historically precedes pantomime; the older the play the less pantomime, the greater dependence upon rite, symbol and gesture. In the evolutionary process, pantomime appears to have kept along with pictorial representation. At the stage at which the primitive would use a straight line abstraction of a bird he would use a sign word for bird, but when he becomes capable of making a true picture of a bird, he will have invented a more or less realistic bird costume. The two modes, that is, sign and representation, may still be seen together in narrative pantomime, in which successive scenes in the life of the hero take place in time and space removed. Here gesture speech serves as a running comment between pantomimic acts, taking the place of captions between motion picture scenes. Thus the gesture as communication proves itself true speech, evolving hieroglyphically into literature, to which pantomime becomes illustration. It is only by keeping in mind this function of gesture as speech, based upon ideation rather than emotional description, and its concurrence with pictorial pantomime, that we can credit the classic statement that Telestes, one of the dancers employed by Aeschylus, represented every circumstance of *The Seven Before Thebes* by gesture alone, and that a performer called Memphis, at Rome, in the second century, "showed what the Pythagorean philosophy could do, by exhibiting, with stronger evidence than they could who professed to teach the art of language." Something of the same sort has been done for Amerindian art and philosophy in the detached dances of the Pueblos, the White Buffalo dance, the Earth Medicine dance and the Eagle dance.

Along with gesture speech, and pantomimic illustration, there occurs a third use of gesture in primitive art, sparingly used in drama, but occurring universally with oratory, and following the solo figure in dramatic *recitative*. This is the type of gesture which is still preserved among us in ballet and solo dancing, in oratory, and in the old Shake-spearian type of acting, particularly accompanying poetic drama. Ges-ture in this case performs the service of orchestration, it is the accom-paniment unconsciously carried over by the solo actor, from the primitive dance which is the matrix of drama. The speaker supplies with arm movements the rhythmic pattern woven by the chorus, by drum beat and rattle stroke, by pounding feet and moving lines of dancers. At various stages of its evolution the oratorical gesture has been ampli-fied by the sword, the wand of office, by banners or scarves as in the modern ballet. There is some reason to believe that the set speeches of tragedy, on down to Elizabethan times, were associated with this type of gesture, while pantomime and word gesture were confined to com-edy parts. Among American Indians I have not seen oratorical gesture used except in oratory, and in the delivery of tribal lays, long, mythical origin tales mixed with tribal law and custom. And as Aeschylus is spo-ken of as having introduced pantomime into the Greek theatre, along with solo dance movements, it seems likely that the primitive canon of gesture extended pretty well into the great Greek tradition. It seems likely, then, that a Greek tragedy should be produced much more in the manner of a Pueblo dance-drama than has ever been attempted. The chorus should execute mass movements while delivering their words in chant or recitative, with sign-word gesture, while the speakers might occasionally use oratorical gesture and pantomimic posture, with great restraint; or if they remained on the stage while the chorus is perform-ing, the speakers would make discreet use of caption gesture following the narrative of the chorus. In comedy both dance and pantomime could be freely used, but with no oratorical gesture. These would be interesting experiments to try in Greek revivals, especially as I am inclined strongly to suspect that the Greek canon of having all killings and other important acts performed off stage, originated not in supreme Greek taste, but in more primitive tradition of the dance drama in which all acts of mystical or violent import are performed in the kiva or medicine lodge instead of in the presence of the tribe.

Beside this brief survey of the relation of primitive gesture to mod-ern theatrical use, it is important to realize that primitive drama—that is to say the evolutionary stages of drama just previous to the drama of dialogue which we begin to know in the Greek and Latin classics,—is invariably a dramatization of man's direct conflict with the great natural forces, sun, rain and thunder, fructification, drouth, disease and death. The powers are thought of as directly present, sometimes in their symbols, but in the higher forms of drama as masked participators, in one or another of their metamorphic appearances. Only occasionally is the force of the conflict mediated in human characters; it is mankind and not man who fronts the gods. Along with man will sometimes be represented his helpers, friendly animals, half-gods, such as the Six Corn Maidens, the Koshare, or sacred clowns, ancestral spirits.

There is in every Amerindian drama the root of the attempt which the Greeks brought to such wholeness and clarity, to define the secret and profound relation of mankind to Immaterial Reality. But it is the tribe that figures, not the individual, and there is no catharsis, because no sense of individual guilt. Neglectful man may have been careless in the performance of rite and ceremony, or even unwittingly an offender, but never a sinner. Gifts may be promised to the Powers for favors granted, dances are sometimes performed as oblations, but in general it may be said that Primitive man does not plead with his gods; he rather commands them. By singing and dancing he raises his own psychic capacity to levels from which he traffics profitably with the Soul of the Universe. This attitude gives urgency to his gestures, but no note of abasement.

In all drama of ceremonial import, gestures, whether sign words or pantomimic, will have dignity and force, and will as a rule carry more words than the voice carries. Many of the songs which accompany dance-drama consist largely of vocalizations merely,—or the words are sung by choruses of old men, while the dancers contribute vowel color and melody, the words being expressed by symbolic decorations, as in the rosettes of green macaw feathers symbolizing the green growing corn, the rainbow *tablita*, the "cloud-calling" head dress of the Corn-dancers. In the rain dances, the observer will note that the hands of the dancers when not otherwise employed are held drooping from the raised forearms, with fingers slightly spread and thrust slightly downward from time to time, which is the sign-word for rain. The Koshare, or sacred clowns, representing the ancestral spirits, will be painted in streaks and splashes of black and white—immemorial guise of clowns—signifying death and life, light and darkness. They will have their hair dressed with dead cornhusks, their necklaces will be of deadly night-shade berries, their other ornaments of rabbit-skin, in which the dead were formerly buried, their other garments, rags and tatters, illustrative of ancient time and the long journey back from the Underworld. They will dance with delicate lightness, uttering those peculiar fluttering cries which since the early stone age we have agreed to call "ghostly," they will draw back their lips, showing their teeth in skull-like grins. But always their hands will say the significant words called for by the occasion on which they are supposed to have come back to earth to help the tribesmen, rain or growth or fructification or defense. In the intervals of their spirit function, they lapse into purely human helpfulness, stooping to tie a dancer's loosened moccasin string, or to disentangle the long blowing hair of one dancer from the armlet of another, or to encourage a timid child making its first ceremonial attempt. But in every return to the character of Koshare, they resume the announcing word gesture. As on these occasions they are supposed to be invisible, the gestures serve as orders delivered to the powers; Rain! Rain! Between the turns of the dance the Koshare perform many amusing little comedies, for it is necessary that both the tribes and the corn be encouraged to laugh that they may fructify, and that their foibles be corrected by whips of laughter.

It is in this clowning that the combined use of word gesture and pantomime is seen at its best, probably very much as in the Greek comedies, since the natural conditions of production are markedly similar. These early comedies are given in the open air in the town plaza, to audiences seated for the most part on the housetops, too far for nuances of voice inflection, or spoken words, to carry with much force. As the players are either painted or masked, facial expression can lend very little aid; but the long, delicately formed, facile hand of the Indian more than supplements other deficiencies. These word gestures are also a defense against too exigent Missionary and Indian Bureau censorship, for the comedy of the stone age is broad—though never salacious—and mostly missed by an audience unversed in sign words. Also in many of the dance-dramas which have for their object the increase of fertility in the earth, sign words may be used, which, because they have not the faintest shadow of indecency in the primitive mind, are not understood by White observers, for, curiously, it is not possible to present by signs understandable to the Whites, any word referring to fertilization which has not some suggestion of indecency in the White mind.

In the Eagle dance in Santo Domingo, the remnant of an ancient mating ceremonial, the eagles are searching the horizon for their mates, and spreading their wings for the nuptial flight while the mud-heads, or first men, encourage them with music, confidently expecting that their own powers as well as all the fructifying powers of the earth will be sympathetically increased thereby, for the evolution of mankind from a state of mud-head stupidity is the Fundamentalism of the Pueblos.

Here, at this point, where gesture constituted a language of communication between man and the Powers in which the relation between man and his universe was friendly and equable, we have to leave the discussion of drama as primitive. Sophistication begins with the use of gesture as expressive rather than communicative.

13

American Indian Dance Drama

1929–30

The first thing that the student of drama learns in an American university, is that all our modern forms of it derive from dance drama of the Greeks; he learns it through the "Poetics" of Aristotle, with whom the passage from the great religious festivals of ancient Greece to greater drama was largely traditional. And the last thing that such an American student learns, if, indeed, he is so fortunate as to hear of it at all, is that here in his own land, accessible from Pullman car and motor bus, Amerind dance drama, recognizably the same type as the pre-Aristotlean mysteries of fertility and increase, trembles on the forward edge of the oblivion of ignorance and neglect. It exists, this primitive dramatization of essential processes between man and his invisible environment, in our Southwest in all the clear brilliance of color, the dignity of ritual, the embroidery of symbolism, and the fervor of religious feeling that characterized the same cultural stages of all Mediterranean life. It proceeds by the same means of rhythmic dance sustained by drum beat and rattle and pounding feet, by symbolic decoration, by choral song and secret ritual act as it did in Athens, in Thebes, in Rome. So close are the fundamental human impulses underlying all man's efforts to consolidate and interpret his relation to the felt but unseen forces of his environment, that here as in ancestral Europe, the symbols, the hand signs, the sunwise turn about the altar, serve as well for Amerind as for Peloponnesian; the altars rise in the same stepped replicas of the high horizons that shut in the celebrants. Here the Spirits of the Ancestors come back to the help of the living in the same livery of black and white with headdresses of tufted vegetation, to cheer them with the quips common to sacred clowns the world over.

Notice of the treasures of dramatic origins which are ours, has come down to us from the earliest explorers of the western continent. From Cortez and Pizarro came accounts of the magnificent and impressive theatricality of the ceremonials of Mexico and Peru. Jesuit missionaries, in the dark forests of the Great Lake country, reported strange and bedeviling rituals of dance and choral song. Almost all we know of certain of the vanished Southern tribes is embodied in accounts of their dramatic celebrations, penetrating even the trail-wearied, frightened sense of French and Spanish exploring parties. Espejo in 1583 saw at Acoma a "dance in the Mexican manner, very impressive." Lewis and Clark crossing the Great Plains were struck by the weird, heart-stirring sun and hunting dramas, which Catlin painted. Emory and Donahue and the Kearny expedition left explicit records and drawings. And yet— perhaps the American sense was dulled to the impact of beauty and strangeness, perhaps American intelligence was enslaved by the European tradition—a few years ago when the informed ones among the American people engaged in a public struggle to save what was left of an unparalleled inheritance, there were voices raised insistently to assert that the Indian dance drama had never had an historic existence, and that such examples as were still to be seen had been "invented with the object of attracting tourist attention." That curious twist of the mind of a conquering people towards the conquered was at work, no doubt, to lessen American offense by belittling the Amerind; and the association of Indian dance with Indian religion operated in the missionary mind to discredit any culture which was not orthodoxly Christian. The early Catholic missionaries in Mexico interdicted the dances and burned the books of the dramas, with the concurrence of political powers who, observing that the dramas were for the most part, based upon historic tradition, discovered them a source of disaffection to the Spanish conquest of the United States, stupidity and neglect worked obscurely and less effectively to the same end.

Only along the Rio Grande, and in the remote pueblos of Hopi and Zuni can the aboriginal drama of North America be seen in anything like its pristine beauty and significance. Now, in this very hour when the Mexican people, realizing their loss, are feeling back along the still living thread of Indian drama in the United States, to revitalize forms towards which the reawakened dramatic impulse of Mexico instinctively turns, there is not one institution of learning or art in the United States which has the knowledge to offer them, or the imaginative strength to commit itself to that adventure. Only Secretary Wilbur's recent gesture towards preserving Indian arts as ART saves us from complete stultification. It will not, however, save the drama without an explicit co-operation on the part of American intelligence.

It is impossible to make any proper approach to our own aboriginal drama without realizing the origins of all drama in man's profound faith in the favorable disposition towards him of the invisible elements in his environment, elements which he could neither touch nor describe, but profoundly felt. That he learned later to see them with the eye of his mind as laws, principles, the law of logical causation, the law of human heredity of retributive justice, did not render them the less portentous, or himself any the less in need of adjusting himself to their operation. There was, for example—long before he came to know it as the law of vegetative growth—that magical association of circumstance by which it came to be known that if, in eating, you threw a handful of seed towards the invisible providers of foodful grass, if, in gathering, you left a few stalks still standing, a few last handfuls of fruit ungarnered, you might safely count, returning to that spot another season, on finding an increase of supply. Thus by experience the cogency of the flung handful, the tabooed portion of food was determined. By much the same empirical discovery, it was established that by the making, in company, of rhythmic noises and the repetition of valorous gesture and boasting word, man fought better, withstood more successfully the onslaught of the visible world. Thus by adding experience to experience, it grew in man's mind that from the thing done, the *drama* of the Greeks, directed towards the invisible environment, there might be expected a flow of events favorable to his existence. Dramatizing his desire by means of rhythmic motion, descriptive gesture, and auto-suggestive words, man felt sure of the attention of the Powers. In time, to dramatic mimicry were added color, form, design; beauty as it was felt in the soul of primitive man was thought of as persuasive to the Invisible Something making for rightness in man's own life. Without some notion of constituting alikenesses between man and his universe, and a transference of activity from one to the other, there would have been no drama, nothing doing between man and Divinity.

It was the thing taking place between men and gods which gave force and form to the Greek dance drama. On the effectiveness of the transaction between the individual and the universe, all drama is to this day judged.

To appreciate a primitive drama, as seen in our Southwest, it is necessary to have a little understanding of tribal mindedness as a factor in the presentation, what we call the "production" of the play. In the primitive mind the validating words and acts, the words and acts which in our sort of drama are said to "make" the scene, constituting its crises and climax, are thought of as magical. Such is their potency that, if performed carelessly or too publicly, the magic evaporates, or can be seized upon by an enemy and turned against the performers. For this reason, the climax of an Indian dance drama usually takes place in the *kiva*, as we know in Greek drama it took place behind the veil of the Mysteries, in the *cella*, off the stage. It was just because Thespis brought the dramatic act into the public view, displaying in dialogue what had formerly been displayed only in secret priestly rite, that his performances were criticized as irreligious. In very many of our Amerind dramas this secrecy as to the validating act is still preserved, and must be inquired into privately by the visitor who wishes to judge it.

The one thing indispensable to the understanding of primitive drama is the nature of the wish which gives rise to the impulse of dramatization. Such obvious wishes as for rain or for an increase of wild game can readily be understood through the pantomime by which they are expressed, of generation, of the hunt, of the falling showers, the sprouting corn. But more subtle desires, as for health, for tribal evolution, for closer identification of the spirit of the performer with the animating Spirit of the universe, these are not easily transcribed in acts. They must be gathered from the multiple rhythms, a multiplicity of which the modern is largely incapable, and from words either sung or spoken, which require translation. Many subtleties of the dramatic medium which we are accustomed to see worked out with the play of light, a whole range of what we know as "stage effects," are, in primitive drama, expressed altogether by rhythm, by gesture and color. Almost the only item with which the inexperienced observer can make immediate contact is the livery and equipment of beauty expressed as decoration. Amerind decoration is everywhere of that salient and essential quality which makes itself felt, even when least understood.

Three things are indispensable to an intelligent approach to our aboriginal American drama; a knowledge of Greek procedure; sensitivity to dramatic mediums either of gesture, rhythm, color or of design; a not too remote sympathy with the tribal mind. Perhaps this last requisite should be extended to include something of the range of cultures among the American tribes. Indian life is never the static affair that popular notion describes it. No two tribes are on exactly the same cultural level, and in any given tribe, ceremonials will be found ranging from the archaic to the modern. The observer who attempts to rest his conclusion as to the importance of Indian drama on one or two, or half a dozen performances, will surely have omitted more than one significant type. To come to any conclusion whatever on the sort of Indian dance which can be seen in a hotel lobby, or between tourist trains, puts the protagonist in the category of trying to understand a Shakespearean play through a Fifth Reader selection from one of its scenes.

For a first contact, I should recommend the Deer Dance, as it may occasionally be seen at Taos, or a variant of it called the Deer Cry, seen early in January at Jemez Pueblo, or a little later in the season, at San Ildefonso. Fragments of this ancient hunting ceremony given at Christmas in honor of the Nativity should never be missed by anyone who cares for the wildness of beauty, but they must not be confounded with the complete drama. The story of the play commemorates a time of great scarcity of game, and with the dual role so familiar to us through Greek performances, guards against a repetition of it. According to this story, the game had all retreated through a rock crevice, into a secret valley where the tribesmen could not follow. Finally, it was decided to send two of the most beautiful of the Medicine women—women strong in that profoundly feminine power known as Earth Medicine—to lure the great game animals forth from their hiding. By the magic of their singing and dancing, the deer, the elk, the antelope, the mountain sheep, are drawn down from the mountains to the valley where the tribesmen lie in ambush.

In the dance as given at Taos, the animal personators have stolen out in secret the night before; the women have spent the night in the kivas where all the Medicine power of the pueblo is gathered up and vested in their persons. As they issue from the sacred ceremonial chambers the morning of the dance, this power is felt emanating from them—the mysterious power of womanhood. They are followed at a little distance by the hunters, dressed and armed in ancient habit. A little to one side the drum sounds and the Ancients reinforce the singing. As the drama proceeds, the great males of the animal tribe are seen advancing cautiously under the spell of the beauty and magic of the dancing women, and are separated from their mountain fastness. Then the hunters fall upon them, with the utmost of realism both on the part of the hunters and the game, with indescribable beauty and wildness. Under all this realism the tribesman feels and the observer perceives the drama of the Power of Women, something reduced in our sort of society to the sentimentality of women being an "inspiration" to men, but void, among us, of the validating fact. As the drama is performed at San Ildefonso, with the "great horned ones" issuing at dawn from the hills to follow the woman lure, it is the despair of poets and painters. Nothing like it has been seen by a civilized audience since the great days of the Peloponnesia. Another more ancient, and, for definite moments, more thrilling version is performed occasionally at the southern pueblos, but so far as I know has been seen by but two Americans, one of whom came away shocked stiff by what is probably the only religiously charged reference to sex he has ever seen dramatically presented, and the writer, who was moved by the performance to depths that lie beyond the relief of tears.

Perhaps the best form of story drama available to the ordinary inquirer is the Dance of the Emergence, to which I once had the honor of conducting Paxton Hibben, and convincing him of much more than I have space to say here of the relevance of Indian dance drama not only to classic Greek but to modern American drama. This was at San Felipe, although if you have friends at Santo Domingo it may also be seen there occasionally by invitation. The story is an important episode in the Pueblo creation myth. Mankind is supposed to have come to self-awareness in the lowest of the four "womb-worlds," as a rudimentary creature—according to one version web-fingered and tailed, according to another as "mud-heads," literally "un-baked ones." Wandering about in cold and darkness, they discover light shining through a hole in the roof of their underworld, and climbing up to it, discover another slightly better world in which they remain until, by a third discovery, they find their way to the third, and finally the fourth world, which is this lovely "land of the sun and the pine."

The play opens simply with the appearance of the first men, abject and miserable, clad in rags, but assisted by the Spirits of the Ancestors—of whom more later. There is the first discovery, carried on by dialogue; the reluctantly begun attempt to reach the second world, presented as a dance across the plaza, at the end of which the dancers arrive in an exhausted condition. This is repeated until the fourth world is reached, upon which the people of the pueblo burst from their houses laden with food and gifts which they shower upon the dancers, and a general fiesta ensues. This is the dramatization of man's evolution and his prayer for its continuing upward direction.

The function of the Spirits of the Ancestors in Indian drama is probably not different from what it has always been in tribal Mysteries. The sheer inability of primitive man to conceive of the extinction of life keeps him surrounded at all times with the sense of uninterrupted companionship, feared in the case of the enemy, unless placated by explicit rites such as the Scalp Dance; feared even in the quarry, to whom conciliatory prayers and tobacco smoke must be offered. Among the Southwestern tribes, the Spirits of the Ancients were revered rather than feared, and by tradition first invoked when the tribesmen struggled through the third of the womb-worlds, a land of fire and quake and fearful monsters, "that the world be made safer for men and more stable." Their special function is to cheer the people with quips and laughter, to cheer the corn that it also may laugh, and by "delight making" insure the fertility of men and crops. This was the use of laughter in relation to love as our ancients understood it.

In Amerind theatre, the work of social correction is carried on by means of little comedies playing up the foibles of the community, performed as interludes—comic relief—in more serious dances, especially those connected with fertility. The two functions of correction and comfort are, in fact, usually combined in fertility dances such as the Corn Dance, the hunting ceremonies, and in commemoration rites. In their sacred function as Spirits of the Ancestors, the Koshare, for so the Delight Makers have come to be called, are supposed to be invisible. They move with spirit-like lightness, uttering ghostly cries, in and out of the dance, with helpful ministrations. In that character no eye is raised to them, an air of reverent tenderness pervades the dance where they are present. In the comic interludes, however, laughter is both permitted and desired, and quips and "gags" pass between the actors and the audiences. The satire of these little comedies is keen, the humor broad, the jesting Homeric in quality, the acting inimitable.

The organization of the Koshare is obligatory; no one elected to its membership may decline without offense. As members are elected for acting talent and humorous invention, these primitive Little Theatre societies represent the highest aggregations of dramatic talent available. Favorite producers of the great tribal ceremonies are often found to be men who had their dramatic training as members of a Koshare society. No written record of the Koshare plays has ever been made, but one gathers, from repeated listenings in, that here is the primitive root of the satiric comedies of Aristophanes as it may be found in "The Birds" and "The Frogs."

Ceremonial drama is not the only type found among Amerind tribes. It has received more attention, as constituting the "best show" of tribal life, and as being the only form of entertainment to which the public is formally invited. Personal friends of the Indians occasionally manage to be present at informal celebrations, feast days, anniversaries; on which occasions historic pageants are carried out with great verisimilitude, often with a spirit of burlesque unexpected from the dignified Amerind. Burlesques of White life and of the manners of neighboring tribes and towns, or of the conflict between younger and older generations are the favorites, and are carried through with side-shaking penetration and aptness. Although such performances are not taboo to the Whites, curiously, one seldom meets them there, and I know of no reference to these pageant performances in print other than my own. Neither have I seen any reference to the dramatic programmes which the Hopi villagers prepare for their own and the neighboring villages in the long winter evenings. The plays thus presented bear a technical relation to the Nō plays of Japan; they might, indeed, be the original primitive form of such plays, not appreciable to the alien mind without much more information than the average White man brings to it.

Thus briefly are enumerated the types of aboriginal American drama which may be found within our borders practically unimpaired. Of technical theatricality, the use of costume, of gesture, of color, of alterations of rhythm, of juxtapositions of tragedy and comedy, to obtain the desired dramatic validation I could, and probably will some day, make a volume. It may be said here that the native material is in shape to be accepted and used by the professional theatre without scholarly intervention. A few notable professionals, such as Robert Edmond Jones, have been able to make valid use of that portion of it which best suits their particular needs. But various representatives of dramatic interests—by that I mean interests connected with the creation of drama rather than its presentation—have approached the Amerind contribution without deriving any public benefit.

The question, then, of what is to be done with this magnificent but vanishing field of dramatic refreshment, is acute. It takes on ironic connotations from the fact that Mexico, profoundly concerned to cast off the imposed Spanish mould of the theatre, and return to its own cultural roots, is looking towards the United States for the best examples of Amerind dramatics. Here at Zuni, in the Hopi towns, and in specific instances at one and another of the Rio Grande pueblos, Mexicans can find unimpaired examples of the ancient Aztec art; in less evolved forms than once existed in Mexico, but of absolute authenticity. How can we preserve what we have until they, and we, perhaps, shall have profited by our inheritance?

That the American people as a whole want our aboriginal drama preserved, there is sufficient evidence. A few years ago when there was danger of losing it through departmental stupidity, public opinion forced a rescission of the Indian Bureau's order forbidding the performance of Indian dances. The present attitude of the Department of the Interior is enlightened and sympathetic towards all Indian Art. What remains to be discovered is the precise method. The profoundly scholarly nature of the problem, suggests the intervention of the dramatic departments of our universities. Just now, when universities are considering the appropriateness of degrees in connection with work in the theatre and drama, one would expect this rich new field to be seized upon with avidity. But the American academic mind seems to be markedly unable to deal with its material directly; to demand before any ingestion can take place, that everything shall be committed to print, in which process much of the dramatic vitality will have evaporated. Almost every week the writer receives inquiry from one school or another for a "book on the subject," but from no one of them an offer to finance the work of collecting and publishing such a volume. Nor from any patron of the theatre has any suggestion arisen that the Amerind drama should be made the subject of such practical stage presentation as is constantly—and so often fatuously—done for European drama.

The problem is not altogether one of ignorance of the factors involved. Much of the difficulty arises from a characteristic reaction of sentimentality on the part of the American individual towards the Indian. Amerind drama is already trembling on the verge of that normal progression away from religious ceremonialism towards the stage, which Greek drama accomplished so successfully. If the American stage were opened to it, Amerind drama would flow naturally, as Negro dramatic talent flows, towards legitimate theatrical expression. Amerind decorative and pictorial art is finding normal outlets; Amerind literary talent is being released in the publishing world. But Amerind drama is prohibited from its evolutionary progression not so much by the lack of proper financing as by the sentimental paralysis which always overtakes the American public when it is profoundly moved. Everybody is moved by direct contact with Indian dance drama, and tends, first, to grow tearful over the frightful violence that is done to Indian integrity by making a public spectacle of religious drama, and then peevish because nothing is done about it. For the average American loves when he is moved, to be able to wave his hand and say Presto Change! and have the thing altered to his liking. What he does not realize is that, with his and the government's connivance, a steady propaganda has been going on for the past thirty years in Indian schools to overcome both the religious and the art values of Amerind drama. In the light of our governmental effort to wipe out Indian culture as such, and to teach the Indian young to ignore and despise their ancestral arts, the sentimental peevishness of a moiety of the Indian dance audience is as objectionable and as futile as the trivial incapacity of another part of the same audience to see it as anything other than "show." What is required for this, as for any other cultural salvage, is the co-operative activity of an enlightened group. And it may as well be stated here as anywhere that any Indian dance drama which the miscellaneous public is permitted to attend has already lost most of its religious implication. If the schools and the missionaries will let him alone, the Indian is perfectly able to maintain his own spiritual integrity.

What is unknown to most Americans is that the Indian himself, the better types of him, is of a scholarly bent of mind. I have never found it prohibitory or even obtrusively difficult to discuss with the Indian his own esoteric meanings, the profoundest implications of his philosophy. He is slow about finding equivalent expression for his spiritual life in our language, in our thought; but I have always found him delicately responsive to the spiritual and intellectual courtesies which we extend to our own artists and philosophers. He appreciates seeing his legends in our books, his pictures in our galleries; he would appreciate seeing his dramas on our stage under the same aegis of artistic integrity and dignity that we afford to other peoples. What he will not tolerate is being admitted as a sideshow, as a mere curiosity of the dramatic entourage. The exhibition of his mysteries to respectful and inquiring groups of our American young people would, other things being equal, please him almost as much as showing them to his own young. Certain religious restrictions are likely to appear for some time—not every ceremonial is sufficiently dramatic to escape being a mystery—but as I personally know the Indian artist, he is homesick for the fellowship of his own kind. If we could forego our rather stupid and coercive campaign to compel him into our competitive economic system, and our purely objective intellectualism, he would come happily into his own place in our art on his own merits.... But if neither the art theatre nor the university school of dramatics is open to him another hundred years will see his brilliant, colorful, and moving drama no more. Christianity, the public school, the stricken consciousness of aesthetic misappreciation, will have had their innings, to our own irreparable loss.

14

Primitive Stage Setting

1928

It is only by keeping in mind that primitive drama was concerned with getting things done, and had nothing to do with story telling that any satisfactory theory of the origin of stage setting can be arrived at. Drama began as magic; as a communal performance for persuading the Universe, under any one of its special aspects, to work together for the advantage of mankind. It was communal in as much as the good of the community as a whole was sought, and both actors and spectators were participants. The performance was rhythmic, since rhythm was an early, empirically discovered method of raising the voltage of group desire. It concerned both gods and men, or if not gods, the invisible Forces which were afterward symbolized as godhead; incalculable, except as they were believed to be alive toward men, and communicable. And this, under whatever shape of the moment, is the function of good drama today; to raise the spiritual voltage of the group, to bring the people into sympathetic communion with the Powers, and thus explicate and inform the particular human need that the occasion shows forth. It is in this shape that primitive drama can still be seen going on before the "medicine-lodge," around the kiva, in Amerindian villages of our Southwest.

The act to be dramatically performed is always one of supreme necessity; that the rain may fall, that game may multiply, that the tribe may increase, sickness be taken away and the arrows of the enemy be turned aside. The community is present in whichever of its aspects is most under consideration, as male or female, as hunter, warrior, farmer, housebuilder, giver of bread. The Powers—afterward deified—were thought of as present in spirit, but were brought closer to the actors by being symbolized, in the phallus, the corn-ear, the bow, later by masked impersonators. Man's helpers also appeared as friendly animals or as the spirits of his ancestors. Still later, when the gods themselves had been specialized and named, the community began to appear not as mankind but as particular men, as Oedipus, Hamlet, Oswald, and the aspiration—or the handicap to be removed—signalized as the madness of Orestes, the nose of Cyrano, the beauty of Melisande.

All of these phases of dramatic presentation had either appeared or been strongly shadowed forth while drama was still primitive; that is to say while movement, color and melody were taking the place that was later occupied by dialogue. This was also before architecture could render any aid, and the play was performed before the huts or tents of the wild tribe. In this period man himself was the only dramatic vehicle. Accordingly he set himself as the stage, the primary object of all stage setting being to isolate the act, to give it cogency and attract the sympathetic attention of the Powers. So man painted himself black to signalize the Earth Power, red and yellow for summer and the sun, turquoise for the sky, or black and white to personate the spirits of the ancestors. Further, he added ornaments and painted or worked designs of appropriate symbol on his skin or his clothing. Very soon he began to isolate the place in which the drama took place; before the tribal altar, on the High-place Shrine, or merely within a sacred precinct variously marked out. Always having it in mind to make an urgent, an unmistakable showing of what he aspired to have or be.

For this is the true use of drama, to make a Showing of Life, that life may be bettered thereby. Thus in the Rain Dance at Sia, men, women and children make a showing of themselves and their desire, "That the corn come up; that the people grow strong; that the people have bread to complete the path of life." In like manner *What Price Glory?* makes a showing of war, that the people may be saved from this madness, *The Silver Cord* makes a showing of obsessive mother-love, and *Abie's Irish Rose* a showing of the folly of race prejudice.

In primitive times man supposed none but the gods able to help life very much. Therefore all drama was what is called religious. It was designed to further the action of men, and so induce the sympathetic activity of the gods. Along this line all stage setting developed. It is not in the earliest stages representative, what is modernly called "realistic," but suggestive. The Papago, before making himself gloriously drunk with saguaro wine as a way of insuring a wet year, fences in the drinking place with "cloud callers," strings of feathers. The Pueblo dancer will sometimes outline near the dancing place, a "god home" in blue cornmeal, or the Navajo erect, for the accommodation of the Yei, a "dark circle of boughs," within which they and the Navajo may meet. But the Navajo did even better. He painted in the floor of the Medicine Hogan or on the open dancing floor, a sand picture of the sacred story which gave rise to his ritual, as bird catchers spread lime on boughs.

When the sand painting is woven into a blanket, as frequently happens, and hung upon the wall of the Medicine Hogan, its relation to stage setting is immediately apparent. It is also from this point that we can definitely begin to spin the threads that connect Amerind drama with what we know of the origins of classic drama in Greece. It has been said that aboriginal drama is not concerned with telling a story. But there is always a story concerned with the play. It is the story of how the ceremonial which is displayed in the dance-drama was originally received by man. Always it is supposed to have been taught to an individual by the Surpassing-Beings, by his totem animal or by one of the animal helpers of primitive man. Sometimes it comes in dreams as the answer to prayer, or in the trance vision of the neophyte, but more often it is given at the end of an adventure with the Surpassing-Ones. It is, in fact, the precious essence of an experience, preserved in song and dance and ritual, remedial for conditions similar to those that called it forth. In the earliest forms, the ritualistic acts and the lyrics or chorals of which the ceremonial is composed, are simply shorthand notations of the story, the story itself being utterly unintelligible to the uninstructed onlooker. To the performers, however, the story has been revealed by the priests, or it has formed part of the childhood instruction of every member of the tribe, and serves to explain the ceremonial as the story of the Nativity explains the Christmas tree to the modern child. Ask yourself how much you would guess of the Christ story if, with no other preparation, you suddenly stumbled upon a group of people singing around an evergreen tree hung with gifts and candles, and over it a tinsel representation of a star, and you will realize how little can be guessed of the origin of an aboriginal dance-drama at the first seeing. You might even suppose in the first case, that the chubby, masked personage in red, with long white whiskers, found distributing the gifts, to be the deity worshipped in this fashion. So you might suppose an explanation of the Navajo Yabetchi which would be wide of the true story of the young man who was stolen by the Utes, and in escaping endured an Odyssey of mythical experiences in the House of the Rock Crystal, or the Rainbow, or behind the Dark Curtain of the Doorway of the Dawn. And having returned home the young man found that his own tribe no longer smelled good to him, whereupon his spiritual guide, Elder Brother, taught him the Yabetchi ritual as a means of restoring him to normal condition. But if you were versed in Navajo symbolism and pictography, you would guess from the accompanying sand painting as much about the play as used to be conveyed by one of George Bernard Shaw's prefaces, or earlier, by such notations as "Towers of Illium in the distance" or "Windsor Castle at the right." It interested me to recall last year, on seeing Robert Edmond Jones' designs for a jazz ballet, that Mr. Jones was directly acquainted with aboriginal art. His method of treating the mechanical background of an amusement park was very much in the Navajo manner, making allowance for the fact that the Navajo is obliged to spread his stage setting flat on the ground, and his medium is colored sands gathered painstakingly from the Painted Desert.

The connection here with Greek Drama is not so instantly perceived. The bulk of Amerind drama is in the condition of Greek drama at about 600 B.C. when historical account of its evolution was first taken. It was composed of ritual acts, dancing and singing, without dialogue; it was confined to one place the locus of which was signalized by the presence of an altar or shrine or other sacred index; it depended wholly on body painting and costume for its explanatory setting. But the most advanced Amerind drama introduces dialogue between the members of the chorus, or between them and a priest or masked personator of the gods. Examples of this can be observed in the dance of The Emergence at San Felipe, The Snake Dance or Flute Ceremony in the Hopi pueblos, and many of the Zuni dances. This means that in the most primitive forms of Greek and Amerind drama the story does not appear, but the ritual is addressed to conditions affecting the community, similar to those in which the ritual arose. But little by little the story emerges, until in the best examples of Greek drama it is the story that makes the play. A precisely similar evolution is demonstrable in the case of Mexican aboriginal drama. The identity of the two processes appears beyond question. In classic drama Thespis is credited with having introduced actors into the dance-drama of Athens; but I strongly suspect that Thespis merely improved upon and formalized a tendency which he had discovered developing naturally in Attic drama.

It is necessary to recall so much of the history of classic drama because it has been supposed that the stage, that is a raised platform for the speaker, was introduced by the Greek tragedians merely in order that the speaker might be better heard. I also suspect that this was not so much the case as that the locus of the play had been modified by the temple which had arisen over the shrine or at one side of the sacred precinct. So long as the fetishes and sacred symbols of the tribe were housed in a tent of skins or a hut of boughs there could be no stage other than the ground on which the audience stood and the dancers performed. When there was a temple or kiva within which the more sacred mysteries were performed, its portico or steps would naturally provide a standing ground for actors issuing from its recesses. This can be seen in the Hopi dances as the Snake Priests or the Katchinas come and go from kisi and kiva. It is more than likely that the rigid stone stage of classic drama originated in the equally rigid temple portico, as it can be shown to have originated among Amerinds south of the United States line. Also it is suggested that the Greek habit of having all acts of violence take place behind the stage originated in a previous habit of having sacrifices and other mysteries take place within the cellar or temple proper, out of sight of, or at least somewhat removed from, the crowd.

On this assumption, which in the case of Amerind drama is simple fact, the altar and wall decorations of the temple or kiva become part of the stage setting. As these are dictated by the particular cult being celebrated, details would be tedious. The one thing that can be said of all these settings is that they are invariably *suggestive rather than representative*. They resemble, making allowance for the primitive vocabulary of art, what Robert Edmond Jones tried to do once in an ultra "modern" setting *for Macbeth*; what was done by Covarrubias in *Androcles and the Lion* with a stylized painted curtain for a jungle background.

This was the evolution of stage setting in the drama which remained religious in character and became tragedy in Europe. But stage setting for drama which was modulated into comedy, proceeded along realistic lines; its setting was representative or, at the outside, tended toward caricature. From the earliest times comedy seems to have been used as a social corrective, and was in the hands of societies or at least of persons as official and as sacred in character as any other. But the comedy "business," necessarily objective, becomes inevitably realistic. Among Amerinds, however, it was never divorced from that economy of means which distinguishes all their art, the innate capacity for occupying space without filling it. In setting the stage for a Pueblo comedy the absolute article for labeling place or period is invariably selected. Once I saw an impromptu farce involving Apache and Keres tribes, in which the Apache country was indicated by three well placed yuccas, while ten feet away the Keres domain was perfectly characterized by a selection of a single young pine tree. When it became necessary to indicate the camp of the white man this was done beyond doubt by a scattering of several rusty tin cans. On another occasion a camp of archeologists was successfully located by an old bone and a few potsherds and an imitation phonograph horn. Extremely clever animal representations are managed for comedy, while for the sacred dances only animal masks and symbolic body paintings are used, along with feathers which have always a prayerful significance. In Pueblo drama the complete absence of feathers in costume or setting would positively indicate the comedy character.

One aspect of primitive comedy, if better understood, might throw a helpful light on the vexed problem of the "sex" play. Many primitive plays have to do with fructification of crops, of wild game, of the mothers of the tribe. And to the primitive mind both reverence and laughter are indispensable concomitants of success. A fructification ceremony entered into as a sacrament is not less acceptable to the tribes than a fructification comedy which can be uproariously laughed at. The sort of sex play which can only be sniggered at or suffered in uneasy silence is never seen in Amerindian camps. It is exclusively served to "civilized audiences."

I am sure that the distinction is a sound one, that an attitude toward sex which is of unbroken solemnity is as degenerate as an attitude

of uniform salaciousness. The probabilities are that our own difficulties about the whole problem of sex drama arise out of our being so
largely bemused by sex obsessions that we do not any more know what
aspects of sex ought to be taken seriously and what can be best corrected with whips of laughter. Any sex suggestion or symbol, even the
sexual act itself, if done in the presence of the gods, is permissible in
aboriginal drama. If done only for or by the people it must be treated
humorously.

15

A New Medium for Poetic Drama

1917

Like those faint trails through the wood to places where wild creatures go to drink, are the paths that lead to the newest fountainhead of Art: first a smooth way into which the foot slips unaware, a barely discernible parting of the grass, and then the broad track that takes on direction and ends suddenly in a huddle of footprints about the spring. And by the time the public has news of the fountain its waters are so roiled and muddied by the multitude that it is impossible for a long time to say whether it is a true perennial fountain or a local puddle.

This has happened recently in America, in the attempt to free poetry from traditional forms. There are those who suppose the movement merely the seasonal overflow of minor poets from the neighborhood of Washington Square; but those of us who were privileged to come stealing upon it through the wilderness of American literary invention of the first decade of this century, believe it to be sprung from that true fountain of youth which somebody or other always hoped to find in America.

It is such a far cry from a Paiute village, called "The-Mush-That-Was-Afraid," to the Sunday-at-Home of a distinguished London critic, that it is impossible for me to say just when I discovered that the half-clue I followed was a trail to Somewhere; but I can recall very well the occasion of my first speaking of it. This was the winter of 1903–04, in an address before the English Club of Stanford University. What I had discovered past any doubt was that the poetic forms of the Amerind (to use the term sanctioned by professional scholarship) reflect to an extraordinary degree the land he lives in, its reach of view; its contours,

sharp or flowing; its fatness, its forest cover. After a reasonable study of
the various forms of Amerind verse, it is possible, on hearing a new one,
to say very exactly whether it comes from mountain or desert region,
Platte River, Great Lakes, or Western Mesa. If one takes musical nota-
tion into account—and tonal quality—it is possible to name the very
tribe, but I am speaking now only of measure and rhythm. People who
have despaired of America producing a distinct art of her own may take
heart at this. The universal reflection of what a man lives and sees, in
what he produces, does not fail here, and river and prairie will work out
their own expression quite as surely through the stubborn European
stuff we send them, as it has already been worked in the native
Amerind. It is not only possible, but it is inevitable that, for any sure
forecast of the future forms of literary art in America, we must look in
our native and aboriginal narrative and verse and drama.

Drama played an important part in the daily life of the Amerind,
but it can hardly be said to have attained a convention of form; or
rather, it was in the form of the earliest Greek drama known to us, the
Satyric dances. Some of the great tribal dramas required several days for
complete production and weeks of preparation. Always there was a
story, sometimes comic, often historical, but the best was, as with the
Greeks, always occupied for its theme with the relation of Man to the
Great Mystery.

It is this religious significance of aboriginal drama which makes the
study of its literary medium important to the modern dramatist. Bear
in mind that the slightest mistake in its performance might have the
most serious consequences to the tribe, and that there was no means of
preserving it except by word of mouth from generation to generation;
then you can easily see that it was necessary for tribal welfare that the
medium of the drama should be as perfect as was humanly possible. It
must be easily remembered, easily apprehended, and have every aid that
could be afforded by rhythm, sound sequence and all those complicated processes which go to make up what we call literature.

Where words are so precious that they must needs be preserved a
thousand years or so, then something must go along with the words,
like amber, to keep their vital form intact long after they would have
in the ordinary use become, as many of Shakespeare's words are, obsolete. Indian drama, which consists of song sequences, dance and inter-

ludes and recitative, was obliged to have such a medium in order to save itself alive.

Here the lack of space makes it necessary to skip the fascinating process of discovering and transcribing into English the lasting fiber of that medium. One must be taken largely on trust in saying that the medium of Amerind drama is like that of all great drama: poetic; and that its rhythms are based on the bodily movements which naturally take their rise in the emotions evoked. It lacks the item of rhyme, and though it exhibits a tendency to flow into form, the form is never controlled by convention, but by the natural accompanying movement. Such a thing as a native drama done all in one kind of verse would be impossible. The verse-rhythm flows along with the action like a river in its bed. Perhaps it is enough to say that I can find you quite as perfect examples of this rhythm in the works of Edgar Lee Masters and Amy Lowell as in the reports of the Bureau of Ethnology. As a matter of fact *all* important tribal affairs are carried on in cadenced speech, nicely suited to the matter in hand, and when I wrote my first Indian play, *The Arrow Maker*, I wrote it instinctively in this medium.

In my innocence I had already tried some examples of this sort of versification on the highest-browed magazine in America, and had had it returned with a top-loftical editorial comment that they "couldn't see any excuse for its being written." Fortunately the more popular magazines proved kinder, and in old files of *McClure's* and *Everybody's* you will find what is probably the first "free verse" published in any American magazine. But when I offered *The Arrow Maker*, written in that form, a horrified agent refused to accept it and said plainly that no New York manager would so much as look at it. So I rewrote my manuscript in ordinary prose form, and later, when it was being produced at the New Theatre, I used to see, both producers and actors puzzling over lines which they could not make up their minds to deliver as poetry or prose. I fancy no one would have that difficulty now, though the lines are still printed in prose form.

Up to this time it had not occurred to me to use the Indian medium for anything but Indian plays, but in the summer of 1909 I was in England, and at the house of Edmund Grosse took part in a conversation on the dearth of modern poetic drama. It was William Archer, I think, who declared that the issue of poetic drama depended on the discovery of a new verse-form capable of carrying modern emotion. Elizabethan forms had been so stamped by Shakespeare as to render them forever sacred to his genius, even if the thoughts of men had continued to keep step with their sonority. Celtic verse, such as had been used so delightfully by Mr. Yeats, was too monotonous, and also too remote for general use; the same ban lay on Maeterlinck's measured phrases. And then Mr. Grosse, with the polite intention of including me in the conversation, suggested that it was up to America to produce the much-needed medium—(no, of course Edmund Grosse didn't say "up to," but that was what he meant). I am sure they hadn't any of them expected anything to come out of the West so apt as that, but they were all interest and appreciation when I began to tell and to give examples of native American Indian drama in its chosen medium. I remember quoting the Pawnee Travel Song, with its long undulating lines like the prairie of the Platte, with the little jog of the pony trot coming in oddly at the end, and also a Paiute Lament that begins so:

> My son! My son!
> I will go up the mountain.
> There I will light a fire to my son's spirit,
> And there I will lament him,
> Saying,
> O my son, what is my life to me, now you are departed!

It was the encouragement that I received that afternoon which led to my writing *Fire*, a drama in three acts, which was tried out at the Forest Theatre in 1912 and produced with much success at the San Francisco Exposition in the summer of 1915. So far as I can learn, this was the first "free verse" drama produced on any American stage. Even so, I found the actors constantly altering the measure, dropping words or filling in, pulling back toward the old, familiar forms. When, in 1914, the Wisconsin Play Book offered to publish *Fire*, further damage was done the original form by the friend who prepared the manuscript for me, I being ill at the time. He worked his hardest to make conventional verse out of it, and offered me in conclusion this valuable hint: "You write splendid plays," he said, "but you really shouldn't try to write poetry. I had a dreadful time trying to straighten out some of those lines."

By this time, of course, the woods were full of writers who had discovered the trails to this new Spring of native verse, and in 1916 the Washington Square Players gave it the "coup" of professional approval by producing Zoë Akins' *Magical City*, a modern drama in the freest of free verse.

It is true that the variety of free verse which is produced in the vicinity of Washington Square lacks the music and tenderness of forms I am most acquainted with among Indians of the Southwest; but who knows, perhaps the early tribe of Manhattan had a truculent temperament.

I have spoken chiefly of the "verse-form" of the Amerind, though I am sensible that some other descriptive word ought to be invented to express the adjustment of form to character and emotion which characterizes aboriginal drama. No such thing occurs there as the king answering the fool in the same measures, or Portia and Falstaff employing a similar cadence for their several emotions. Every man's speech proceeds from the center of consciousness of that man, and the fluency of the form can be seen in any ordinary Indian pow-wow when, as emotions are excited and gradually lifted to the same plane by a community of interest, the cadence of the speeches keeps pace with it, so that at the high moments everyone speaks more or less in the same key. When dramatic interest drops, the manner of speech tends to greater diversity.

There are many striking likenesses between original Amerind and modern magazine narrative forms, and it may be possible that the recent tendency toward community masque and the dramatization of man's relation to his job, in pageant and play, may be quite in line with this influence of the soil. Out in the West, where the climate permits it, Raisin Festivals, Tournaments of Roses, Grape Harvests, and Cherry-blossom Fêtes, seem to fall naturally into the aboriginal Festival of Green Corn, Piñon Harvest Dance, and Mountain Festivals. These are items which stare every student of local art influences in the face. Yet, no longer ago than two years, I wrote an article for one of our best known magazines on Art Influences in the West from which the editor forced me to delete what I have said here about the relation between modern American drama and native American drama, and permitted the mention of the festivals only in connection with early

Greek celebrations. This sort of shallow snobbishness is quite as much to blame for retarding indigenous development as is our much-decried commercialism. Free verse has, I believe, like the wolf in the ancient nursery tale, got one paw in the crack of the stage door. The next moment it will come shouldering through.

16

Letter to the Editor of
Theatre Arts Monthly

1929

You ask me what I am doing in the dramatic field besides my work in the Indian dance drama. What I am trying just now is to restore the Spanish drama in New Mexico, probably the only genuine folk drama still productive in the United States.

You know, forty percent of our population in the Rio Grande country is Spanish speaking, which means of course that they are congenitally dramatic. Every little town far enough away from the railroad to be untouched by American influences still has its little theatre society. Every year these societies give certain traditional plays in connection with the holiday seasons; and in the long winter evenings they still compose and enact amusing and touching little dramas, sometimes wholly original and wholly New Mexican, and sometimes merely remembered and localized versions of moving picture dramas and seldom-seen American entertainments. A number of years ago I became interested in collecting these plays, especially the traditional ones which go back to the time of Lope de Rueda and Lope de Vega and other dramatists flourishing about the time New Mexico was settled.

Many of these plays have not been committed to writing since they were brought over by the military from Spain, or if written down, usually by young people who have never learned to write or spell the language that they speak; so one has to collect them part by part from the families in which the parts are hereditary along with the costumes and properties and the traditional business. It has been a rather tedious business to get them onto paper intelligibly. But on the whole it is an exciting and rewarding undertaking. My very first prize was the manuscript of the first play ever performed on the soil of the United States, July 10, 1598, and which is still played on Holy Cross Day within ten miles of the location of its original performance. My next discovery was that many of these plays have genuine literary quality, in the folk *genre* of course. And it goes without saying that there is a surprising amount of acting talent as well as playwriting ability.

Of course these manuscripts are all in the condition of the treasure that archaeologists dig up, earth and time-encrusted, and it's been a task requiring patience and time as well as a knowledge of the folk method to restore them to anything like their original condition. However, while I was at Yale last winter, with the help of Mr. Alexander Dean and his students, we produced one of them with the primitive business, and found to our surprise that it had power to charm and to move the very sophisticated audience of Yale University. It isn't, however, to provide little theatre groups with a new and natively American medium that I am primarily interested. What I am trying to do is to restore to the Spanish people the opportunity which they once made and we Americanos stupidly destroyed. I'm quite sure that these simple people here have it within them to make an important and exciting contribution to the American theatre. All they need is a little encouragement and financial aid. They are so desperately poor. Most of the performances have to be given out of doors, or in the church or the school house with such a poverty of dramatic equipment that I am often moved to tears to see the way in which their native genius is able to make itself felt. What I am trying to do here at Santa Fe is to reinstate the original Teatro de Corral, an open air stage set up in one of the town's little plazas or *placitas*. When I think of what I could do with a few thousand dollars to reanimate this earliest American form of folk drama I feel quite desperate. Why doesn't some one of the wealthy patrons of the drama who is willing to sink hundreds of thousands of dollars in musical comedy and doubtful Americanizations of indifferent European dramas see his opportunity to immortalize himself in the history of the American theatre by opening the way to the New Mexican folk drama? I think I'll have to burn a candle to San Luis de Gonzaga! And in the meantime if you see anybody who has any money to spare for a perfectly ripping adventure in the drama, please tag him for me and New Mexico.

17

A Drama Played on Horseback

1928

When the two great streams of colonization came into the country that is now the United States of North America they behaved after their racial kind. The Nordics reaching the northeast coast fell upon their knees and prayed. The Latin-Iberians entering the desert regions of the Southwest bestrode their horses gallantly and played. The English came trusting none too confidently in God, and the Spanish celebrated their *entrada* with a pageant play which demonstrated that God was already on their side.

This was in July of 1598, at the junction of the Chama River with the Rio Grande, where their first capital was decreed. That they found the site already occupied by two Indian pueblos, called Yuque-Yunge, in no wise disconcerted them. The Spaniards speedily changed the name to San Juan.

About the twelfth of July the founding was celebrated with the performance of "The Moors," so far as known the only play ever performed entirely on horseback. One wonders how the expedition had the heart for it after their seven months' trek from Santa Barbara in old Mexico; but play they did, while the aboriginals of Yuque-Yunge watched from the housetops as a measure of safety against being eaten by the "long-tailed elk" of the caballeros. Every year or two since that day the descendants of the Spanish colonists of New Mexico in the district of Rio Arriba (Upper River) have entertained themselves and their neighbors with a revival of "*Los Moros.*" Not more than three miles from Alcalde, the site of the original performance, I recently saw such a revival.

The original manuscript of the play was undoubtedly brought from Spain—not written in the New World, as was the comedy with which

Oñate's expedition celebrated its arrival at the south bank of the Rio Grande. But Captain Farfan's little play was enacted near the present city of Juarez in old Mexico and was not actually done on territory belonging to the United States, which leaves that distinction to the play of which I write.

"Los Moros" is a play of Spain's conquest of her enemies the Moors. The action revolves about the theft of Holy Cross by the Infidels, its recapture by the Christians, and the reduction of the Moorish army to humble acceptance of the Catholic faith. The original must have been written in conventional blank verse of the period, but in existing manuscripts, set down from memory, there is only the rhythm of the dialogue to prove the poetic form.

It was from one of these memory transcripts that the Alcalde performance was played. The characters of the drama are Don Alfonso, the general of the Christians; *El Gran Sultan*, general of the Moorish army, and several of their captains. The armies are equally divided and as large as can be conveniently assembled. At Alcalde, New Mexico, the part of Don Alfonso was played by Estonislao Borego, while Valentin Martinez carried off the honors of the Christian host. Other names as musical and as honored in New Mexican history as Winthrop and Standish are in Massachusetts figured in the cast.

As is usual with these ancient folk plays of the Spanish colonies, the actors, many of them, appear in parts their fathers and grandfathers played before them. Parts are often handed down by word of mouth from generation to generation along with the traditional business, which, so far as I can discover, never has been written down. Nevertheless the order of sally and attack and mimic battle is so completely ritualized that it is probably that in just this fashion the gentlemen of Oñate wheeled and raced and reined their horses and clashed their swords in 1598.

At the Alcalde performance there was no costuming except the use of white sashes and bandas and banners for the Christians, and crimson for the Moors, though it is known that there are still preserved in ancient chests many handsome relics of the colonial period. There were swords, however, ancient Spanish blades, slender buffalo stickers, rusty cavalry sabers of the period of the American occupation and beautiful, free sword-swinging gestures such as one imagines will always go with Spanish blood.

The stage setting was of the simplest; a white covered altar topped with a white cross for the camp of the Christians, set in the open plaza, and a smaller rosy cross for the Moors to steal and race away with to their own camp under a cottonwood tree. During the play the prompter leaned against the altar and not infrequently lost his place in the excitement of the action, thus holding up the play, as unselfconsciously as the property man in a Chinese theater. The audience was about equally divided between black-shawled and wide-hatted descendants of the Spanish colonial families and modern American spectators. The note of formality was given—for this was on the thirtieth of May—by the truck load of the local members of the American Legion, with *their* banners over them. Half a dozen guitars and violins made a strange half-Spanish, half-jazz accompaniment. Over all was the wide New Mexican day.

It is necessary to witness one of these naïve folk plays to realize their charm. It is not all in the aesthetic consonance between the setting, the actors and the drama. Nor is it entirely owing to the dramatic instinct that goes with the blood of the Spanish-speaking. There is a subtle something in the effect not only of entertainment but also of aesthetic satisfaction which cannot be described. It can only be felt and enjoyed. It is perhaps the thing that is now drawing such numbers of the aesthetically inclined to New Mexico, the demand which it all makes on the recipient for participation. You may not care for what the cross symbolizes; you may think war too awful for this mimic play; you may be quite indifferent to the conversion of the Moors. But if you happen to stray into the plaza of one of these little Rio Arriba towns when they are playing "The Moors" you will not leave it until the last Christian has led captive the last infidel and the audience with a long sigh of satisfaction follows after.

18

Story of the Guadalupe Play, Matachines Dance

1933

The apparition of Our Lady of Guadalupe in the form of an Indian maiden to Cargadero Juan Diego, on the Hill of Tepeyac, occurred on the 12th of December, 1531, in the first third of the 16th century. The Hill of Tepeyac which is in the suburbs of the City of Mexico, was a place already sanctified to the Mexican gods of fertility, and the spring which is still gushing at the foot of the hill was one of the sacred wells of the locality.

The play tells the story of how the apparition appeared to Juan Diego. He was on the way to secure a doctor for a sick uncle; when the virgin insisted that he should proceed at once to the archbishop in Mexico and make known her request that he build her a chapel on the spot of her appearance; and the play tells of how the archbishop demurred and insisted on evidence; of how finally roses were produced on the bare rock of Tepeyac as evidence for Juan Diego to take to the archbishop, and how when he reached there, a picture of the appearance was seen painted on the front of his tilma. This picture is still reserved at the chapel of Our Lady of Guadalupe and bears certain superficial evidences of its authenticity, as it seems to be painted on a piece of native homespun material.

Many Plays Written

There are various references in early Mexican history to the miracles which were wrought at the Chapel of Our Lady, even as early as the manuscript of Bernal Diaz. A number of plays have been written about this incident, but the most of them go back to a manuscript produced by Don Jose de la Pena, which is a rather long and complete drama in three acts. This was not printed for some time and was handed about by manuscript copies and shortened. Also, everybody who produced it felt at liberty to make alterations in the text to suit the group who participated in the play. But the version which is being produced by Manuel Romero in Santa Fe is not only very much shorter than the de la Pena manuscript, but Mr. Romero has himself worked at it in trying to increase the clarity and the dramatic quality of the play itself.

I have in my possession one of the few, perhaps the only exact version of the de la Pena play, and from it I made an English translation which was produced by the dramatic department of Yale University two years ago, with great success. And I also took some liberties with the original, cutting out the sermonizing on the part of the archbishop, which was conspicuous in the third act.

The Matachines Dance

It may not be known hereabout that the dance known as the Matachines is by tradition connected with the Guadalupe incident, and is older than the drama. Matachines is a Spanish word indicating a story telling dance, a dance in which a story is indicated, and the tradition is that when the chapel was built and the sacred evidence of our lady of Guadalupe established, a dance was performed there by the Indian bishops who had already been appointed by the Catholic bishops in old Mexico. The Indians in Mexico were still very primitive, so that a sacred dance was their most effective way of presenting their religious sentiments. The Guadalupe dance was supposed to have been already in existence as an Aztec religious dance and was somewhat modified by churchmen of that period to represent the soul's progress. A good deal of confusion arose in the native mind about what was actually meant by the dance, and it is believed in some quarters that there was a deliberate effort to satirize the conquest.

Original Characters

The actual original characters of the Matachines consist of el monarco; two capitanes; a girl who from the fact that she is usually dressed in white communion robe is called the Bride or the Soul, but is also called Marina, who was the mistress of Cortez. Then there is the character called El Toro, who represents the old pagan spirit and a figure of lust or sensual pleasure, along with a number of dancers. In support of the tradition that this Matachines was danced by the early Indian bishops, there is the fact that the head-dress worn by the dancers represents the bishop's mitre, and that the costumes are rude approximations of priestly robes. For a number of years the Matachines dance was the only ceremonial belonging to Our Lady of Guadalupe, but it was finally replaced by various attempts at drama until the drama of Don Jose de la Pena was written and became the standard play. It is not known how early the play and the dance were imported into New Mexico, but probably they came in with the first settlers who had attached to them a number of Mexican Indians.

I should say in conclusion that both the Matachines dance and the Guadalupe play are found here in New Mexico in a purer and more exact condition than in old Mexico, and I heartily recommend Mr. Romero's performance of Los Cuatro Aparicones as of genuine interest to the people of New Mexico, being probably, with the exception of Los Moros y el Cristiano, the oldest play produced in the whole United States and intimately connected with the history of New Mexico.

19

The Trail of the Blood:
An Account of the Penitent
Brotherhood of New Mexico

1924

Don Juan De Oñate, explorer, settler, and *Adelantado* of the province of Nueva Mexico, was also a devout man.

Faithful son of the church and member of the third Order of St. Francis, he writes himself down as keeping Lent with his men after the fashion of the whipping brotherhoods.

Thus the furthest ripple of the spiritual intensity which showed itself first in whipping brotherhoods, flowered in the art of the *Cinquecento*, and bore the colonization of the western hemisphere as its fruit, was absorbed into the Spanish-speaking settlements along the Rio Grande and its tributaries, to reappear as *Los Hermanos Penitentes*, whose annual penance ends in the realistic and sometimes fatal crucifixion of one of their number.

Every year about the time Arcturus leads the herdsman over the eastern hills, and the willows redden along the stream-borders, you can hear in the neighborhood of the mud-walled towns the fall of the lash on bared backs, and the eery tootle of the flute as the *pitero* leads forth the procession from the local chapter-house. It is a heart-and-ear piercing tune the flute plays, wailing through the quarter-notes of the native Indian scale to the breaking-point, and falling off to passages of plaintive sweetness in pure Gregorian intervals. Behind it the ghostly light of lanterns bobs level with the tops of the young sage, and the shadowy forms of men move in unison with the chant that is led by the *pitero* almost up to the door of heaven, and dropped into the very slough of human despair. If you are fortunate in your choice of location, and not too much of a "bounder," you may be permitted to see the whole of a native American passion play beside which Oberammergau is a tourist's interval.

To understand how the practice of the Third Order has been reworked into an American community drama, one must realize the nature of the human material worked upon. Oñate not only brought with him the most exigent stuff of Spanish stock, Aguilars, Ortegas, de Herreras, Guiterres; he brought also a considerable company of old Mexican natives, chiefly Thalascans, in whom, as well as in the native New Mexican stock absorbed by them to make the present Spanish-speaking population, there was a long-seasoned disposition to express man's own sense of his relation to the Saving Powers by dramatic mimesis. Later there came Chauves, Armejos, Vegils, Lunas, Oteros, continuing the rich strain that produced in old Spain the magnificently theatric era of Lope de Vega. If anything of the mother country's abundant creative energy spilled over to the colonies, it was bound to be dramatic in quality, as whatever they absorbed from the Pueblos was mimetic in form—deer dance and corn dance and races of the swift-coming rain. With every contributory strain of Indian blood came memories of whipping rites, of fastings and of gashings and expiation by the maddening prick of the cactus thorn.

Items of this sort emerge obscurely between the record of Oñate and September of 1794, at which date, by a report made by Father Bernal to Governor Chacon, the order of *Los Hermanos Penitentes* is shown to have been in existence for some time. Then no more mention until 1886, when the French Bishop of Santa Fe is discovered issuing an order forbidding the performance of mass in the *penitente* chapels.

From this we understand that in the interim the drama that the dark-whites of the Southwest had made for themselves had become more sacredly familiar than the formal observances of the church. It was perhaps not wholly because they had made it for themselves that still, in the Rio Grande villages and in the flat lands about Las Vegas, north across the Colorado boundary and south into Old Mexico, a narrow space, you find the tall, gaunt crosses of the *Calvarios*, and every season when the wild plums whiten the creek-borders, out of the squat, shuttered chapter-houses hear the rise and fall of the blood-soaked *disciplinas*.

The *morada*, or chapter-house, identified among the other flat-topped buildings by its cupola and the cross over the door, exists wherever there is a brotherhood. Always there are two rooms, one of which is a chapel, the other housing the implements of the order. Occasionally there is a third, serving as office and club-room for the members. There is never more than a single entrance to the *morada*.

Straight away from it leads the *Rasto de la Sangre* to the stark-lifted arms of the cross on the nearest hill, the *Calvario*. In the more accessible, tourist-tormented settlements, both chapter-house and *Calvario* will be secret, removed from observation; but in the older communities you will find them placed in the same relation to the community life as the *kiva* to the pueblo. At Trampas the brotherhood occupies a room in the loft of the church, its walls spattered with the blood of generations of scourgings. At Abiquiu the children play under the *Calvario*, and the women gossip as they linger there over the drawing of water. That the true evaluation of *Los Hermanos Penitentes* in the life of the people should have been persistently missed by most writers about it, from the time that Charles F. Lumis first broadcast his young Harvard horror of what he saw in Taos in 1891, is perhaps due to our inherently American disposition to look upon every sort of social differentiation as a "sight," to be gaped at and judged for its quality of diversion rather than to be understood. It is always so much easier to dispose of phenomena like the *penitente* crucifixions in the current Freudian phrases than to penetrate far enough below the surface of history and our common nature to discover that the *morada* is an instinctive reversion to the council lodge and the *kiva*, the self-established pivot of community relations. Something of the cult and something of the clan shows in its organization, which is without central government, the good of the order being maintained by occasional conferences of the local *hermanos mayors*, the elder brothers, presiding over the local chapters.

2

Of the historic progressions by which the Third Order has become a fraternal benefit society, incorporated under the laws of New Mexico as provided for all such organizations, little is recorded, but much may be inferred from the social background of the people among whom it is still cherished.

Not originally a secret society, it became so first under the moral necessity of protecting its penitents from spiritual pride by concealing their identity under the black garb which is still worn by *flagellantes* in all public processions. Finally it was driven to conceal itself from the deeply rooted ill breeding of the American public, which, not to emulate, constrains me to set down here far less than I know of what goes on in the *moradas* and in the hearts of the penitents. Besides the *hermano mayor*, there are three officers whose function is so public that to name them violates none of the secrecy under which the society still maintains itself, the *infermo*, who looks after the sick, the *resador*, who accompanies the penances of the members with the necessary prayers, and the *pitero*, whose flute leads forth the processions on the Trail of the Blood.

Of the times and occasions by which the flagellations of the Third Order passed into veritable crucifixions with nails nothing is preserved. The modern substitution of cords, and the reduction of the time from the traditional three hours to forty-five minutes has taken place within the last quarter of a century. The change means less than might be supposed. It is necessary to recall here that death was not ordinarily supposed to ensue of the actual wounds of crucifixion, but, after two or three days, of loss of blood and starvation. Three years ago I saw a young man in khaki with wound stripes on his sleeve following the *Rastro de la Sangre*, and I would have given much to know what he thought about it. Whether, for instance, he found the emotional phases which make war bearable very different from the ecstasy that sustains the *Cristos* through his agony, whether, indeed, the charm of war for men does not partly lie in its office of expiation.

Like every communal art, the New Mexican passion play is more or less shaped by its environment. The intensely dramatic landscape and the introverting effect of isolation have their part in it. For three centuries after Oñate the distances of New Mexico were stupendous. Even in this day of high-powered motors the roads about Abiqui, Terra Amerilla, and Picuris are difficult to negotiate. Always there were too few priests for the people. In Taos County, which is exactly the size of the State of Maryland, there are still only three parishes.

In the dark interval after the crass, new-made Republic of Mexico abolished the Franciscans, the only centers of organized faith for scores of settlements among the wild gorges of the Rio Grande and the plains of Las Vegas were the little chapels of the chapter-houses of *Los Hermanos Penitentes*. Spanish-speaking New Mexico was never a reading community.

3

Hardly yet does the power of print run to the well-swept *placitas*, and in the middle years of the nineteenth century that primer of Americanism, the mail-order catalogue, had not yet been invented. One source they had of art and drama and mystery, of spiritual energization and culture, the story, every detail of which had been worked into the fiber of their lives by the brown-skirted *frailes*, of the passion and death of Jesus. Not the social philosophy of Jesus as we modernly conceive it, not the esoteric teaching, but the drama of a dying and resurgent Saviour. Finding themselves in the dark of a social submergence lasting more than two generations, *Los Hermanos Penitentes* hugged their possession to their breasts and erected around it the shrine of their annual performance.

Special saints days, the first and second days of May, and funerals of the brothers are observed ceremonially, but the avowed purpose of the penitents is to keep alive the memory of the suffering and death of the Saviour. It begins with the first Friday in Lent, with the gathering of the *hermanos de luz*, the whole body of officers, at the *morada*. To them, singly and by twos and threes, the brothers assemble from the *placitas*, from low huts on the *loma*, from sheep camps and woodcutter's fires. There is a pungent smell of sage-brush in the air, the smell of the rain-freshened earth, and the evening star like a torch in the green streak of sky beyond the mountains.

The high windows of the *morada*, too high to afford any glimpse of what is going on within, are shut and barred.

From time to time the sound of singing can be heard, like bees droning within a hollow log. Late, usually about midnight, the first procession issues, making its way with the help of fitful lanterns and the feel of the ground underfoot, toward the *Calvario*, which is set on a low hill about half a mile from the *morada*. By the rise and fall of the lanterns and the intermittent droning, you make out that they are telling the stations of the cross. The squeal of the flute is high and keen, like the glimmer of the skyline along the mountain-tops made audible.

These early demonstrations are all singing processions. As Lent advances, however, strange ripping sounds, intermittently in fives and threes, can be heard issuing from the *moradas*, and to the midnight processions will be added figures of men clad only in white-cotton drawers, naked to the waist, bare arms rising and falling as the *disciplinas* are laid on, first over one shoulder and then over the other. Later they may be seen drawing huge, unhewn crosses, staggering and falling, whipped to their feet again by the zealous *sangrador*. Often the crosses are so heavy that the bearer must be accompanied by a brother to ease the long beam to the ground when the *penitente* faints under it, lest it slip and crush him.

As the season progresses, the penitential passion rising with it, one is likely to meet anywhere in the deep lanes between the fields, or in the foottrails of the wild, sharp gorges, the solitary penitent, dragging his bloody cross, or two or three making their way from *morada* to *morada* on their knees, accompanied by the *resador* reciting the prayers that make the office effective. On one such occasion, just at the edge of dusk, I met one of these private processions headed by a youth carrying aloft, in an almost unseeing mood of exaltation, a huge and pathetic effigy of the crucified, followed by the *resador*.

After him two men staggered under crosses, and a third, half naked like the others, clasped between his breast and arms, manacled at the wrists against any temptation to let it fall, a heap of *cholla*, that wickedest of barbed cactus. Around the heads of all of them were bound tight fillets of wild rose-brier, beaded with drops of blood. This was early in my acquaintance with the strange brotherhood, and I had been many times warned by my American friends against letting myself be seen in the neighborhood of their rites. But the procession had come upon me so suddenly that there was no retreat, and by a swift reach of spirit, making myself one with them, I dropped on my knees on the moist earth between the budding thickets of the wild plums, offering with uplifted palms my sincere respect to the symbols of their faith. With only an instant's check and a side-glance, the procession swept by me, and the wailing lost itself in the immensity of the mountain shadow.

But with that brief moment on my knees all the sense of wild strangeness in the Lenten rites went from me. The shiver the sound of wailing flutes and the rattle of the thunder-twirler excited in me, breaking the midnight, is the shiver of recognition of what my blood remembers. Whatever was brought to the surface of consciousness by that act must have been of perceptible quality, for never afterward, when I went among the *penitentes* alone, did I have anything but deeply recognizing glances that ended in my being admitted at last into several of the chapels, and in coming into possession of one of the ancient manuscript books of hymns, much thumbed and blood-spattered. But lest I give a false impression of revealing mysteries, it must be said that the *penitente* hymns can be heard at any funeral watch night, and the prayers as they are read in procession, by any bystander who has the wit to understand the quaint, sixteenth-century Spanish in which they are sung. It meant, my coming into touch with them in this fashion, that I was admitted to the community mind on this matter, and to the gossip of the wives and sisters of the Brotherhood, who participate in many of the purely religious functions of the order.

The formal Easter drama begins on the evening of Holy Tuesday when the brothers, on entering the chapter-house, receive the "seal of obligation," the three gashes down and across, made by a flake of obsidian or broken glass, set just deep enough in its wooden handle to miss severing the muscles of the back. After the seal, the penitent asks for and receives the three strokes in remembrance of the three meditations of the passion of Our Lord, and according to his fortitude or the depth of his repentance, strokes for the five wounds, the seven last words, and, if he holds out, for the forty days.

Ash Wednesday is spent in prayers and confessions and private penances. Day and night the sound of the steady blows of the *disciplinas* can be heard from the *morada*, drowned from time to time by the wailing anguish of the hymns.

Originally the *disciplina* seem to have been of ancient iron ringwork, such as may still be found occasionally in the *moradas*, but all that the modern spectator sees are the white whips braided of leaves of the yucca whose white bells swinging above the leaf cluster a little later in the season make incense of the air. By use the leaf matter is stripped from the fibers, leaving the stinging flail to which in excess of fervor bits of metal are sometimes attached.

From hour to hour on Holy Thursday processions go out, to the *Calvario*, to the *campo santo*, or to neighboring *moradas*. Bareheaded and singing, they pass between the pale thickets of rabbit-brush and sage. Welcoming delegations come out to meet them, and after brief sessions of prayer inside the chapel, set them on their way. The singing is led by the *cantador*, proud of his office, and referring constantly to the well-thumbed notebook in which the *alvados* has been written by hand and spelled by ear from generation to generation.

Always the flute-player accompanies the official processions, and his wailing tune is punctured by the skirl of the *metraca*, the wooden rattle, the "bull roarer," the "thunder twirler," of which the bell that signals the elevation of the host is the last, most Christian reminder.

In this country the towns hug the skirts of the mountains. Rounding the *prados* they spread from point to point of rising land, having always a friendly eye one upon the other, so that the flow of processions between the *moradas* takes on an effect of community pageant. Gradually as Holy Week advances, the whole community is swept into the fervor of atonement. Children leave their play to follow the master of novices, Raphael-eyed cherubs lifting their sweet trebles and altos, learning the stations of the cross as they plod back and forth between the *morada* and the *Calvario*. In some such fashion all affairs are left for *penitente* week. It is more than likely that the saints flock there at that season for the savor of willing sacrifice, as we go into the desert to see the Palo Verde bloom.

The height of spiritual frenzy is reached by midnight of Holy Thursday, when the procession, led by the chosen *Cristo*s of the year, with head veiled for humbleness, staggers forth from the *morada*, the hymns shrill with pain, the wet whips falling steadily, followed by that most desolating sound—the slither of the crosses in the dust. The direction of this midnight trail is never known to outsiders. Guards are stationed to prevent its being followed to its lonely destination in the hills. Forth in the midnight he goes, whipped by the *sangrador*, and back he comes in the dawning, dragging his heavy cross, often in a fainting condition and leaning upon the *compañeros*. Years when Easter comes while the ground is still frozen the way of the cross can be tracked by blood from the torn feet of the penitents.

For an hour or two the *morada* swallows up the weary group of flagellantes. Then, as the great red sun comes over the mountain and the
friends and families of the *penitentes* begin to collect about the door to
join in the morning procession to the *campo santo*, the keen flute and
the skirling rattle call forth the still-fasting and only half-conscious
brotherhood.

The blood is stiff upon the *disciplinas* that fall on flinching backs
with the steady sound of rain; the heavy crosses rake the stony ground,
the voices rise wavering and charged with homely, human passion.

> "Por el rastro de la sangre
> Que Jesucristo derrama,"

they sing.

> "By the trail of that dear blood
> Which by Jesus Christ was shed,"

and again, as they near the great cross standing sentinel among the
village dead,

> "There is no one now
> Who is not worth something,
> Since now Christ is dead."

Drawing over my head the black shawl which is the universal outdoor wear of matrons in that country, to join the "women following
afar off," my thoughts followed those who, down all history, have taken
the Trail of the Blood to our ultimate gain in peace and spiritual insight.
There were women in that procession whose own sons had walked in
another bloody trail that same year in France, and as we knelt among
the little crosses painted heaven blue, as with eternal hope, I was thankful to be able to cry quietly with them behind my shawl, while the
voices of the men rose piercingly:

> The rose has dried,
> And the garden has withered!
> The common flower of the field,
> And my white lily,
> On the cross have found their fate.
> *Dios, ten piedad de mi!*...

My son is no more;
The dear of my soul
Has gone and forsaken me!
Dios, ten piedad de mi!"

It is not until after this sunrise observance that the weary brothers break their fast with coarse food, and rest in preparation for the passion play, which formerly took place at the prescribed third hour, with faithful realistic detail. But in the early eighties the church instituted so active a protest against the traditional practice that it has been many years now since a veritable crucifixion with nails has taken place. In the remoter villages the *Cristos* is bound upon the cross with ropes so tightly drawn that the strongest man can not safely endure it for more than about forty minutes. The body of the *Cristos* is covered with a sheet, and his head encased in the customary black bag to prevent recognition, and, as a protection from tourist curiosity, the elevation of the cross seldom takes place until after dusk.

At Talpa three years ago we saw the last stage that human experience travels on its way from being a propitiatory rite to legitimate dramatic art. Here an effigy was substituted for the living *Cristos*, and the involved emotional complex was released in dialogue and mimetic acts, restrained by the compass of attention of the audience. Talpa lies at the upper edge of the loma, where the *rillito* comes out between round, detrital hills, having Ranchos de Taos hidden in the cañon below it, and Fernandez de Taos in the fertile *bolson* toward the west. It looks across as the crow flies to Taos Pueblo, at the foot of Pueblo Mountain. In between, the fields were starting green, and the pink of peach orchards melted into the warm tones of adobe walls. Three *moradas* had turned out for the occasion, with their assembled women folk, and about the traditional hour began the stations of the cross.

In that clean, bright air, between the most majestic mountains, the black shawls of the elder women gave almost as insistent a note as the clear cerise and orange and green scarfs of the young girls. For an hour the shifting procession moved down the hollow of the valley and up the little hill of the *Calvario*, rising and falling in slow rhythm to the stations as they passed. *Cantador* and *resador* walked in grave responsibility at the head, close behind them the young scions of the blood of the conquistadors, with dark, handsome faces, simply serious and devout. Behind them young girls, black crape over their white communion dresses, carried on a platform the chief treasure of Talpa, Our Lady, also swathed in black, from whose outstretched waxen hand drooped one of the webby, wheel-lace handkerchiefs which are not made anywhere now in this country outside of the mud huts of New Mexico. Last of all the brothers dragged the *carreta de muerte*, with its grinning image of the Angel of Death, arrow laid to bow in its skeleton hands. Formerly this carriage of death was the ancient New Mexican ox-cart, with solid rounds of cottonwood-tree for wheels, loaded with stones and drawn with chains or horsehair ropes, which the penitents took across their naked breasts, or, in excess of contrition, their bare throats, and the Death was life size. It is related in the annals of the brotherhood that on one occasion the arrow was loosened by a jolt, from the grinning angel, and found its mark between the shoulders of a *penitente*. But every decade of *penitente* history shows a shrinkage in the size and importance of the figure of Death. On one occasion, I was offered one, about half life-size, most horribly realistic, for a price, to add to my collection of curiosities.

Meanwhile, as nearly the whole population of the village surged down the valley toward the *Calvario*, the older brothers had set up the three crosses a few paces from the chapel door, and laid the implements of the passion in order.

The effigy was brought forth in its blue-painted casket, a most deplorable life-size figure, and with the utmost reverence, as though it had been a beloved body, affixed to the central cross.

As the procession returned from the *Calvario*, the hymns changed from the wail of penance to the poignant note of human sorrow, and the drama of the passion began. They were all there, the historic characters; the Roman centurion with his spear, the Jewish constabulary, the three Marys with their lanterns, the soldiers that diced for the seamless robe. This being a war year, and the passion of patriotism being scarcely less in New Mexico than the passion of penance, Caiaphas–Pontius Pilate, the two parts rolled in one, in his white robe, had mounted on the very tip of his high priest's hat, an American flag, which fluttered and flapped brightly amid the solemn scene.

All that could be heard—and understood, for the Spanish of Talpa is not the Spanish of the books—of the dialogue seemed superior in literary value to the Oberammergau drama. It had the true folk quality, and something of the rhythmic elegance of phrasing which characterizes as much as I have been privileged to hear of the ritual of the order. Until he comes unexpectedly upon something of this kind, the casual observer is likely to forget that the age that fed the cultural life of the Spanish colonies was the resplendent age of Spanish literature. But it will not be by me that the interest and charm of the American passion play will be handed over to an American public, still in that undeveloped stage in which appreciation too often takes the form of tearing a lovely thing to tatters. When I think of what American people do to much of the beauty and strangeness of which they find themselves possessed, I hope there is some truth in the gossip of mysterious disappearances and burials alive visited on the violaters of the enjoined secrecy of the order. But my acquaintance with the friendly, simple folk among whom it flourishes gives little color to the hope.

The formal drama of crucifixion and laying in the tomb closes about the hour that the sudden glory of high altitudes pours about the mountains from the level sun.

Through its rose and lilac veils the penitents return singly and in twos and threes to their homes, the goatherd beds the flock, lights come on in the huts along the *loma,* and the great day is over.

A few of the brothers will return to the *morada* after dark for the *tiniablas* commemorating the dreadful three hours of Jerusalem. There seems to be even among the celebrants some confusion of mind about this act of the drama, confounding it with the night of Holy Thursday, in which the disciples desert the Saviour one by one, and the bitter hour of betrayal closes the scene. Probably both the betrayal and the hours of darkness were once kept, but now the two scenes, by a device familiar to the drama, are telescoped and kept by choice usually on the night preceding the crucifixion. During this celebration the little chapel is dark, and there is great rattling of chains, roar of the thunder-twirler, shrieks of devils in hell and gibbering ghosts. I have had men tell me with rueful laughter, that they can remember as boys being half scared out of their wits by the too realistic performance of the *tiniablas.*

4

For the ordinary sight-seer the business of *Los Hermanos Penitentes* ends here, and gives rise to the erroneous impression that its sole function is of emotional release. In the spirit of our own worship of dead levelness, which we are pleased to call consistency, we are even led to speak contemptuously of a religious experience that runs to a yearly climax with the recurrent rhythms of the earth. But the work of the order in the lives of its members is no more over with the annual flagellations than the work of nature is over with the resurgent glory of the spring.

The chapel of the *morada* is open on Lady days, on days of the local saints, and on all Christian festivals. In communities where there is no resident priest, it becomes the repository of the village Santos. From it they are carried to houses of sickness and mourning, and the body of Christ is borne about the fields on Corpus Christi day. The ritual of the order gives the touch of divine consolation to funerals in lonely neighborhoods, which may not be visited by the priestly office oftener than once in the year, and the infermo is the recognized source of neighborhood relief in sickness and affliction.

In the dark period after the removal of the Franciscans, prolonged into the first thirty or forty years of the rule of the invading *Americanos,* when civil processes were all in the hands of interests alien, or even hostile, to the natives, many matters which might otherwise have been brought to the courts were settled by the local *hermano* mayor. Gossiping in the twilight with the wives and mothers of the brotherhood, one hears how *Tomacito* was made to pay for the damages his cow committed against the corn of Pablito, of how Ascencio was required to withdraw his membership from his own *morada* to one six miles distant because of a too conspicuous interest in the wife of Bartolomé, and how at Questa, after the visit of the national representative of the Anti-Tuberculosis campaign, a penalty of two strokes with the *disciplina* was prescribed for spitting on the floor. One Assumption day at Fernando de Taos I was a party to the visit of our Lady from the *morada* there to one at Prado, newly established and not yet furnished.

Forth she went in the morning with garments reverently kissed by the escorting brothers, and back she came in the twilight in a new silk gown bestowed by the women of Prado.

A happy custom this, of visiting with the blessed dead, for my part more improving than the inanities of the ouija-board.

There was a time, beginning in that dark period to which I have referred, and after lines of political cleavage between the native New Mexicans and the invasive Americans sharply showed, when the order became the instrument of political intrigue, but that is passing with the growth of mutual understanding and the advance of the English press. Everywhere among the more foreseeing of the present population there is an increasing appreciation of the social value of an organization which shows itself possessed of the seeds of self-help and the vital spark of community spirit. A year or two ago on the day of the Assumption of the Virgin, when I had gone into the little chapel at Fernando de Taos to pray, with full courtesy of the brotherhood, a party of curiosity-mongers undertook rudely to force their way in after me, with the result that there were pistol-shots exchanged and a narrow escape from a tragedy. Promptly, however, on the part of the Protestant community, and on the part of the Taos Indians, on whose land the *morada* stood, there was a general rally in defense of the right and dignity of the order. For this is more than a question of the right of free worship. It is a question of our general attitude toward those native spiritual impulses out of which great national art must spring. It is because I am not able to think of *Los Hermanos Penitentes* in any more important connection than this, as often as Lent comes round and my mind goes visiting the high valleys of the Sangre de Cristo and the *placita*s of Abiquiu and Rinconada, I think also of the young soldiers walking in the Trail of the Blood with the stripe of their own wounds on their sleeves, and the little flag that flapped so gaily from Pontius Pilate's hat.

20

The Delight Makers

1929

It has escaped the observer that professional Merry Makers wherever they are found, all fools, zanys, clowns, pierrots, tend to present themselves in black and white garments, top-knotted, with wide mouths of fleshless grinning, with garments shapeless, often tattered, foreign at least to the fashion of their audiences, and that they make foolish, gibbering noises. At Zuni in New Mexico they go further and show by their crudely shaped masks their derivation from human forms less evolved, mud-heads, the first men come back for the entertainment of their successors. And everywhere in New Mexico it is known that the black and white daubed clowns are the spirits of the ancestors, black and white for life and death, for light and darkness, dressed in the tatters of their ancient rabbit skin shrouds, their hair tied up with dried corn husks, and yet always somewhere about them a sprig of evergreen spruce, the sign and symbol of life everliving, even in the grave. It is told in the creation myths of the New Mexico Pueblos, that before the struggling tribes had arrived at this pleasant land of the sun and the pine and the maguey, while they wandered affrighted in the perilous worlds between, that so the ancestral spirits were permitted to return to aid and comfort them, to give force to their ceremonies and cheer their hearts with laughter. It is not at all unlikely that clowns of every country had some such origin. At any rate we find them in some such guise emerging out of the past of Greece and Rome and of those European peoples who have contributed most to our existing notions of professional entertainment. Probably in the beginning the clowns of Europe had a two-fold function not differing greatly from that of the Koshare of New Mexico. They are visible symbols of that universal half apprehended sense of men that the spirits of tribal ancestors are ever with us, and they serve blamelessly as the means of social correction by the whips of laughter.

It is important for the modern to realize that in primitive society, in which ridicule, if not the sole social corrective, is the one most easily exempted from quick tribal resentment, it is indispensable to give to ridicule which embodies the tribal idea of behavior, some such formal authority. By this means the virtue of fortitude is encouraged in the victim of quip and jest in which the sting is more than half condoned by cleverness. By putting official fun making in the hands of personators of the ancestral spirits, and by attributing to these a less developed mentality, the element of ill nature in personal criticism is minimized, and the audience is freed to the greatest possible enjoyment in seeing one of their members singled out for a good drubbing of ridicule.

Just how early in the history of the southwestern tribes the function of the Delight Makers, or Koshare, became part of the social organization, can be determined only by the fact that drawings of them have been found etched in the sooty walls of cave and cliff dwellings, and that their forerunners are found in more or less institutionalized form in most tribal groups of less developed cultures. Among the Pueblos they have more social importance and more sanctity. The Koshare group in every Pueblo constitutes a society the members of which are generally appointed by the religious council of the tribe, their personnel not being known to the village in general, except as it can be guessed through the thick daubings of black and white paint of their make up. They become an integral part of all ceremonial occasions which have to do with fertility and with the tribal past.

In their spirit function the Koshare are ritually invisible and are so treated, when, early in the morning of great ceremonial days, they run lightly about the village seeking those "whose hearts are bad, whose thoughts have left the straight road." No eyes are lifted to them and small boys with guilty recollections of stolen melons or neglected ceremonial obligations creep behind their elders until the ghostly visitors have passed.

When they associate themselves with the clans upon whom devolve the ceremonies of the day, Corn Dance, Rain Dance, Buffalo or Deer Dance, as they move in and out of the dance, incredibly light upon their feet, uttering and fluttering, hair-raising cries which ghosts are universally supposed to make, their function is wholly helpful. They support the special prayers of the occasion with compelling gestures, stoop to tie an unlaced moccasin, to fasten a slipping arm band, to fetch a trembling bashful youngster on their backs to his coveted place in the line. During the intervals of the four times perfected ritual, especially at the mid-day meal, when they bless the household by dipping their finger in the sacred meal bowl and accepting a bite and sup with the house-holder, the sense of their presence runs like a warm smile about the village. They are the beloved dead come home again.

It is not until the ceremonial act is quite over, or has at least passed its peak, that the function of the Delight Makers becomes of interest to the inquiring Modern, for it is then that it branches directly out of the root of tragedy which Aristotle discerned in the tribal dance, and produces Comedy. It would be interesting to know why Aristotle failed to apprise us to the debt of Tragedy to the Comic Muse, when he describes the introduction of dialogue into the tragic dance as though it were an original, unused device; whereas there is every reason to suppose that comic dialogue among the Greeks was, as it is among the Amerindian tribes, much earlier and more explicitly developed. Amerind drama, as we find it today in New Mexico, has reached the development of part acting, "things done" by solo actors, hunters and hunted, gods and their worshipers, men and spirits, but no Indian Thespis has yet appeared. And at the same time non-sacred drama, especially comedy, is discovered with fully developed story plot and original dialogue. It is possible that this development has been assisted by the observation of White entertainment, of which all Indians are inordinately fond, but it is also quite certain that its inception was much earlier than White influence. In the Southwest the Koshare have carried formal Comedy to the point that demands consideration as a characteristic item in the development of the American folk theatre.

Primitive Comedy begins no doubt with buffoonery, and includes burlesque of animal behavior as well as of men. The Koshare, to whom social correction is an obligation, go seriously about the business of abating a village nuisance; the braggart, the bully, the too willing victim of sex appeal, the gossipy woman, the scolding wife. In the secrecy of the underground ceremonial chamber the butt of the performance is selected, the order of presentation determined and the dialogue composed. There may even be two or three castigations in one comedy, and any number of local hits. These little plays are always short, and the story developed with simplicity; they resemble, in fact, the spoken bits of musical comedy, occurring as they do in the intervals or at the end of serious ritualistic performances. As the membership of the society of Delight Makers is probably selected for skill in such delineations, they are always supremely well acted; for all primitives possess in some degree the gift of mimicry. It is part of the hunting way of life, and properly interrogated pushes the primary root of drama back upon the instinctive self protective mimicry of animals; the instinctive way of self education, the attempt to get inside a situation by imitating it. Observing the Delight Makers at work it is impossible to avoid the conclusion that the theatre rightly understood has been man's natural way of realizing society.

Attempts to transcribe Koshare Comedy in English have not yet resulted in anything that can be successfully instanced, since the point so often turns on the violation of tribal mores utterly unintelligible to the White mind. The single exception to this rule of unintelligibility is the humor that turns upon the universal factor of sex. Even to understand this it is important to realize that your genuine primitive is profoundly aware of the relation of fecundity to laughter. Sex is both a sacred cooperation of created being with Uncreated Spirit, and a joke played upon man in his human capacity to bind him to the purpose of the gods. That is what constitutes to the Protestant Missionary, with his borrowed shock over the alleged "immorality" of Indian ceremonies, a social nuisance in the West. However it may appear to moderns who have lost all sense of the sacred mystery of procreation, sex in the primitive theatre is treated either with reverence or with jocund, thigh slapping laughter. The sex comedies I have seen among the tribesmen, deal with the aged women who, in an Apache raid are discovered to inquire with ill concealed and excruciatingly funny anxiety, when the atrocities are to begin; the impotent man in a situation which makes his condition embarrassing to conceal; the too easily deceived husband; the farcical uncovering of his betrayer; the woman who pursues men, innocently unaware of her failure of appeal, and other stock figures of ribald farce. But the proportion of such subjects to matters of general appeal is not excessive. Every sort of human frailty and humbug that can occur in the Stone Age receives its due attention; and when these fail there is the inexhaustible fund of White stupidity. The tourist, the archeologist, the missionary, aspects of our social life most of us suppose secure behind a veil of unapproachable superiority, are expertly butchered to make a tribesman's holiday.

As with us, the Delight Makers employ certain traditional plots and devices for displaying their humor; the visiting members of a rival tribe; the burlesque test of skill or endurance; the Stone Age equivalent of the gold brick—a fake "Medicine" or false fetish. At Taos the favorite "obstacle race" centers about a greased pole to the top of which has been affixed a net containing a substantial prize, usually contributed by the War Captain, the only Pueblo official whose privilege is normally subject to political intrigue. It has been rather widely assumed that the Taos pole is a White innovation, but it is equally possible that it is a burlesque of the pole that figures in the Sun Dance of the Plains tribes by whom the Pueblo of Taos has been harassed in times past. At any rate it makes the pivot of some excellent fooling, as, at the southern Pueblos, the ancient menace of the Navajo is made to fill the place once occupied in our theatre by the stage Irishman.

Other factors, such as the prevalence among all primitives of the commemorative pageant-drama, contributing acting technique and the handling of stage equipment, have undoubtedly had something to do with the earlier evolution of Comedy as an established dramatic form, much more closely resembling sophisticated Comedy than any form of Aristotlean tragedy resembles tragedy today. But undoubtedly the chief factor in establishing Comedy as the more advanced form among Amerindian tribes has been the importance given to Comedy as an effective ritual in assisting the powers of nature. For among our native tribes, Comedy is recognized as a direct aid to fertility. Even the corn must be made to laugh in order that it may increase. Among the earliest discoveries of the Southwest tribes in relation to the social function of increase, was that it is not advantageous for society to be always thinking of sex in its socially responsible aspects. The more the personal experience of fecundity assumed seriousness, the more necessary it became to keep its jocund aspect to the fore in the one wholly public medium in which it was then, and still is, permissible to treat it humorously. Even among us, encumbered as the subject is with salacity and pathology, drama is still the medium in which most liberty can be taken with the conventional mores of sex among civilized tribes. So that our acquaintance with the Delight Makers in their spiritual function comes just in time for us to rescue this most ancient social instrument from its accumulations of filth, and keep clear under all its avatars the face of the laughing god. This is not the only item making for the renewal of our understanding of the sacred social use of Comedy, which can be learned by a study of the technique of the Delight Makers, but it is the one which most commends itself to the present hour.

What American Comedy needs just now is to be freed from the years of its bondage to the salacities of barbarism and restored to the fruitful simplicities of social correction through the mediation of the priests of laughter.

21

Native Drama in Our Southwest

1927

The landing of the Pilgrims on the coast of Massachusetts was dramatic in situation; the entrada of the Spanish Colonists by way of the Chihuahua Trail was so by intention. There is all the difference in the world between the cultures that might be expected to spring from such beginnings. Arriving at the crossing of the Rio Grande amid hardships before which the Pilgrim crossing pales, the expedition sat down on the bank of the Rio Grande and witnessed a comedy of their adventure written by Captain Farfan and played by his company. Thus on the 29th of April, 1595, modern drama began in our Southwest, which was taken possession of next day with a pageant of banners and ritual in the name of all the Blessed Personages, the King of Spain, and St. Francis. The founding of their first capital, now Chamita, New Mexico, was celebrated by a horseback pageant of Christians conquering the Moors before an audience augmented by two pueblos of Indians who sat securely on their housetops against the possibility of being eaten by the "long-tailed elk" on which were mounted the strange bearded men. From this gallant beginning the chief entertainment of New Mexico has been, aside from horse-racing and cock-fighting, dramatic, and almost exclusively native.

The century of extensive Spanish colonization along the Rio Grande was also the "golden" century of Spain, in which Lope de Vega wrote his thousand comedies, Pedro Calderon wrote his religious plays, and Lope de Ruega regenerated the Spanish theater, introducing music between the acts and sometimes into them, thus opening the way to grand opera. In that happy age the king also wrote plays and the people took as much interest in literature as in bull fights. It was the century marked in its beginning by Cervantes's *Don Quixote*, and distinguished toward its end by the substitution of the guitar for the viola as the popular musical instrument of Spain. Most of what came over in the saddlebags and in the memories of the Colonists of that period was wiped out by the Pueblo Revolt of 1680. But after the reconquest by DeVargas in 1698 every settlement began to have societies of players whose performances became social institutions, existing in some of the outlying towns to this day and in others rapidly reviving under the sympathetic reevaluation which has been the gracious result of the most recent invasion of New Mexico by working artists. Collections of the various local versions of the more popular plays are being made, and the privilege of attending their presentation is eagerly sought. It is still impossible, however, to trace out the entire connection between what goes on in New Mexico and its possible derivation from drama in Old Mexico and Spain. Quite certainly nothing much came from Spain after the first half of the eighteenth century, and after the first quarter of the nineteenth the slender trickle of cultural influence from Mexico definitely ceased. A generation later the American invasion, with its characteristic bargain-counter rush, forced the Spanish Colonial culture back upon itself, and almost succeeded in causing its complete extinction. Only under the conserving influence of the church, careful of what is ritualistic and symbolic in culture, the Spanish Colonial drama has survived in whatever was definitely of religious significance. At present only one of the native plays of that period which is not religious in theme is still being played or has been collected in entirety. This is "Querneverde," sometimes known as "Los Comanchos," a drama which seems to have been written in Taos County about the middle of the nineteenth century and which deals with the exploits of Querneverde (Green-Horn), a Comanche chief who harried the Spanish settlements of that time.

One is entirely within the fact in speaking of "collecting" these Spanish Colonial plays. Writing among the New Mexican settlements was never much practiced, and so seriously were the dramatic societies taken that membership because hereditary; parts as well as costumes and properties were handed down often from father to son, and in many cases passed from generation to generation without once being written down. I have heard, for example, of manuscript copies of the play "Nuestra Senora de Guadaloupe," but my own version was taken down entirely from word of mouth; and of the less popular plays, which may yet be performed from memory, there is not even a tradition of a written version. One must collect a part speech by speech—with its clues—from an old man at Ranchos de Taos, another from a great-grandmother somewhere about Socorro, and missing fragments where they can be found. There was, of course, marked preference for the "fat" parts, such as Lucifer in "Los Pastores" (The Shepherds) or the Chief in "Los Comanchos," and these can often be found letter perfect, as the player learned them from his father forty years ago. People who do not trust much to print have excellent memories.

"Los Pastores," as may be guessed, is a Nativity play and still frequently played on *Nochebuena* (the Good Night), first before the priest's house and then in the patio of the local *rico* or other influential citizen. In remote villages where there is no resident priest and no *sala* large enough, the performance will take place in the schoolhouse or the church, and the interest and appreciation of the audience is never a whit dimmed by the fact that most of them have been present at all the rehearsals. The costumes are traditional and suggest the period in which Agamemnon might be played in a powdered wig with ruffles and Lady Macbeth in hoopskirts. I have seen "Our Lady of Guadaloupe" done at Santa Fe with no setting but a rock of crumpled paper, a few tissue roses, and a single ecclesiastical chair; the long journey between the rock of Tepeyac, where the Vision appeared to Don Diego, and the Bishop's palace, indicated by the chair, being so completely presented by the actor in fifteen feet of flat space that the audience missed nothing of its mountainous character, its fatigues and misgivings. In these native players the power of entering into the part, which is shared by a native audience, is quite capable of so completely engaging even the sophisticated attention that it is only afterward that the observer recalls that the Star of Bethlehem was an evil-smelling oil lantern hitched along on a rope, and that the audience has united in helpful suggestion when the mechanism by which the Angel of the Annunciation is let down from heaven has been unaccountably stalled. And with both audience and players one has relapsed into reverential awe when the difficulty has been overcome.

Such plays as "Los Pastores," "Our Lady of Guadaloupe," and "Las Estrallas," and "Los Comanchos" show literary quality with an explicit folk flavor, and such variations of style and handling as suggest Colonial origins. Even the Nativity play is so completely localized that no one has yet been able to trace it to a Spanish derivation. But if such origin could be predicted it could probably only be proved out of old monkish manuscripts. "Los Pastores" and the "Guadaloupe" are both found south of the Rio Grande, and may have originated there, but "Los Comanchos" could not have arisen south of Santa Fe.

Also of distinctive New Mexican origin is the yearly "Passion Play" of the Penitentes, now so rapidly disappearing before the assaults of the bargain-counter spirit which incites Americans to rush in wherever there is rumor of beauty and strangeness, to tear it to tatters of sensation. This American version of the drama of the Crucifixion is played out in entirety between the first Wednesday in Lent and Good Friday, and its source is obscurely traced to the Dark Hours of the Spanish settlements between the withdrawal of the Franciscans by order of the newly established Republic of Mexico and the coming of the French priests in the 1880's. It is possibly a local revision of the Third Order of St. Francis, which came into the country with Oñate, or fragmentary recollections of whipping brotherhoods such as were common in Europe throughout the period of Spanish colonization. Unquestionably it drew from penitential practices of various Indian tribes; for by that time Spanish and Indian blood were well mingled in New Mexico. More than anything else it drew from the dramatic urge that brought the Spanish settlers over the sea and up the whole arduous length of the mountains of Mexico, along the Jornado del Muerte (Journey of Death), to face the wild hills and wild tribes of the Rio Grande. And not only from that impulse, rooted in the love of conquest and adventure, but from the world-embracing missionary spirit of the century. It was most deeply informed with what is in some measure at the root of all art, man's profound, incurable passion for expiation.

The Penitente play culminates during the last three days of Holy Week in what was formerly a detailed realistic crucifixion. But after the church resumed its direction of its Spanish-speaking membership in New Mexico, many realistic features disappeared. The Cristo is no longer nailed but tied to the cross, and the most dramatic penances take place within the morada, or are screened by midnight and remoteness. Within the past four or five years there has been a disposition to substitute a painted life-size image for the Cristo, and to enlarge the dialogue until it approaches the proportions of literary drama. As much as I have been able to hear of this dialogue is far superior in directness and simplicity to the pretentious blank verse of the Oberammergau "Passion Play." Such is the reverent purity of spirit in which this humble rendering of the dramatic climax of the Christian story is made that it was not until hours after the effect of seeing it at Talpa had worn away that I remembered how the three Marys chewed gum in the pauses of their parts, and how the two parts of Pontius Pilate and Caiphas had been combined into one by the simple expedient of a Roman robe and a Hebrew high priest's hat. This was the first time the whole story had been presented at one session, the usual method being to represent the betrayal and abandonment of Jesus, with which are often curiously combined incidents of the hours of darkness, on the evening before Holy Thursday; the Via Dolorosa with the meeting and parting of Jesus and his mother, on the afternoon of Holy Thursday, and the crucifixion at the traditional hour on Friday, each one at appointed places. Left to itself, the Penitente performance would inevitably develop into a true passion play of considerable power; but it seems evident that the tourist passion will prevail over every other and that the beautiful occasion will pass without a trace.

This Penitente play, with the Matachina, links the Spanish Colonial theater with the Pueblo Indian dance-drama. For still in New Mexico the Puebleños keep up the annual mask dance typical of that on which all European play-acting is founded. In the corn dance, the deer dance, the fire dance, and a score of masked, ritualistic performances all the forms and devices of the dramatic vehicle before it split into the allied but definitive arts of dance, song, and dialogue, may be studied. The Penitente play, besides being communal and ritualistic in character, as Indian dances are, and expiatory, as we now know Greek drama was at its best, mingles whippings, genuflections, solemn processions, and other modulations of the dance impulse with its dialogues and spoken prayers.

Midway between the dance-drama of the Puebleños and the miracle play is the Matachina. Matachina is a generic name applied in Spain to an old type of ballad dance, reapplied in Old Mexico to more than one modified survival of native dance-drama. But along the New Mexican border the name refers to one specific dance which has all the earmarks of Indian origin with super-imposed Christian handling. The costumes are unquestionably derived from Roman ecclesiastical robes, particularly the head-dresses; the wands used by the dancers are three-branched, such as are used in many Indian-Catholic ceremonies to signify the Trinity—and in many Mexican-Indian rites for the fruitful corn-mother. There are not wanting hints that the use of these things might have originally been derisive; and more than a hint that the aboriginal foundation of the local Matachina was of phallic significance. For what else was the miter, of which the Matachina head-dress is plainly reminiscent, but the phallic crown? But whatever the original intention, the Roman influence has triumphed since the matachina is recognized as a dance suitable for exclusively Christian festivals, such as Christmas and Easter.

At the same time there are reasons for suspecting that this might have been one of the native Mexican dances which the church in the beginning of the Spanish conquest undertook to repress because it was found that they keep a sense of nationalism alive among the conquered tribes. For the leading characters of the matachina can be found both north and south of the border, with two sets of names: El Monarch, Montezuma; El Toro, Cortez; the Bride, Malinche (mistress of Cortez); and sometimes a hair-and-horn masked figure which is recognized either as the Devil or as one of the Sacred Clowns familiar to dance-drama audiences. Altogether it seems probable that this was an aboriginal fertility dance made over by the church into a masque of the Soul's (the Bride's) struggle with the world, the flesh, and the devil. For which violence to their traditions the tribes compensated by reading into it secretly their own forced acceptance of Spanish rule. As an example of transition from dance-drama to popular entertainment the New Mexican Matachina is worth more study than has been given to it.

So much has been written of late about the beautiful and inspiriting dance-drama which may be seen not only in the pueblos of the Southwest but at the tourist festivals of Santa Fe and Gallup, that description here would be superfluous. To the student the chief use of these ceremonies, besides providing a high type of aesthetic entertainment, is to enable him to divide the several elements of gesture, both realistic and symbolic, from the literary components of drama. Beautiful enough to engage every aesthetic reaction, even that least worthy and by the average onlooker most coveted one of sensation, the fire dance, the buffalo dance, the Yebetchi challenge the intelligence at every contact. As if all the primitive life of man from the very earliest were gathered up in them, about to burst into the final flower of art expression. To the uninstructed, however, they remain largely unintelligible because the explicatory acts and incidents of the drama are many of them performed in the *kiva*, as in the Penitential drama they take place in the *morada*, as in the best Greek tragedy they took place off stage. So that one wonders if the Greek habit of having the killings and other acts of violence done behind the scenes, instead of springing, as popularly supposed, from a Greek sense of propriety, did not rise from an earlier ritualistic custom of having them happen in the secret ceremonial chamber. The whole dance-drama complex is thus a mine of information and illumination as to dramatic origins and as to the possible use of elements of form and expression that in the modern theater have gone as flat as uncorked champagne; synthetic gesture, significant setting, the use of masks, of climax, of sacred clowning. Indian comedy, a subject too vast for more than descriptive mention, is sufficiently close to modern comedy to be easily understood by any audience. It springs from the tribal need of social correction by laughter and is the business of the Koshare, the Society of Sacred Clowns personating the spirits of the ancestors. Historic events, such as the entrada of Coronado and the killing of Estevan, the first Negro, are often used as pegs on which to hang corrective farces, and of late the absurdities of modern white life are satirized for the benefit of the younger generation.

While at present the office of native drama in the Southwest seems to be that of reinstruction in the fundamentals of dramatic and theatrical practice, it cannot be seen as providing other than the securest groundwork for a type of dramatic writing which will be inevitably fitted to carry all that the Southwest has to express. In so doing it will probably be found to be more expressive for what we call American uses—meaning by that the concurrent output of our mingling strains and local environment—than anything derived from purely Nordic sources, such as Greek and Elizabethan playwriting. Already the incursive interest of creative workers occupies itself with the separation of Indian dancing from its tribal elements in order to save it for aesthetic service, as Greek drama was saved. On this point public opinion is somewhat at fault, arguing that apart from its tribal significance Indian dancing will cease to have meaning and power. But the whole history of plastic art goes to show that the only way any of it was ever incorporated into the evolutionary history of culture was to cut it out cleanly from the creedal and mythologic root as poetic tragedy was cut off from Hellenic pantheism, as European drama was excised from the medieval theology. Several movements have begun looking toward such a saving result; an association for the revival of Spanish Colonial Arts at Santa Fe, Witter Bynner and Camilo Padilla for the encouragement of Spanish Colonial lyricism, and Indian Art Museum for Indians. The emergence of a native Southwestern drama is only a matter of a little time and intelligent fostering.

In particular I expect to see a new school of gesture—taking the word in its widest sense in which the human personality can be used as a vehicle of expression. Here alone, in Indian drama, do we approach the condition in which gesture is speech, as in the Spanish Colonial plays we rediscover something of the provocative relation between manners and art. And if such evolutionary processes go on, screened as they are by little-understood languages, so much the better for their successful escape from the present gaucheries and dullness of American drama.

PART IV

A Southwestern Rhythm:
Introduction to Poetry

Although poetry is the last section in this anthology it is certainly not making its first appearance. A strong poetic influence surfaces regularly in the first two sections as the essence of experience in the one-smoke story or as imagery and rhythm in dance drama. Austin explains that, like Aristotle, Southwesterners often regarded poetry as comprising several arts. She believed poets often bogged themselves down in form, pattern, and rhyme, restricting their ideas to established molds, and that much of what poets strain for in order to produce poetry intellectually should come naturally through deep regional roots, with the environment serving as the underlying force for an entire literary tradition.

During the years when Austin was a young teacher in California, she was dismayed that the poetry she was supposed to teach to the children of the Mojave Desert, Death Valley, and the Eastern Sierra could not create images in their heads because the images came from wet, green Europe or the American east coast. So she and her students simply made up their own poems, with their own rhythms, images, words, and characters. These children's poems were later published in a collection called *The Children Sing in the Far West*, including this one, which she called "Western Magic":

There are no fairy-folk in our Southwest,
The cactus spines would tear their filmy wings,
There are no dew any where for them to drink
And no green grass to make their fairy rings.

But sometimes in a windless blur of dust
The impish twins of War and Chance go by,

Or after storms the Spider Woman mends
With thin drawn cloud, torn edges of the sky.

And there is One who plays upon the flute
In deep rock crevices where springs are found,—
'Twas at To-yallanne they saw him first,—
In April youths are magicked by the sound.

Hot dawns the turquoise horse, Johano-ai,
Races the sun in dust of glittering grains,
Or round Pelado Peak the Rainbow Boy
Goes dancing with the many-footed rains.

There are no fairy-folk in our Southwest,
But there are hours when prairie-dog and snake,
Black beetle and the tecolote owl
Between two winks their ancient forms will take,

Clad in white skins with shell shield glittering
The sun, their chief, the Ancient road will walk,
Half in her sleep the mothering earth
Of older things than fairy-folk will talk.[1]

Through this children's poetry, Austin says she "set about the business of providing my pupils with verse that would serve the immemorial purpose of poetry in linking them with their natural environment and evoking through it that mystical feeling for the land which is the root of what goes by the name of culture."[2] Several of Austin's articles on children's poetry contain her clearest explanations of poetic development.

One of the recurring images in Austin's own work is the color black.[3] In *The Land of Little Rain*, Austin wrote that from black shadows often comes music:

Singing is in fact the business of the night.... When the moon comes over the mountain wall new-washed from the sea, and the shadows lie like lace on the stamped floors of patios, from recess to recess of the vine tangle runs the thrum of guitars and the voice of singing.[4]

In many places, shadows and recesses conjure murder and fear, but in the Southwest, shadows are life giving. In most climates the sun symbolizes life, goodness, and God. In the desert, however, the sun is often the killer. All creatures and plants must use their wits to avoid its relentless destructive forces. So from the blackness of shade comes comfort, peace, sustenance, and life. Is black shade the place, Austin wonders, where the lion may actually lie down with the lamb: "There was a fence in that country shutting in a cattle range, and along its fifteen miles of posts one could be sure of finding a bird or two in every strip of shadow; sometimes the sparrow and the hawk, with wings trailed and beaks parted, drooping in the white truce of noon."[5] Even the black buzzard, usually a symbol of death, is, to Austin, a symbol of life: "In mid-desert where there are no cattle, there are no birds of carrion."[6] So, in the sun-scorched world of the Southwest, she found that black is beautiful.

Some Indian tribes also considered black one of their spiritual colors. Black feathers, black dirt, and black pebbles were often considered "good medicine." In Arizona's Sonoran desert, small, smooth, almost transparent black rocks are called "Apache Tears." The best arrowheads were often worked from this same rock: black obsidian. According to a snow-coach driver/guide in Yellowstone National Park, surgeons are now experimenting with obsidian scalpels because obsidian supposedly leaves fewer scars. Did American Indians know? Austin explains that the penitentes used obsidian to scar their backs. Did they know their scars would miraculously heal? Did Mary Austin know?

Black rock is usually volcanic, the blood of the earth. In the desert it often represents a natural boundary, and most importantly a place where water might be found. Even water—clear and white when frozen, rushing, or held in one's hand—in nature, especially in the desert, often appears black. Springs, seeps, and cienegas are usually found around black rocks, since volcanic action is usually associated with faults that collect and allow water to move freely. Because black rock comes from the "fiery furnace down below," it also makes a wonderful place for Austin to begin questioning the white culture's color symbolism and religion. From the Greeks to the Aztecs, from the Bible to Emerson, rock has represented God, Christ, altar, and foundation. It has also conjured visions of weapon, sacrifice, and tomb. Carl Jung explains black as nothing less than the shadow side of God.

A serious student of Oriental literatures, Austin found parallel subtleties in much of the Indian's poetic imagery. To people living among
them, cacti, mirages, irrigation ditches, and buzzards conjure deep
thoughts and waves of emotion, as did cherry blossoms, dragons, foggy
moors, and swans to people who lived among them. Students of literature go to great lengths to study the symbolism of European and Oriental poets, and Austin believed American regional writers deserved the
same serious study. She believed the Southwest was brimming with rich
images upon which to draw, like those she describes in "Cactus Country": the creosote's tail waving in the sun, the blossom crown of the
yucca, and the sotol's saw-edged leaves.

She said Southwestern poetry should not be approached with traditional literary tools because it was not created for the printed page,
explaining that Indian images were not only visual but auditory: heart
beats, animal sounds, weather. But these subtleties were not always
obvious to other literary critics of her day.[7] In an extensive exchange of
arrows, Austin chides one reviewer of a collection of Indian poetry for
his "New Yorkish" literary judgment, saying, "If Mr. Untermeyer could
get his mind off the Indian Anthology as a thing of type and paper, he
might have got something more out of it,"[8] and unless he "knew something of the genius of the aboriginal Indian language, unless he knew
something of Imagism besides what it looks like on paper, he had no
right to review this book." She goes on to apologize to him with
tongue-in-cheek for having "drawn her fire" saying he was "not the
only poet who has reviewed the book under the impression that Imagism was invented in West Twenty-Third street and perfected in
Chicago."[9] Fiercely defending native literatures, she often pointed out
that Indian poetry relied on free verse and imagery long before these
"new" styles became popular in "those temples of Imitation, the Universities."[10] Carl Van Doren, supporting Austin's prophetic abilities,
says, "A decade before the newer forms of verse came into fashion, she
had forecast them and practiced them, deriving her methods from those
of the primitive Americans near whom she lived."[11]

Because Indian poetry was always suggestive, and a small word contained complicated meanings like a form of shorthand, she said, "the
greater part of a man's life may thus be sung in a simple sentence."[12]
She called this kind of minimalist and symbolic language a "glyph" (as

in petroglyph), explaining it in such a way as to help readers understand her own attraction to "divided narrative":

> Mold or rhyme-pattern, so far as it exists for the aboriginal exists only as a point of rest for the verse to flow into and out of as a mountain stream flows in and out of ripple-linked pools. It is this leap of the running stream of poetic inspiration from level to level, whose course cannot be determined by anything except the nature of the ground traversed, which I have called the landscape line. The length of the leaps, and the sequence of pattern recurrences will be conditioned by the subjectively coordinated motor rhythms associated with the particular emotional flow.
>
> This landscape line may of course involve several verse lines as they appear on the printed page, and it is best described by the modern term, cadenced verse. In the placing of this line, and the additional items by which it is connoted and decorated, the aboriginal process approaches closest to what is known as Imagism, unless you will accept my term and call it glyphic. Once having adopted a definite space of consciousness for the purpose of realizing it poetically, the supreme art of the Amerind is displayed in the relating of the various elements to the central idea. Like his cognate, the Japanese, the Amerind excels in the art of occupying space without filling it. Sometimes the whole area of experience is sufficiently occupied by a single undecorated statement.[13]

To the Indian, she says, poetry was sometimes very private and personal, and not something contrived to impress others by flaunting artistic craft or style. Austin discovered that aboriginals often created their songs to memorialize important moments in their own lives—a great hunt, finding love, the death of a son—and it was understood that no one else could sing that song without the owner's permission. The aboriginal values it, she says, "for the reaction it produces within himself rather than for any effect he is able to produce on others by means of it."[14]

The unique rhythms created by Indian poets especially fascinated her and led her to compile her thoughts and observations into her most significant book-length critical analysis of poetry *The American Rhythm* (1923). For an excellent overview of the controversies, major players, influences, and errors surrounding publication of *The American Rhythm* see Michael Castro's *Interpreting the Indian: Twentieth-Century Poets and the Native American*.[15] Castro summarizes his own efforts as an attempt

> ...to demonstrate the characteristics and the appeal of Indian poetry and to record that several poets and editors understood their interest in Indian poetry not as antiquarianism, but as vital concern with the development of a new American poetry that could speak in ways that would serve the literary and spiritual needs of modern America[16]

He concludes that "None of them understood or articulated this better than Mary Austin."[17] However, he explains that after publication of her book *The American Rhythm*, critics were basically split into two camps, those who defensively dismissed her ideas as destructive to development of good poetry modeled after European classics and those who saw her ideas as a breath of fresh American air.[18]

In *The American Rhythm*, Austin explains the general fundamentals of rhythm and lyricism as keys to understanding the influence of the land on the people. She believed natural poetic rhythms emerged directly from an intimate relationship with the land flowing directly into the food and then the body and then the literature. Preceding the "new" field of ecocriticism by over half a century, Austin believed that the "poetic faculty is...the most responsive to natural environment," that the "poetry of the forest dwellers is more lyric than the songs of mountain and mesa."[19] Austin claimed she could listen to phonograph recordings of Indian free verse and correctly identify the "landscape line," which picked up the rhythms from the place where the poet lived. She said indigenous people had no intellectuals to imitate or intimidate, so their rhythms were instinctive, but this did not mean that they suffered from inferior intellectual development. She labels this instinctive response as neither substandard nor immature, but rather freer and more natural, a source of rhythm inspired by experience and environment.

Austin also believed natural rhythms arose from humble vernacular occupations or transportation activities like riding in a rocking stagecoach, or striding across the prairie beside an ox team. She claimed to hear the rhythms of "hog butcher of the world" in the poetry of Carl Sandberg, the axe-stroke in Abe Lincoln's Gettysburg Address, the horse's hooves in cowboy poetry, and the push and pull of women grinding corn on a metate in Indian verse. She believed these natural rhythms were our very own American Rhythms—our poetic roots— and was convinced that "American poetry must inevitably take...the mold of the American experience shaped by the American environment."[20]

She said we would have "come into our heritage of rhythms based on the tug and heave of constructive labor much earlier, if all the time the common people were learning them, the intellectual caste had not been, in an environment artificially created for that purpose, sedulously putting the young through the ancient carpet-treading, crosier-bearing paces."[21] Llewellyn Jones calls Austin's ideas on rhythm "controversial" and "dubious" and says that Austin obviously means cadence.[22] But Austin carefully differentiated between cadence and rhythm.[23] She was also, according to Lewis Mumford, anxious to make clear that she was "not interested in the influence of rustic occupations and experiences on poetry, but the influence of *American* occupations upon *American* poetry."[24]

Mumford, however, finds this one of Austin's "weaknesses" and says she seems to be "letting her imagination run away with her."[25] Sometimes her theories seem to imply that Indian poetry is produced too easily or that Spanish geographical terms seem almost accidentally poetic: However, she explains that poetry can develop naturally, not that it comes without intellectual effort:

> All primitive speech is immensely more poetic to the sophisticated ear than it has any intention of being. When a Paiute speaks of the 'moth hour' he means something about as commonplace as 'six o'clock in the evening' and when he makes an appointment for 'the moon of tender leaves,' he refers merely to the first week in April. Almost anybody is forced to become a poet by the loss of mechanical exactitude."[26]

In *The American Rhythm*, she also discusses the Indians' superior sense of awareness, explaining their attention to detail: "The Indian sees no better than the white man, but he sees more, registers through every sense, some of which have atrophied in us, infinitely more."[27] By using her own unique blend of story with literary analysis, she explains that this trait could be found in all Southwesterners who lived close to the land, remembering how in May and June the Sierra shepherds

> ...would go peering along the edge of the down-pouring rivers for the floating yellow scum, pollen drift from the forest hundreds of miles away on the uplifted flanks of the Sierras. By the date of the first appearance of the floating pollen, and the quantity, they judged whether the summer feed would be full or scanty, and on indications as slight as these they bargained with the dealers who came out from San Francisco for their spring lambs. Intimacies such as these between the land and the people breed poets faster, and much better than do universities.[28]

Poetry was a matter of observation, instinct, and experience to Austin—not imitation—and she realized it would be difficult to capture the full quality of this complicated poetry on paper. Many of the literary critics of Austin's day never looked beyond words on paper, failing to appreciate the full spectrum of rhythm, image, gesture, ritual, experience, and emotion in these oral forms of poetry. No matter how well she or anyone else worked to bring Indian verse to the literary public, she lamented that it could not be fully appreciated without the physical presence and vibrant rhythms of its makers, their holophrastic language, and the place where it was produced. She called her own efforts "re-expression" rather than translation. Ford explains that Austin's method was to "absorb the culture, seek out the thought, and then re-express it in terms faithful to the Indian version, yet intelligible to the white reader." But he warns that "It is possible that she read something into the poetry that was not there."[29] Austin may have agreed since even she was wary of her re-expressions:

> Our easy newspaper habit of ascribing authority where there is no more than an informed and intelligent interest, has credited me with being an authority on things Indian, which I am not,

as a translator which I never pretended to be, and as a poet which I am only occasionally, and by induction.[30]

This rare attempt at humility did not last long, however, as she soon goes on to defend herself:

That I should make mistakes in a field where so little had been done before me was to have been expected. That the only mistake I have ever had publicly to correct came of my trusting to the ethnologists too implicitly is my excuse for occasionally venturing beyond their findings on ground where nobody but a poet could have ventured at all.[31]

Castro says that unlike the Transcendentalists, Austin found a "holistic awareness" not by going to India but by going to Indians. This, he argues, answers "Emerson's call for a uniquely American poetry" and is important to "modern poets in search of mythopoetic roots or the spirit of place."[32] Austin was often the first to recognize the unique value of Southwestern poetry, protesting that there was no reason to look beyond our own land and people to find not only our own poetic roots, but perhaps the roots of all poetry as well. However, her efforts have almost been forgotten, and even in her own day she often complained bitterly that no one seemed to remember her contributions:

I am a little tired of furnishing stepping-stones for other people to utilize; especially as most of them seem to forget anything they might possibly have owed to me. Of the half a dozen or so people now adding to their own reputations by adventures into Indian poetry, only one has ever had the grace to admit that I was first in the field. Most of them try to forget that I even exist in that connection.[33]

She was the first to seriously discuss cowboy poetry, to seriously study the various forms of Mexican poetry such as the *copla* and *corrido,* or to attempt to trace the rhythms in Indian tribal lays. Although all of these genres are American born, American scholars largely ignore them, or as Austin derisively says, "Americans have been more interested in *being* 'cultured' than in *creating* cultures."[34] Although Castro says Austin's influence is "limited today," he also says,

The central figure in the movement to bring Indian poetry to non-Indian Americans was Mary Hunter Austin, who pioneered the exploration of Indian consciousness in this century as a poet, playwright, essayist, and anthologist. Austin was one of the most active and influential of the early twentieth-century writers who redefined the meaning of the Indian for American culture. Though she is regarded as a minor poet today, Austin's efforts were extremely important in stimulating many of her contemporaries to consider the Indian's relevance to American cultural identity, poetry, and poetics, and in anticipating the concerns of more talented and influential poets later in the century.[35]

According to Austin the Southwest possessed great poetry and a great poetic legacy. We hope that by reading her words again we might yet produce a new generation of critics who will discover her, and who might recognize from their own experience that where there's smoke, there's fire.

Notes to Poetry Introduction

1. Mary Austin, *The Children Sing in the Far West* (Houghton Mifflin, 1928), 55–56.

2. Mary Austin, "Poetry in the Education of Children," *Bookman* 68 (November 1928): 270–75.

3. Esther F. Lanigan, *Mary Austin: Song of a Maverick* (New Haven: Yale University Press, 1989; Tucson: University of Arizona Press, 1997), 185). Lanigan describes Austin as possessing dexterity in "composing verbal pictures."

4. Mary Austin, *The Land of Little Rain* (New York: Houghton Mifflin Company, 1903; New York: Penguin Group, 1988), 102.

5. Ibid., 6.

6. Ibid., 14.

7. Thomas W. Ford, "The American Rhythm: Mary Austin's Poetic Principle," *Western American Literature* 5.1 (Spring 1970): 3, 14. Ford calls her ideas "astonishing" and thought she might be guilty of reading "something into the poetry that was not there."

8. Mary Austin, Letter in *The Dial* (May 31, 1919): 569.

9. Mary Austin, Letter in *The Dial* (August 23, 1919): 163.

10. Mary Austin, *The American Rhythm* (New York: Harcourt, 1923), 7.

11. Carl Van Doren, "Mary Austin Discoverer and Prophet," *The Century* 107.1 (November 1923): 154–55.

12. Mary Austin, "Medicine Songs: Transcribed from the Indian Originals," *Everybody's Magazine* (September 1914): 413.

13. Austin, *American Rhythm*, 55–56.

14. Mary Austin, Introduction to *Path on the Rainbow*, ed. George W. Cronyn (New York: Boni and Liveright, 1918): xv–xxxii.

15. Michael Castro, *Interpreting the Indian: Twentieth-Century Poets and the Native American*, with Foreword by Maurice Kenny (Norman: University of Oklahoma Press, 1983).

16. Ibid, 38.

17. Ibid.

18. Ibid, 45.

19. Austin, Introduction to *Path on the Rainbow*, xxiii.

20. Austin, *American Rhythm*, 42.

21. Ibid., 15.

22. Llewellyn Jones, *Bookman* (August 1923): 647.

23. See letter to "Hal" (Witter Bynner) dated 5–29–30 in Center for Southwest Research, MSS 31 "Mary Austin Letters, 1932–1933)" Fray Angélico Chávez, Chavez History Library, Box 1, Folder 1.

24. Lewis Mumford, "*The American Rhythm*." *The New Republic* 35.443 (1993): 20.

25. Ibid.

26. Austin, Foreword to "Fire," 6.

27. Austin, *American Rhythm*, 29.

28. Mary Austin, "Art Influence in the West," *The Century Magazine* (November 1914–April 1915): 831.

29. Ford, 14.

30. Ibid.

31. Austin, *American Rhythm*, 37 and 64.

32. Castro, 6.

33. Mary Austin, Letter to Arthur Fiche, August 8, 1929, Center for Southwest Collection, MSS 31 "Mary Austin Letters, 1927–1930" Box 1, Folder 5.

34. Mary Austin, "Regional Culture in the Southwest," *Southwest Review* 14 (1929): 475.

35. Castro, 5.

22

Introduction to *The Path on the Rainbow*

1918

Not often does there fall to the writer of prefaces an opportunity equal to this, in introducing the first authoritative volume of aboriginal American verse. Probably never before has it occurred that the intimate thought of a whole people should be made known through its most personal medium to another people whose unavoidable destiny it is to carry that thought to fulfillment and make of that medium a characteristic literary vehicle.

To those unaware until now of the very existence of such a body of aboriginal verse, this may seem a large claim. But unless the occasion has some such significance, it has in this year of nineteen eighteen, no excuse. This is no time in which to divert public attention to mere collections of literary curiosities. Arresting as single examples of it are, a greater interest still attaches to the relationship which seems about to develop between Indian verse and the ultimate literary destiny of America.

That there is such a relationship any one at all familiar with current verse of the past three or four years must immediately conclude on turning over a few pages. He will be struck at once with the extraordinary likeness between much of this native product and the recent work of the Imagists, *vers librists*, and other literary fashionables. He may, indeed, congratulate himself on the confirmation of his secret suspicion that Imagism is a very primitive form; he may, if he happens to be of the Imagist's party, suffer a check in the discovery that the first free movement of poetic originality in America finds us just about where the last Medicine Man left off. But what else could he have expected?

The poetic faculty is, of all man's modes, the most responsive to natural environment, the most sensitive and the truest record of his reactions to its skyey influences, its floods, forests, morning colors. It is the first to register the rise of his spirits to the stimulus of new national ideals. If this were not so there would be no such thing as nationality in art, and it is only by establishing some continuity with the earliest instances of such reaction that we can be at all sure that American poetic genius has struck its native note. Therefore it becomes appropriate and important that this collection of American Indian verse should be brought to public notice at a time when the whole instinctive movement of the American people is for a deeper footing in their native soil. It is the certificate of our adoption, that the young genius of our time should strike all unconsciously on this ancient track to the High Places.

Poetic art in America at the time it began to be overlaid by European culture, had reached a mark close to that of the Greeks at the beginning of the Homeric era. The lyric was well developed, the epic was nascent, and the drama was still in the Satyris stage of development, a rude dance ritual about an altar or a sacrificial fire. Neither poetry nor drama were yet divorced from singing, and all art was but half-born out of the Great Mystery. Magic was sung, and songs had magic power. Both were accompanied by appropriate bodily movement, so that an Indian will say indifferently, I cannot sing that dance, or I cannot dance that song. Words, melody and movement were as much mixed as the water of a river with its own ripples and its rate of flowing. Hum a few bars of a plainsman's familiar song, and he will say, puzzled, "It ought to be a war song," but without the words he will scarcely identify it. Words may become obsolete so that the song is untranslatable, but so long as enough of it remains to hold together the primary emotional impulse out of which it sprang, the Indian finds it worthy to be sung. He is, indeed, of the opinion that "White man's songs, they talk too much."

This partly explains why most Indian songs are songs for occasions. The rest of the explanation lies in the fact that songs have magic power. Tirawa, Wokonda, The Friend of the Soul of Man, is in everything; in the field we plant, the stone we grind with, the bear we kill. By singing, the soul of the singer is put in harmony with the essential Essence of

Things. There are songs for every possible adventure of tribal life; songs for setting out on a journey, a song for the first sight of your destination, and a song to be sung by your wife for your safe return. Many of these songs occur detached from everything but the occasion from which they sprang, such as the women's grinding song, measured to the *plump, plump!* of the mealing stone, or the Paddle Song which follows the swift rhythm of the stroke. Others, less descriptive and retaining always something of a sacred character, occur originally as numbers in the song sequences by which are celebrated the tribal Mysteries.

Back of every Indian ceremony lies a story, the high moments of which are caught up in song, while the burden of the narrative is carried by symbolic rite and dance. The unequal social development of contemporaneous tribes affords examples from every phase of structural development from the elemental dance punctuated by singing exclamations to the Mountain Chant of the Zuni in which the weight of the story has broken down the verse variants into strong simple forms capable of being carried in a single memory. Half-way between them is the ritual sequence of the Midwan.

The practical necessity of being preserved and handed on by word of mouth only, must be constantly borne in mind in considering the development of Indian verse forms.

It operated to keep the poetry tied to its twin-born melody, which assisted memory, and was constantly at work modifying the native tendency to adjust the rhythm to every changing movement of the story. Ancient Chippeway singers kept ideographic birch bark memoranda of their songs, and wampum belts commemorated the events that gave use to them, but the songs themselves came down from their ancient sources hundreds of years in the stream of human memory shaped by its limitations.

From the Zuni Creation Cycle with its sustained narrative style to the Homeric Epic is but one poetic bound, the space between them, represented in old world literature by the Norse Sagas and the Kalevala, indicated but not filled, in America, by prose relations. It is probable that if we had anything like adequate records of the literature of vanished tribes, this pre-Homeric period would show notable examples of epic stuff. Nobody really knows how the Walam Olum or the Creek Migration Myths were recited. They embodied whole epochs of tribal history, to which the known literary remains were merely the mnemonic key, a tally of significant items. In every tribe are floating songs which appear to be fragments from a story sequence the key of which has been lost, and it is not unlikely that records like the Red Score would have owned complete, if detached, narratives of the historic events so slightly indicated, some of which may yet yield themselves to the patient researcher.

For the casual reader more interest attaches to the personal songs, the lullabys, love songs, most of all the man's *own* song which he makes of his great moment. This is a peculiar personal possession. No one may sing it without his permission. He may bestow it on a friend, or bequeath it to the tribe on his death, but it is also possible that he may die without having sung it to anyone but his god.

On one occasion in the high Sierras I observed my Indian packer going apart at a certain hour each day to shuffle rhythmically with his feet and croon to himself. To my inquiry he said it was a song which he had made, to be sung by himself and his wife when they were apart from one another.

It had no words; it was just a song. Wherever they were they turned each in the direction he supposed the other to be, when the sun was a bow-shot above the edge of the heavens, and sang together. This is the sort of incident which gives the true value of song in aboriginal life. It is not the words which are potent, but the states of mind evoked by singing, states which the simple savage conceived as being supernally good for him. He evoked them therefore on all his most personal occasions. Poetry is the Path on the Rainbow by which the soul climbs; it lays hold on the Friend of the Soul of Man. Such exalted states are held to be protective and curative. Medicine men sing for their patients, and, in times of war, wives gather around the Chief's woman and sing for the success of their warriors.

"Calling on Zeus by the names of Victory" as Euripides puts it.

It is this inherent power of poetry to raise the psychic plane above the accidents of being, which gives meaning to the custom of the Death Song. As he sees his moment approaching, the Indian throws himself, by some profound instinct of self-preservation, into the highest frame of mind attainable. When men in battle broke into the death song, they had committed themselves to the last desperate adventure. Dying of enfeebling sickness, their friends came and sang around them. One such I heard, the death song of a Yokut Song Maker. It was very simple:

"All my life
I have been seeking,
Seeking!"

What more than this have the schools taught us!

Of Indian meters there has been no competent study made. The whole problem of form is inextricably complicated with melody and movement. The necessity of making his verse conform to a dance, probably accounts for the liberal use of meaningless syllables. To our ear no specific forms seem indicated, yet that the Indians recognize a certain correspondence between form and meaning is certain. They will readily classify songs of other tribes in unknown tongues into songs of love or war or magic. The genius of the tribal language is a determining factor. No clumsiness of translation can quite disguise the—from our point of view—superior singableness of Chippeway verse. In general, poetry of forest dwellers is more lyric than the songs of mountain and mesa. An inquiry which I once made into the psychology of the Indian sign language with a view to discovering a possible relation between it and Greek manual gesture as displayed in ancient graphic art, led to the conclusion that Indian rhythms arise rather in the center of self-preservation than of self-consciousness. Which is only another way of saying that poetry is valued primarily by the aboriginal for the reaction it produces within himself rather than for any effect he is able to produce on others by means of it. This is true even of that class of songs which originates wholly in the desire to affect the fortunes or well being of others, songs of healing and magic formulae.

The first stage of Indian magic is the rise of the singer on his own song to a plane of power; only while he is in this plane is he able to bring the wish of his client to pass. It is a natural process of deterioration which leads to the song being thought of as having potency in itself.

Magic songs can generally be recognized by the form of affirmation in which they are cast, as in the Winnebago Love Song, which is not really a song of love, but a song to secure success in love,

Whosoe'r I look upon
He becomes love crazed.

or the Cherokee formula to insure the constancy of the beloved, and
the Micmac vengeance song

Death I make,
Singing.

Among the Navajo the magic effect is made certain by the four-fold
repetition of the affirming phrase, four being a sacred number.

These are all items which have to be taken into account in interpreting American Indian poetry. It is in the very nature of primitive
verse that it should require interpretation, even among the audiences
for whom it is originally intended. For verse is to the Red singer but a
shorthand note to his emotions, a sentence or two, a phrase out of the
heart of the situation. It is the "inside song" alone which is important.
Says the Medicine Man, explaining these matters, "You see Injun man
singin' an' cryin' while he sing. It ain't what he singin' make him cry;
iss what the song make him think, thass what he cryin' about."

This inside song may be a fleeting instant of revelation, or a very
long story... as if one should try in the Zuni fashion to compress the
whole Christian myth into one bitter cry,

My God! My God!
Why hast Thou deserted me?

Hi-ihiya, naiho-o,
It is finished,
In beauty it is finished
Nai-ho-o!

Whole cycles of tribal or personal experience can lie behind some
such simple but absolute phrasing. It is this hidden beauty for which the
interpreter must dig deep into aboriginal life....

The single line which identifies the song of Tiakens as intrinsically
American is that one which inquires: "Didst thou understand her signs
when she danced to thee?" Embodying as it does a very widespread
aboriginal belief that in the dance and song, more than in any other
medium, a maiden revealed the physical capacity and the power of sus-

tained emotion which fitted her for marriage. Since when, and with what unhappy results, have *we* forgotten that creative emotion is a qualification for marriage! We do shallowly indeed when we dismiss the dance and song as mere millinery of courtship. They are the speech of the spirit identifying itself with cosmic forces. I do not know whether or not the Tenasa had the custom known on the Pacific Coast as the Dance of Marriageable Maidens, but I know that if you cut deeply into any Indian poem it yields that profound and palpitant humanism without which no literary art can endure.

Failure to realize the living background of Indian art has led to singular misinterpretation, in a class of songs common to every tribe, and almost invariably translated as love songs by the novice. These are the songs of the Mystics, Songs of Seeking. They record the unavailing search of the soul for the Absolute, for touch of that Great Mystery which is the object of the Indian's profoundest aspiration. Two such songs may be found in Frederick Burton's collection of Ojibway music, done into rather sentimental love ditties, the "Lake's Sheen" and the "Birch Bark Canoe," though their character as religious songs was so plainly marked that Mr. Burton himself commented on the singularity of Indian sweethearts forever getting themselves lost and requiring to be sought. It is well to remember before attempting the interpretation of an Indian love song, that the great Mystics have always appropriated the intimate language of the heart for the soul's quest . . . .

23

Letter to the Editor of *The Dial*

1919

SIR: I am asking for a little space in which to protest Mr. Louis Untermeyer's review of the anthology of American Indian verse in your issue of March 8. Or perhaps it amounts to a protest against giving a book of such national, one might say international interest to be reviewed by one whose mind has so evidently never visited west of Broadway.

Mr. Untermeyer describes himself as a "mere man of letters," a more limiting title than I should have chosen for him, but it begins to be a question in America whether a man is entitled to describe himself as a man of letters at all who so complacently confesses his ignorance of and inability to enter into the vast body of aboriginal literature of his country, literature that rises to the saga form easily comparable to the great works on which European literature is built, and to epics that for sonority and richness of figure approach and at times equal the epics of Homer. That these treasures of native literature are not yet available in that easy edition de luxe which Mr. Untermeyer appears to desire, is very largely due to the large number of persons who, like Mr. Untermeyer, apparently can not get at literature in any other form. The movement, however, to aid the average American to understand what his own land has to say through the medium of a homogeneous race, will not be helped by making such reviews a mere statement of limitation.

I agree with Mr. Untermeyer that The Path on the Rainbow might have been accompanied by explanatory notes to the advantage of most readers. I may say here that the only thing that has prevented me from publishing such an edition of American verse, is the difficulty of finding a publisher for anything that smacks of scholarship in that direction.

But I feel that the failure to get anything out of the edition as it stands is wholly Mr. Untermeyer's. It would be a great deal, for instance, to have fully established, as this volume does, that vers libre and Imagism are in truth primitive forms, and both of them generically American forms, forms instinctively selected by people living in America and freed from outside influence.

I feel quite sure that I said enough in the introduction to enable the thoughtful reader to discover that Imagism is an *incomplete* form, as recognized by the Indian, requiring melody and the beat of drum or pounding feet to fulfill itself. It should have been fruitful to the thoughtful poet to consider just how far the Indian could carry this form, as instanced in the Marriage Song of Tiakens, which I am sure I could have passed off as Greek by the simple change of name.

Even more interesting it is to note how stanza structure is built up out of the unrhymed, unmeasured lyric, as is shown in the collection of songs from the Southwest. And what a lot of discussion might be saved us if Mr. Untermeyer could have made the observation which this volume suggests and further inquiry could but confirm, about several things that Imagism is *not*. It is not, with the aboriginal, merely descriptive, and never merely decorative.

The incident which the reviewer recounts as related to him by Mr. Robert Frost is true enough; it may be found by the curious in Burton's Ojibway Songs, and since Mr. Burton so frankly admits his error, he would not object to my saying that it is not the only mistaken translation he made. When one considers how many readings of Sappho and even of Shakespeare are in doubt, it is not surprising that Indian verse should occasionally suffer at the hands of the translator. It is also true and ought not to seem surprising, as Mr. Untermeyer suspects, that Indian poets are like other poets, occasionally banal and commonplace, but it is again pertinent to suggest that something more than a "mere man of letters" is required for the appreciation of literature which is different from one's own, or the fashion of the hour.

It is not necessary to read banality into the particular examples given by Mr. Untermeyer, any more than one reads triviality into an army singing John Brown's Body because the words are trivial. I did not translate the particular verse instanced by Mr. Untermeyer, but what must always be taken into consideration behind Indian songs is democracy of thinking and feeling. The communal life of the Indian leads to a community of thinking which made many words unnecessary, made the words a spring for the release of emotion which might be anything but banal. Ten thousand American boys in a foreign land singing Home Sweet Home is a very moving thing, and twice ten Indians at the ragged end of winter, when the food goes stale and their very garments smell of wood smoke, singing the maple sugar song might sing a great deal of poetry into it, poetry of rising sap, clean snow water, calling partridge, and the friendly click of brass bowls and birch bark sapbuckets. If Mr. Untermeyer could get his mind off the Indian Anthology as a thing of type and paper, he might have got something more out of it. He might even have launched into a dissertation on the horrible banality of poetry under complete democracy, and have further supported it by turning over a few pages to songs of the Southwest where everybody knows the aboriginals live in terraced houses, and the stanza form advanced with the increase of privacy and individuality of living. No one who reads the Hako ceremony of the Pawnees, realizing that the Pawnee country is open, rolling prairie, lifting toward long level mesas, can fail to be struck with the way in which the shape of the lines is influenced by the contours of the country. It was in order to show just such local influences that the poems in the Anthology were grouped sectionally rather than tribally.

That all these things seem to have been missed by the reviewer raises again the question as to whether we can ever have anything which is American literature, *sui generis*, until literary judgment begins to be American and leaves off being thoroughly New Yorkish.

24

The Meter of Aztec Verse

1929

When the poet Longfellow, actuated by the first stirrings of authentic feeling for an American literature which should be native not only in material but in form, selected for his projected aboriginal epic the form of the Finnish *Kalevala*, his action was generally excused as the resort of desperation. Whether or not he had already discovered the fact, known to two or three scholars of the time, that American Indians had tribal lays made up of sequence-cycles of hero myths, it is now impossible to determine. At that time at least, there was only one such cycle of which anything approaching a translation existed. This was the Red Scroll of the Lenni-Lenape, or Delaware, Indians; and of this it is still impossible to say whether or not, as recited by the Keeper of the Lays, it had a distinctive meter, or even whether it had a traditional form which could be recognized as poetic. Of other Indian verse, there was at that time nothing extant which could be said to follow in translation the original form or to exhibit a characteristic poetizing tendency.

What was known, however, to students of poetics, was that tribal lays in general did have such form as had already been recognized in *Beowulf* and the *Kalevala*, and that poetic form, even if it served no other purpose than that of making the subject matter easily rememberable, could safely be assumed for any long primitive narrative. Moreover, the Finns were, of all European primitives, ethnically nearest to the Amerind tribes. In making, therefore, a choice of Finnish meters for *Hiawatha*, Longfellow was doing the best that the scholarship of his time permitted. That he was at the same time, by his unscholarly mixing of story elements and cultures from two or three unrelated tribal groups, confusing the most inspiring and dramatic of all aboriginal hero cycles, troubled neither the poet nor his critics. The story of *Hiawatha* as Longfellow conceived it is probably as accurate as any American reader of the time could be made to accept, and at present the poet's selection of the Finnish trochaics appears as one of those prophetic flashes which only poets dare trust. For, although nothing exactly corresponding to the childishly reiterated *tumpty-tumpty-tumpty-tumpty* of *Hiawatha* has been uncovered within the tribal territory of the United States, recent investigations into the form of Aztec poetry in Mexico seem to confirm the poet's guess.

Professor John Hubert Cornyn of the National Summer School of Mexico has long been making an extensive study of the remains of Aztec literature as presented in Spanish translations made during the period of conquest. It has been known to scholars that such Spanish translations were made, but since they were made without much sympathy and with little understanding of the native aesthetic, they have not been taken very seriously as representative of the genius of the Aztec people. Until the revival of national interest of the Mexican people in their own past history and Indian inheritance, a movement which followed the late revolution, the great mass of existing manuscripts and of authentic tradition had been largely neglected. Professor Cornyn, however, has recovered scores of versions of ancient lyrics and story cycles, both in the original Aztec and in Spanish translations, which enable him to declare that they were almost wholly couched in the meters known to the American reader generally as the meter of *Hiawatha*. It is true that the Spanish versions do not always scan so smoothly as Mr. Longfellow's trochaics, but Mr. Cornyn feels certain that in most cases and particularly in the long *Song of Quetzalcoatl* (which, when translated into English, "equals about one hundred ordinary book pages") the want of metrical correspondence is due to hasty and incompetent translation. In Professor Cornyn's English version of a war song the identity of the Finnish and Aztec meters is not to be questioned:

> I the master song-composer,
> I the singer, beat my war-drum
> That its stirring notes may waken
> The dead souls of my companions.
> In their souls a fire I'd kindle,

Souls that ever sleep the death-sleep;
Souls that never yet have journeyed
O'er the Pathway of the Dawning;
On whose gloomy night the Dawning
Never yet has poured her glory.

That this is also authentically Indian no one who has acquainted himself even casually with published translations of tribal verse in the United States can question. The incremental thought rhythms, as Nellie Barnes has so competently shown, are indeed the fundament of all Amerind poetics. The following invocation from an Aztec Hunting Ceremony might have come from our own Navajos:

Come, O priest-enchanters,
You the sacred Tlalocs,
From the four directions,
Where you have your stations,
Where you have your dwellings,
Where you hold the heavens!

The Song of Quetzalcoatl is the most important single work which Professor Cornyn has translated, one of the few of which the Aztec original exists along with the Spanish version, illustrated in colors by native artists of four hundred years ago. It opens with a description of the honors accorded the Fair God in ancient Tula (which is probably the now ruined city of San Juan Teotihuacan), says Professor Cornyn in his own account of it in a recent number of *Mexican Folkways*. I give both the Spanish and English translations of a fragment which illustrates both the metrical incompetencies of the Spanish and confirms Professor Cornyn's assumption of the original form:

Y su pueblo, los toltecas,
Eran hábiles en todos los asuntos,
En las artes y artificios
De tal suerte que nada ignoraban;
Trabajaban como obreros maestros.
Tallaron las sagradas esmeraldas;
Esmaltaron así la plata como el oro.

It must be recalled, however, that in all Amerind verse the latitude of what we call "poetic license" was much greater than is permitted in English, so that it is unlikely the original Aztec in every instance ran so smoothly as Professor Cornyn's English of the above:

And his people, they the Toltecs,
Wondrous skilled in all the trades were,
All the arts and artifices,
So that naught there was they knew not;
And as master workmen worked they.
Fashioned they the sacred emeralds;
Smelted they both gold and silver.

I have purposely chosen obviously objective and prosaic passages, not to raise prematurely the question of the poetic value of these Aztec literary remains aside from the light the quotations throw on the evolution of verse form. It is to be remembered that tribal lays are no more than tribal annals cast in poetic mould for better preservation in the tribal memory. They contain few ornaments and figures, and those often repeated as frequently as the "wine-dark" seas of Homer. But even with this in mind, the *Song of Quetzalcoatl* is inferior in poetic content to our own Zuni *Creation Myth* as translated by Frank Hamilton Cushing, supposing of course that Cushing's version owes nothing to Cushing that a translation should not owe. For judgment on both these points we must await the completion of Professor Cornyn's studies.

That the esoteric content of the songs and odes is worked out to a point at which it will be possible to institute comparisons with similar compositions of other peoples seems likely. This too awaits the publication of the whole recovered treasure of Aztec verse, which it is hoped will not be too long delayed....

25

The Road to the Spring

1926

Twenty years ago those of us who were in a position to assert our faith in the relevancy of Amerind poetry to the evolving American aesthetic did so in the face of a general skepticism as to its authenticity. Improbable, said editors and critics, that verse so limpid and explicit could be the work of ignorant "savages." Today, unable longer to deny the fact, reluctant critics defend their failure to appreciate the significance of the increasing bulk of credible translations, on the ground that it is none of it sufficiently pleasing as poetry to be taken into the national account. Both of these attitudes are eminently characteristic of our American—or should I say democratic?—disposition to rate art values by their concurrence with the immediate intellectual prepossession. As a matter of fact, except for less than a score of individual lyrics, the absolute rendering into English of what Witter Bynner has called "the serenities, the simplicities, the grave and happy mysticism of Indian song" has not yet been made. Probably it can not be made until, at least among people who concern themselves professionally with poesy, there exists toward our aboriginal literature such a cultural perspective as we give to the Greek Anthologies.

For the present, however, it is not necessary that such translation appear, since it is evident that for the people who do interest themselves in Indian song it serves a purpose other than and—for the time—more important than aesthetic appreciation. It serves for the untwining of the three-plied cord of rhythm, melody, and ideation of which poetry is made. For in our time all three of these modes of poetic expression have so altered their form and relative values that the modern poet, when not inhibited in the use of one or the other of them, is at least staggered. Not only have the sword-waving, crosier-bearing, lute-plucking gestures that accompanied the dance of life for the elder poets changed to the movement of a machine-timed, crowd-swayed age, the key of poetic inspiration, the plane of consciousness from which poetic perceptions arise, has been transposed to regions unfamiliar to the young muses. So much so that the whole art of poesy, from being the special mode of youth, promises to become, as it was in the beginning, the preoccupation of the grave and wise, the medium of truth to be apprehended only at levels beyond the reach of sense and sentiment.

Poetry is a medium of expression which requires the whole man; body movement, concreted in the drum and the rattle or, as with us, in the stress and fall of syllables; voice, tempered to musical pitch and interval and these modulated finally to the flow and succession of vowels and consonant; and ideation, controlled by the precise choice and dexterous use of words. The various kinds of poetry take their technical names from the several manners in which these elements are employed. In the passage of poetry from its aboriginal expression by the whole man—pounding feet, shaken rattle, singing voice, leaping body—into the printed page, poetry has taken on an infinity of devices. Many of these, such as assonance, alliteration, rhyme, both internal and terminal, and stanzaic pattern, the modern poet tends to discard in the effort to renew his footing on the bare and salty earth; some of them no doubt to be picked up again with new insight into their value and use. But what now to discard, what to maintain as fundamental amid the clanging alterations of the national expression? Rhyme and fixed stanzaic pattern, as substitutes for melodic effect, are being rather widely let go. But what of rhythm, the printed modulation of body gesture? To what extent will the machine-rhythm, rapidly reducing the gestures of the whole world to uniformity, prevail against the local rhythms of natural environment, the landscape line, the seasonal succession, race, climate?

The poet, who sings more or less under the pressure of such readjustments subconsciously taking place in the racial matrix of his group, will accept with what dignity he can the handicap of a fumbling uncertain age. But the critic and the teacher, while they wait for sheer genius to produce the absolute rearrangement of the technical elements, must resort for forecast and example to the unselfconscious song of the

American aboriginal. American for choice, not only because it is the only *living* body of primitive verse easily accessible but because it has, binding it to the modern condition, the inescapable natural background, all that the soil, the scene, supplies. Students can find, if they know where to look for them, rhythms of the corn lands, of the great plains, the desert and the wooded ranges. But Amerindian verse has more than this which is intrinsically American in the modern sense. It has that preponderance of the communal impulse over the personal which is beginning to be hopefully and yet so menacingly the American note. And it has this advantage over every other body of primitive literature which can be conveniently studied in schools—racial purity of expression; nothing borrowed, nothing engrafted. Altogether an admirable medium in which to study the movement of the poetic impulse working from within outward to clothe itself with literary form.

The true use of poetry is to the makers of it. It serves others, if at all, by giving pleasure, the pleasure arising from the absolute welding of force and form which we call aesthetic. Anybody who is expecting from our aboriginal verse, or neglecting it because it has not, the quality of giving rise to poetic impulses in others announces himself by that expectation as lacking in the original strain from which poetic impulses immemorial take their source. He is showing himself to be, if a poet at all, merely an induced poet; a state from which, like the soft iron which becomes a magnet when subjected to the electric charge, he will, when the inducting charge is cut off, find himself returning to the condition of soft iron. No one can by taking thought or by reading the works of other poets become more poetic than he naturally is. The most he can hope for is the illumination of form. For what is all art, all manners, but the experimental search for form adequate to the animating impulse? And when the current forms of a given art are no longer found equal to the current inspiration, to what source could the artist more hopefully turn for such illumination than to a society in which man has not yet shorn himself of any of his possibilities of expression? The Amerind, if he requires it to complete his poetic form, may stamp the earth, leap in the air, shake a rattle, or, for the announcement of his title, paint himself red and yellow, as a Song of the Sun, or black and white and green, as a Song of the Earth Needing Rain. He is not only free of all possible rhythms and patterns but he is not even bound to the word.

He may add or interpolate syllables until the words are "lengthened for singing"—that is, until they fit properly into the rhythmic pattern which his poetic emotion naturally takes. By the fresh observation of this instinctive choice among the elements that make up poetic form the perplexed modern, tormented by ideas which he cannot make at home in traditional verse forms, may see his way in his own work to a choice nearer to his desire. It has never been so much as suggested, by any of us who have been in a position to make such observation, that modern poets should write in the Indian manner. Only that, by studying the manner in which the untutored mind displays itself among its materials—stress, movement, color, pattern, sounds, and words—we may make a new and more satisfactory alignment of the modern equivalents for such material. It is the road to the spring that we travel, to the source of man's medium, rather than to his emotions; a road which every people must take from time to time if it would not see its own most intimate expression smothered in staleness, ossified by tradition.

Not that Amerindian verse has not aesthetic charm when successfully rendered into English. It is a wicked waste of a national resource that we make no move to finance the translation of the best of it by students poetically endowed, instead of trusting it to ethnologists who make no claim to poetic gifts, or to scholars...whose interest is scholarly rather than poetic. Nevertheless, it is in the work of faithful students that the treasures of Amerindian poetry are most usefully preserved. In these unpremeditated motions of man's mind toward the use of his whole self in the expression of the deepest impulses of that self is the root, sound and nourishing, of the sum of all those affective impulses which we know as culture. Only when we come around again to the Amerindian capacity for putting the whole man into any cultural expression shall we achieve its ideal.

26

Indian Poetry[1]

1931

Indian poetry is the key to Indian design, perhaps to all art among all peoples everywhere. But when we speak of primitive poetry we mean a little more than the word "poetry" means among us; we mean the formal expressiveness into which a man puts the whole of himself, his thought, his heart-beats, his breath, his voice, the movement of muscles rippling in the emotionally controlled effort of the "inside man" to explode into something which signalizes his experience of the moment. Poetry for primitive man is a thing done, precisely as a decoration on a water-jar is done: the abstraction of an experience sketched upon the audience with the poet's self as the tool. He uses the pound of his feet, the movements of his body, vocables, both melodic and articulate, and if these are not enough he will add to himself other means of expression: paint in various colors, feathers, rattles, drums, anything which will communicate himself to the hearer. He does all these things and does them movingly before he has any word meaning poetry, as distinguished from dancing, singing, and dressing up expressively. He does them before he makes anything in wood or clay or textiles, and often his poetry is so far advanced in expressiveness that by the time he arrives at decorative design and the beautification of useful things, all these are strongly marked with the moods and the methods of poetry.

Primitive design always tends to poetic significance; it undertakes to say something rather than to picture something. Even when a picture is introduced, as it often is in Pueblo pottery, it is not the picture as portrait which interests the Indian, but the picture as idea. Thus the remarkably life-like drawings of deer or skunk or whatever, but to say food, vitality, summer, good hunting, fecundity, spiritual power, ideas and experiences associated in the tribal mind with the animal represented.

But if you go further back into the use of these animals in poetry, you will find this association of ideas worked out into what we call figures of speech, as in the Paiute song, in which the poet means that he is beset by unhappy events but says

Truly buzzards
Around my sky are circling

or the Plainsman sings

The sharp hawk (of death)
Is over me.

Other elements carried along from poetry to later arts can be clearly traced. Rhythm, of course, as the fundamental of poetic form, rhythm of number, especially of sacred numbers; incremental rhythms, the phrase repeated with slight additions or alterations; rhythms of symmetry, sounds patterned in a verse by much the same principles that color is patterned in a blanket. Indian poetry seldom rhymes, perhaps never intentionally, but it chimes. It has no formal measures, but agreeable sound clusters tend to recur at intervals according to patterns deep within the Indian consciousness, which are not reduced to rigid rules as with us. It is possible that if as much study were given to Indian poetry as to Greek, or French, definite underlying patterns would be discovered, but the Indian poets themselves can not help much. They have taste in respect to their own productions, so that the poems they tell us are most esteemed among them, when translated, exhibit those characteristics which make the best poetry everywhere, but they know no rules.

It must always be remembered in connection with all Indian art, that it is racially akin to the art of the Chinese, and that the local influences are all American. Running through all Indian poetry and all Indian decoration, there is that subtle network of the association of ideas which makes Chinese poetry so difficult to translate. Words and phrases do not only mean literally what they say, but refer to myths, to religious beliefs, to stories and tribal incidents which the reader unfamiliar with Indian thought would never suspect. Or they may refer to associations of fact in the background of a particular tribe, which could not be guessed by one unfamiliar with that environment. This often leads to amusing errors when people not acquainted with the Indian's life try to translate his songs.

27

Poetry in the Education of Children

1928

M any years ago, having done nothing all my life but go to school, I went on inevitably to teaching school. That was in our Southwest, in the southernmost stretch extending back from the California coast into the desert and mountain country, imperfectly explored and incompletely described. Its landmarks were still largely unidentified, a few of its wild flowers had common names and its wild denizens were unfamiliar to a teaching force recruited chiefly from the severer climates of Back-East. For neither teachers nor children was there any written word which linked them with the environment.

Few people realize how long and intricate is the process of weaving a new environment into the common thought and common speech of the people. Perhaps two hundred years are under ordinary circumstances little enough to allow for the development of an adequate popular vocabulary of natural things in an unfamiliar region. The circumstances, however, were not ordinary. Population increased at incredible rates. Moreover, the Southwest is a country that excites the beholder almost to infatuation with the desire of mastery, of which the earliest evidence is the calling of it by familiar names.

The process of interweaving the natural environment and the consciousness of the observer is one of the fundamental processes of poetizing. To express a peculiar and precious intimacy between the observer and the thing seen, that is the first social service of poets. But in the late eighteen-nineties, there were more and busier realtors in the land than there were poets. For a long time there was no poetry more pertinent to the need of children in the Southwest than Wordsworth's *Daffodil,* Longfellow's *New England Mayflower,* and Bryant's *Waterfowl.*

Deliberately, and with a sense of high excitement, I set about the business of providing my pupils with verse that would serve the immemorial purpose of poetry in linking them with their natural environment and evoking through it that mystical feeling for the land which is the root of what goes by the name of culture.

I could hardly have had all the convictions then that I now hold about what constitutes good school verse, but I am certain that one of them was that it is verse and not poetry which is demanded by very young children. Otherwise, so high and romantic was that young teacher's appreciation of the quality and function of poetry, she could hardly have persuaded herself to subvert the muses to the plain purposes of pedagogy. But almost anybody can write verse, and few people can go to school all their young lives without realizing that children have in themselves a criterion of acceptability in verse to which the best poets oppose themselves in vain. The project was also made to seem possible by the restriction of subject matter to the aspects of wild nature which engage, by their inherent interest, the versifying faculty of young westerners. For, from its inception, the idea was not for the teacher to compose verses, but to draw them out of the children by skillful manipulation of their own observations and feeling-reactions. What, indeed, did I know of the response of youth to a West to which I myself had so recently arrived!

It was not necessary to waste any time rediscovering that verse for children must first of all be rhythmic, with the sort of rhythm natural to body movement—hopping, marching, swinging, pounding rhythms such as are common to nursery verse everywhere. Also, there should be good singable vowel tunes, with repetitive and incremental consonances. The material should be objective, with an objectiveness native to the child's range, competent to serve as pegs upon which to hang the emotional reactions characteristic of child life. These need be neither moral nor reasonable as morals and reasons are understood by the adult; might even defeat their own object in presenting moral or logical fronts such as would check the natural flow of sympathy with and for the common objects of the child's environment. The purpose was simply to create that rapport between the young westerner and the familiar aspects of the West which ties the reactions of interest and delight in nature to things seen and experienced rather than to things read about.

Mother Goose rhymes were the earliest models we used. But, oddly, they proved, with two or three exceptions, so unsuitable as to be promptly rejected by the children themselves. They are perhaps purely domestic rhythms, derived from mother-craft, not self-originating child rhythms. We had to go back to hippity-hops, to stamping and rope-skipping and desk-pounding accompaniments for natural expression of reactions to wild nature. One of the exceptions had a nature beginning and derived its pertinence from an intimate concern of the children's own lives. At that time adult attention was centered on the adventure of the Australian lady bugs which had been imported for the destruction of San Jose scale, an insidious pest threatening the growing orchard industry. The public schools had been impressed into the service of educating the orchardists. Out of this emergency we produced, in my school, the following dramatic recital:

"Lady bug, lady bug, fly away home,
The scale bug is down in the orchard alone!
He's eating his way to the topmost limb,
Lady bug, lady bug, go and eat him!"

This had an immense popularity such as was not equaled by any other attempt to combine instruction and literary recreation. And here I may say that the children, left to themselves, usually declined informative verse of every description. Poetry, to please, must, it unmistakably appeared, confine itself to the outgoing rather than to the receptive impulses. The only "educational" purpose which I was ever able to serve with my experiments in the versifying activities of children was that of encouraging explicit expression, the finding of apt and exact figures and descriptive phrases, and, of course, of stimulating observation by public examination and comparison of such expression. One of our first experiments in this direction centered about the Sandhill Crane who used to hunt every morning about eleven, and every afternoon about three, by the weir in the *Acequia Madre,* a hundred yards or so from the school-room window. Pupils who had done their lessons were permitted to stand quietly observing. The result of this and later similar adventures was built up line by line into the pattern of verse determined by the first two or three statements, answering what? where? when? and how?

Probably the most popular, and the nearest approaches to poetizing, as distinguished from versifying, arose out of the play impulse, in the world-old play of children known as "I'd rather's," or as the teacher never succeeded in inhibiting, "D'rathers." These were chanted to an accompaniment of bare palms on desk tops under the inspiration of the moment. In these spontaneous exhibitions no criticism other than that of the children themselves was ever admitted. (Neither grammar nor the dictionary was allowed to interfere with the poetizing tendency. It was not until years afterward, when I had grown more familiar with primitive poetic processes, that I understood the spontaneous variations of syntax, the perverted constructions, the chromatic rhymes and invented words which the children introduced into their own compositions, as part of the language-forming process which in our precise age is too much inhibited in the young.) The gorier and more unchristian the "D'rathers" were the better the children liked them. On one occasion local attention had been engaged by the misadventure of a sheep herder, who on a trip to town for supplies had become too drunk for discretion, and had been severely mauled by a bear he had found visiting his flock in his absence, and mistakenly attempted to punish. We had a long and deliciously horrible description of the "rathers" of bears, in which the line

"Their bones I'd crunch"

hung up the flow of versification lacking a suitable rhyme. But not for long. Somebody supplying the need with

"Their bodies I'd squnch"

which the teacher had not the heart to decline on so flimsy a pretext as that *squnch* failed to appear in the school dictionary. It seems to me still a word any poet might be pleased to have invented.

Somewhat later it became evident that as children advanced in the grades they welcomed a closer approach to poetry. The poetic approach to life is an evolutionary phase in which intuitive penetrations and assimilations by the observer of the thing observed naturally occur. The path of these assimilations is not yet intellectualized but is routed through the sympathetic organism, beginning to function with the approach of adolescence. In general the objects of such intuitive reactions are selected by a mind still juvenile, but they are of the same nature as reactions which will later be aroused by objects of adult interest.

What this means is that the subject of pre-adolescent poetry will be much the same as the subjects of child verse, but that the emotional reaction will take on adolescent character. This can be seen in the pleasure which children of from eight to ten will take in verse like Milne's *When We Were Very Young* or Stevenson's *Child's Garden of Verse*, their appreciations touched with reminiscence and a sentimental color absent from the appreciations of the very young for whom the same verse was written.

Many of the verses were originally written for primary grades and reworked by the children themselves for intermediates, with more complicated rhythms and a more emotional and imaginative content. In this undertaking I became a pest to the community, digging up out of everybody's past all possible reactions, and all the popular phrasings for the subject in hand.

Form and stanzaic pattern were left to be determined by the movement of the child-observer's mind. The children showed an untroubled aptitude for bending the verse to a preferred rhythmic pattern by emphasis and repetitions. No repetition or variation of stanzaic form ever troubled them so long as the rhythmic tune was not broken. Syncopation did not trouble them at all, but was met with almost the musician's facility for absolute pitch. Rhyme was lavishly employed out of pure enjoyment, and unrhymed verse was almost unanimously rejected by children under ten. In the pre-adolescent years however, it became in many instances a preferred mode. In rhyming, subtle dissonances—chromatic rhymes, I have called them—seemed actually to give pleasure, so that I came to realize that they did not necessarily spring from incompetence in the rhyming faculty but probably from that universally human procedure by which the complete ablaut is accomplished. Later I was to find this "lengthening the song for singing" by the addition of vowel color was a pronounced characteristic of aboriginal song making.

Children's Songs of the Far West

Rathers

I know very well what I'd rather be
If I didn't always have to be me!
I'd rather be an owl,

A downy feathered owl,
A wink-ity, blink-ity, yellow-eyed owl
In a hole in a hollow tree.
I'd take my dinner in chipmunk town,
And wouldn't I gobble the field mice down,
If I were a wink-ity, blink-ity owl,
And didn't always have to be me.
I know very well what I'd like to do
If I didn't have to do what I do!
I'd go and be a wood pecker,
A red-headed wood pecker
In the top of a tall old tree.
And I'd never take a look
At a lesson or a book,
And I'd scold like a pirate on the sea,
If I only had to do what I like to do
And didn't always have to be me!

Or else I'd be an antelope,
A prong-horned antelope,
With lots of other antelopes,
Skimming like a cloud on a herd grass plain,
But if I were an antelope,
A bounding, bouncing antelope,
You'd never get me back to my desk again!

Or I might be a puma,
A singe-colored puma,
A slinking, sly-foot puma
As fierce as fierce could be.
And I'd wait by the waterholes where antelope drink
In the cool of the morning
And I *do*
            not
                    think
That ever any antelope could get away from me.

But if I were a hunter,
A red Indian hunter—
I'd like to be a hunter—
I'd have a bow made of juniper wood
From a lightning blasted tree,
And I'd creep and I'd creep on that puma asleep
And I'd shoot him with an arrow,
A flint tipped arrow,
An eagle feathered arrow,
For a puma kills calves and a puma kills sheep,
And he'd never eat any more antelope
If he once met up with me!

Thanksgiving

When we sit down to turkey, roast turkey,
—A plump and crispy drumstick or a tender piece of
breast—
When we sit down to turkey on a Thursday in November
To cranberries and celery and gravy and the rest;
With second helps of everything so savory and hot,
When we sit down to turkey there's something to remember,
And someone to be thankful to that's usually forgot.

When we sit down to pumpkin pie and maple syrup sundae,
To potatoes and tomatoes and to luscious lima beans,
To succotash and peanuts and clams and popping corn,
There's something to be thought besides what Thanksgiving
means—
And Puritans and Presidents to whom our thanks are due—
About a thousand years before a Puritan was born,
Among the first Americans who gave these things to you—

There's something to be thought of with gratitude and
wonder
Of the grass called *teosinte* which the patient Red-man
found,
Which he loved and labored over till it answered with a yield

That has saved a world from famine; and the tuber small
and round
Which he coaxed to be potatoes, and the seed whose snowy
fleece
Makes the half of all our clothing, and the smoke that, going
round
In after-dinner comfort, spells a full-fed people's peace.

When we sit down to turkey, roast turkey,
There are thanks too long ungiven, and things that must be
thought
About the first Americans whom so seldom we remember,
And whether we've repaid them for the things they gave and
taught,
And if not, is there something we could do to make amends,
When we sit down to turkey on a Thursday in November
On the day that all Americans should be the best of friends?

A Feller I Know

His name it is Pedro Pablo Ignacio Juan
Francesco Garcia y Gabaldon,
But the fellers call him Pete,
His folks belong to the Conquistadores,
And he lives at the end of our street.

His father's father's great-grandfather
Was friends with the King of Spain
And his father peddles hot tamales
From here to Acqueia-madre lane.

And Pete knows every one of the signs
For things that are lucky to do,
A charm to say for things that are lost,
And roots that are good to chew.

Evenings we go to Pedro's house
When there's fire light and rain
To hear of the Indians his grandfather fought
When they first came over from Spain.

And how De Vargas with sword and spurs
Came riding down our street,
And Pedro's mother gives us cakes
That are strange and spicy and sweet.

And we hear of gold that is buried and lost
On ranches they used to own,
And all us fellers think a lot
Of Pedro Pablo Ignacio Juan
Francesco Garcia y Gabaldon.

Texas Trains and Trails

Whenever I ride on the Texas plains
I never hear the couplings cluck,
I never hear the trains
Go chuck-a-luck, chuck-a-luck, chuck-a-luck,
I never hear the engine snort and snuffle.
I never see the smoke plume, I never watch the rails,
But I see the moving dust where the beef herds shuffle,
   And I think I am a cowboy,
   A rope and tie 'em cowboy,
   Punching Texas longhorns
   On the Texas trails.

   And the engine goes *Whoop!*
  Whoopee, whoopala!
  And the cars go *Ki-yi,*
 Ki-yi, ki-yi, coma-ya ky-yi,
   Whoopala,
 Ki-yi!
   Whoop!

No, I never hear the bell, nor the brakeman call
When I ride on the Texas trains;
But I hear the steers bellow and the yearlings bawl,
And the lone wolf howl on the wire-grass plains.
And I never play I'm fireman, or anything like that,
  For I'm playing I'm a cowboy,
  A bronco bustin' cowboy,
  Riding Texas longhorns
  In a ten gallon hat.

  And the trains go *Youpi-ya,*
  Get a-long, doggies,
  Get a-long, get a-long
  Youpi-yi, youpi-ya,
  Youpi-youpi-youpi-ya
  Get a-long, get a-long
  Youpi-ya,
    Yo-o-u-u-p!

28

Excerpt from "Cactus Country"

1924

It is only by taking thought that you will get anything more than a poet's or a painter's notion of plant life in the arid regions. For there is no such thing as a desert science of botany, no special desert way of flowering and bearing fruit. There are only highly specialized adaptations of the stem- and leaf-bearing generation by which the reproductive generation is supplied, under conditions of extreme aridity, with the necessary water. The journey's end of such successive adaptations is found in the sahuaro.

It is probable that the country below the Rim has not changed much since the little Eohippus ran about there on his toes. Since there are no fossils of arid region plants, it seems more than likely that previous to Pleistocene times, since which our Southwestern desert has undergone no essential modification, there were no such types.

They have, in fact, evolved there in the places where we find them, out of the ceaseless operation of the vegetable complexes in contact with desert conditions. Of the moisture-loving plant forms, only such types survive there as are able to compress their flowering and fruiting processes into the curtailed seasons of quick rains. But out of some forgotten ancestry there have sprung tribes of plants that survived not by hurrying their processes, but by holding them through rainless periods, in arrested states, similar to those in which the great bears pass the winter's snows. Of this type are the creosote, the mesquite, cat-claws, smokebush, and palo-verde. By varnishing its leaves or dropping them altogether and filling its bark with the green substance of leaves, by reducing its branches to stubs and thorns, each in its own fashion establishes an equilibrium between its necessities and the water supply. For so much water there is so much growth, and then no growth at all for indefinite periods, prolonged sometimes over several seasons. By thus suspending the functions of growth, the whole life cycle has been indefinitely extended in shrubs like the mesquite and the creosote. I have reason to believe that the mesquite, in the neighborhood of Death Valley has lived to be centuries old, and as far as our knowledge goes, the creosote is immortal. Times when I have had to destroy one of these ancients to prop my tent or cook my food, I have wished that I knew some such propitiatory rite for the appeasement of its Spirit as the Navajos taught me to use before and after the killing of a bear.

To appreciate a creosote plantation one must be able to think of the individual shrub as having its tail waving about in the sun and wind, and its intelligence under ground. Then the wide spacing of the growing crowns is explained by the necessary horizontal spread of the root system in search of the thin envelope of moisture around loose particles of the gravelly soil. In the rainy season the roots drink by means of minute hairs that are cast off when the last drop has been absorbed after which the soul of the creosote sits and waits.

Plants of this type will run successfully through the average rainfall from century to century, but for growths of a shorter life cycle and a more exigent bloom, it has been important, possibly more important in the early Pleistocene than now, to meet conditions of great irregularity in the water supply by water-storage. For this the yucca and agaves developed in their pithy stems and the thickened bases of their bayonet-pointed leaves storage capacity that enabled them to send up with magical rapidity great spikes of waxen bloom to grace the rainless years. The difference between a yucca and an agave is that the yucca produces its blossom crown from a lateral bud, and may go on doing so for indefinite periods, but the agave blooms from the central stem, and blooming dies. The great *Agave americanus*, called the century plant, a visitor across our Southern border, out of its stored energies, which by no means run the hundred years with which it is popularly credited, throws up in the course of days a flowering stalk three or four times the heights of man, bearing seven thousand flowers on whose fragrance the whole life of the agave is exhaled.

It is the yellow-flowered *Agave palmeri*, taken just before the expanding growth begins, while the leaf bases are still packed with the sugary substance of the flowering bud, that is known as mescal among the Southwestern tribes.

Anywhere about the three or four thousand foot levels of the mountains of southern Arizona you may come upon the pits where mescal is roasted, or even surprise a group of Indians feasting on the nutritious, but not very attractive, mass. When I calculate the seasons through which, drop by drop, the agave has collected the material for its stately bloom, eating mescal is to me a good deal like eating a baby.

The long central stem of the yuccas enables them to make much more of a figure in the landscape, particularly the one known as "Joshua-tree," whose weird stalking forms can be found farthest afield in pure desertness, or the sotol (*Dasylirion wheeleri*), whose dense plumes of long rapier-like, saw-edged leaves and tall pyramids of delicate racemes are visible like companies of bandoliers far across the mesas.

This sort holds its dried flower-stalk aloft long after the fruit has been eaten and scattered by the birds, even on into the next season's bloom. There is a humbler variety which goes everywhere, like the prickly pear, and under the name of amole, furnishes those who know enough not to despise its narrow, yellowish rosettes, with an excellent fiber and substitute for soap. But the final most successful experiment of the vegetative spirit on its way up from the sea borders to the driest of dry lands is the great sahuaro, *Carnegiea gigantea*.

In the economy of the sahuaro branch and twig have been reduced to spines, the green of its leaves absorbed into its skin. The need of woody fiber has been perfectly met by the stiff, but stringy, hollow cylinder of semi-detached ribs that hold the stem erect, and its storage capacity rendered elastic by the fluted surfaces, swelling and contracting to the rhythm of evaporation and the intake of the thirsty roots. After successive wet seasons new flutings are let into the surfaces, like gores in a skirt, or after shortage has taken up with the neatness of long experience. By such mechanisms the cactus plant surpasses the stonecrops, the "hen-and-chickens," the "live-for-evers" of other arid regions, so that until some plant is found making water out of its gaseous constituents in the air and soil, we may conclude that here in the great sahuaro, the vegetative spirit comes to rest. Here it has met and surmounted all the conditions that for our cycle menace on this planet the vegetative type. Passing, I salute it in the name of the exhaustless powers of life.

29

Geographical Terms From the Spanish

1933

To any one interested in local nomenclature in America, it must have occurred many times how fortunate it was that the early settlers in our Southwest came from a country mountainous and desert, dramatic and picturesque, people who would have on hand a supply of geographical terms eminently suitable to that sort of topography, as plain English would never be. And one can see readily enough how the descriptive Spanish terms would win acceptance from the later coming English settlers because of the very paucity of suitable name words in their own tongue, for canyons, arroyos, sierras, and the like. The very plentitude of suitable terminology for a dramatic scene such as the American southwest provides must have afforded considerable aid in communicating an intelligible account of the exploratory adventures of the first comers, as can be easily seen in the list of aptly descriptive terms which the direct confronting of that scene calls to mind.

Take for instance the term *Cordilleras* for the outstanding geographical feature of the southwestern landscape. The word is from *cordel*, string or rope, so that the full term comes to stand for Strings of Mountains, which is the aspect of the continental axis most completely presenting itself from north to south of the new world. Next comes the word *sierra*, saw-tooth, for the single ridge, sharp pointed as most of them are, so that all that is needed for identification is a precise adjective, such as *Sierra Nevada*, snowy range, *Sierra Madre*, mother range, *Sierra Prieta*, dark colored range. For the lifting crest of a range, or the long rounding top, the word is *cumbre*, related to the root from which we derive a descriptive term for the lifting tide. Then comes *picacho* for the solitary peak, and *cabezo* or *cabezon* for the round, head-shaped hill. This is a term most commonly used for the type of hill which is formed of the hard basaltic plug of an extinct volcanic vent from which the volcanic ring has been worn away. *Cerro* is a hill and *cerrillos*, little hills.

Canyon is the absolutely indispensable term for the gash between two bulks of mountains, whether due to erosion or earthquake fault. *Cañada* describes the wide shallow mouth of a canyon, and *cañoncito* is a little canyon, while for that vast gulch in the midst of which Boulder Dam is being erected, no better name has been found than the original *Grand Canyon*. For the dry gash in which erosion has not been specially at work, which is consequently narrower than a canyon proper and usually clothed with brush on either side, the term *barranca* answers admirably, being closely related to a word which signifies an interruption, a difficulty. For shallower clefts between hills, down which water intermittently runs, the word is *arroyo*, *arroyo seco* for a cleft which is on most occasions dry, and occasional qualifying words pointedly suggestive such as *arroyo vuelto*, or *arroyo rodeo*, for winding arroyo, or *arenoso*, sandy. *Hondonada* or *arroyo hondo* is a deep cleft.

A large stream of water is called a *rio*, *Rio Grande*, *Rio Gila*. A tiny creek or rill is called *rillito*.

A word which has been in use as a place name, but has only recently become generally descriptive is *bajada*, descent. This is quite explicitly applied to the abrupt break-off of a lava flow. It is the professional botanist who has contributed the general use of the word, since owing to the character of the broken rock, special types of plant life find their footing there which can best be described as bajada inhabiting. But when lava flow is found encircling the long closed vent it is called an *encierro* (inclosure).

One of the earliest terms adopted by the American settlers was *mesa* (table) for the high flat tablelands so characteristic of the western landscape. But a mesa, when it spreads too far for its square cut edges to be taken in at a glance, is called a *llano*, usually associated with a qualifying term such as *Llano Estacado*, Staked Plain. Or when the mesa is small and not quite level, especially when it is plainly one of a series of stepped banks, it is called a *loma* (hill), such as *Loma Prieta*, dark hill, *Loma Colorada*, red hill.

For special landscape features there are particularized words. For instance, for the flattened roundish space at the bottom of a shallow dip where the runoff of rain collects and shortly dries, the term *playa* (beach) is used; but when the water has stood for some time before drying it is called a *laguna seca* (dry lake). The open spaces between very old, worn-down mountains, which have filled in flat with detritus, are called *abras* (openings). Where high mesas are edged with sharp narrow points, these are called *potreros*, colt pastures, since they can be lightly fenced with sticks and stones across the broad end, and colts are afraid to venture down the steep sides. A nook in the hills is a *rincon*, but if broad and open, a *rinconada*.

A marshy place is called a *cienaga*, but if small is a *cienagita*, while a collection of small marshy spots is known as *cienguillos*. If water stands at the surface, the place is known as a *laguna*. A spring is always *ojo*, literally an eye, but usually carries a qualifying word, as *Ojo Gigante*, giant spring, *Ojo Verdoso*, verdant spring, *Ojo Caliente*, warm spring. *Vega* is the word used for meadow (*Las Vegas*, the meadows).

If a pool or spring is well grown with reeds, it is called a *carrizal* (place of reeds) from *carrizo*, a reed, or if with cattails, *tulare* or *tularosa*. This termination "al" (place where) is often used with words denoting a characteristic growth as *chaparral*, place of the brush, *chamisal*, place of the chamiso (a plant woody below and herbaceous above), *chollatal*, place of the cholla cactus, *encinal*, place of the encinas oak. *Bosque* is the general term for thick woody growth (*bosque redondo*, round wood), as *selva* is for forest.

Practically all the above words are anglicized for general use in the Southwest. Perhaps not bosque and selva, abra or vega except when used as a place name, or encierro. There are also a great many geographically descriptive words commonly used as place names and consequently anglicized, of which the following are most in use:

Abajo—lower. Rio Abajo, lower river.

Arriba—upper. Rio Arriba, upper river.

Alto—high. Pino Alto, tall pine tree.

Ancho—broad. Rinconada Ancha, broad corner.

Arena—sandy. Llano Arenoso, sandy plain.

Algodones—cotton fields.

Alamogordo—round (or fat) cottonwood trees.

Bonito—pretty. Pueblo Bonito.

Chico—small. Rio Chico, little river.

Campañas—fields.

Escondido—hidden. Rincon Escondido, hidden corner.

Hondo—deep. Arroyo Hondo, deep arroyo.

Hermoso—beautiful. Ojo Hermoso, beautiful spring.

Hueco—notched. Pena Hueca, notched mountain.

Jicarilla—little cup.

Mesilla—little tableland.

Mimbres—place of willows.

Oro—gold. Cerro Oro, gold hill.

Oscuro—obscure. Rio Oscuro, river difficult to find.

Pajarito—bird. Pajaritan Plateau, bird plateau.

Peña—rock.

Peñasco—rocky.

Puerco—dirty. Rio Puerco, dirty river.

Quemado—burnt. Cerro Quemado, burnt hill.

Questa—hill. Questa la Plata, silver hill.

Salado—salty. Ojo Salado, salt spring.

Soledad—solitary. Peña Soledad, lone rock.

Tierra—earth. Tierra Amarilla, yellow earth.

Verdoso—verdant. Ojo verdoso, verdant spring.

Yeso—gypsum. Cerro Yeso, gypsum hill.

30

Rimas Infantiles of New Mexico

1930

If any doubt existed that the *poblanos* of Spanish New Mexico have a strong mixture of the native Indian strain, it could be settled by a glance at the multitude of tender, whimsical, exquisitely wrought verses and songs current among them for the comfort, the entertainment, and the moral instruction of children. Overlaid as Spanish Colonial culture is in our Southwest by later Americanization—and where does Americanization *not* mean the loss of tenderness and whimsicality and the delicacy of design?—charming examples of all these things may still be picked up there, fashioned with all the sympathetic care that Indians in old Mexico give to the miniature household equipments which they love to make for their own. . . .

Many of the cradle songs undoubtedly came over from Spain and were sung by pioneer mothers trekking up the four-months' horseback journey to the valley of the Rio Grande. I suppose that the first time any of them were heard there, was as they were sung by that intrepid mother of the first white child born in New Mexico on the Espejo expedition of 1583. One familiar with the lullabies of peasant Spain can trace the shapes of the originals through changes of expression that are wholly New Mexican, or perhaps old Mexican, since many of them had had a century of domestication in the southern country before crossing the Río. A four- or six-line verse is the form most in use, with strongly assonanced terminal syllables, occasionally amounting to the exact rhymes by which their sprightliness can be best translated to English; and all of them are peculiarly singable, a quality which they owe in part to the genius of the Spanish language. Just as

A la ro-ro; niño, ro-ro!

is inevitably more tuneful than

Rockaby, baby,

so

Quiere el coco, quiere?

has a more playful sound than

Do you want the booger-man?

There is also an effect of tenderness and gravity in many of these *rimas infantiles*, due to their preoccupation with other-worldness and to the host of saints and blessed personages who crowd out the fairies, elves, and sprites of our own child-lore; as in the following finger song:

This little child asks for bread,
This one says: there is none to be had,
This one says: what shall be done?
This one says: I'll steal some,
But this one says, Oh, no, no!
That would break God's heart!

It is, indeed, almost impossible to select any of these New Mexican nursery songs of true poetic values, which are not also religious in their implication, especially this Spanish version of our "letting the little colt go bare." The two given below are undoubtedly of continental origin:

I

At the gates of Heaven
They sell shoes
For all little angels
Who have none to use.

II

Señora Sant' Ana,
Why does the Baby cry?
Is it for an apple He has lost?
I will give you one,
I will give you two;
One for the Christ Child
And one for you.

There are as many versions of the latter as there are counties in the state. The following, I suspect, originated in Old Mexico, where Christmas and roses are not so far divided as with us. It must be remembered that for the first hundred years of New Mexican colonization, more Mexicans than Spanish came into the country:

Run little shepherds on the hillside,
Gathering the roses of spring;
    Sing little birds
    With joy and delight
Diverting the Christ Child
    On his birth night.

The following was found in New Mexico:

Nodding on the rosebush
Sleeps the little rose.
Now that it is evening,
To sleep my baby goes.

In translating, originally I have had it in mind to make these songs available for American children in a region that is more nearly bilingual than any other state in the union, so that in any case where the Spanish is as easily understood as the English equivalent, and better suited to the uses of poetry, I have not hesitated to employ it. "Mr. St. Joseph," which is the obvious rendering of the first line below, is obviously impossible:

Señor San José
Is a carpenter so fine;
He made a pretty cradle
Of oak wood and pine.

He made a pretty cradle
Of clean wood and new,
Where sleeps the little Jesus;
And so, sleep you.

Like our own nursery rhymes, many of the New Mexican favorites are topical in their origins. Here are two of a score or more quatrains which deal with the Comanche tribes that during the eighteenth century harried the Río Grande colonies. All the Comanche rhymes, most of which are banal and many of which are ribald, are designed to lessen fear by inducing contempt. These two have to do with the lack of sufficient commissary equipment, by reason of which the hunting tribes were finally overcome by the settled agricultural groups. Of course, every New Mexican child knows that a Comancha is the female of a Comanche:

> The Comanche and the Comancha
> Set out to go to war,
> The Comanche carried his bow
> And the Comancha her griddle.

> The Comanche and the Comancha
> Went out to dig *amole*,
> They had to turn back on the road
> Because they forgot the *pinole*.

Pinole is the extremely concentrated corn food on which the Río Grande campaigns were fought and won. The Comanche quatrains were sung to the tune of "The Buck and the Doe," of which there are also many versions:

> The Buck and the Doe

> The buck and the doe,
> Set out for Santa Fé,
> To buy for their little fawns
> Sugar and café.

> The buck and the doe,
> They went to Santa Fé.
> The doe wanted sugar,
> And the buck, café.

> The buck and the doe
> They argued all the way;
> The doe all night
> And the buck all day.

The buck and the doe
They walked with anxious care,
For fear that the hunters
Would take them in a snare.

The buck and the doe
They went to Santa Fé,
To buy for their little fawns
Sugar and café.

Tecolote, of which *tecolotito* is the diminutive, is the small burrow-nesting owl of the Southwest, which was first named in Mexico, as the word indicates—a universal folk-lore favorite:

Tecolotito

Tecolotito, from where do you come?
Tecolotito, from where do you come?
From Pueblo in Colorado,
From Pueblo in Colorado,
Ai——I, Ai——i!

I bring to you a notice,
I bring to you a notice,
That you have lost your true love,
That you have lost your true love,
Ai——I, Ai——i!

Little owl, coo, coo, coo;
Poor little, dear little animalito,
Are you hungry, Tecolotito?
Coo, coo, coo!

The neighbor across the way,
The neighbor across the way,
Take care, he keeps a butcher shop,
Take care, he keeps a butcher shop.

To the married ones he sells for cash,
To the married ones he sells for cash,
To the single ones he gives credit,
To the single ones he gives credit.
    Little owl, coo, coo, coo!
    Poor little, dear little animalito,
    Are you hungry, Tecolotito?
    Ai——i, Ai——i!

31

Sources of Poetic Influence in the Southwest

1933

There are invariably two sources of poetic influence in any given region; one of them the shape, the rhythm, and procedure of the land itself, and the other, the contributions to the life lived there made by the experience and racial qualities of the people, out of whom the body of native verse proceeds. In our American Southwest both of these sources are abundant and varied. The land itself contributes magnificent sculptural form and rhythm, color and enticement, and out of its history are gathered not only the most vital passages of primitive experience, but also the most fertile traditions of two great peoples, English and Spanish; so that it is impossible not to expect from it a rich and exciting fulfillment of its poetic promise. In that section of our country lying along the Mexican border and spreading well into the north are to be found not only native tribes, stemming out of the most primitive hunting cultures, but the most advanced agricultural communities achieving the highest cultures known to tribal peoples. Along with this, on the part of the dominant race, goes a degree of scholarly understanding of racial psychology that elucidates the whole psychic movement underlying the poetic mode of expression. Never before have we had an emerging literary mode co-existent with the means of completely realizing its progressions.

The relation of fundamental body movement to verbal rhythm is nowhere else so explicit as in a social background where there is no word for poetry which is not also a word for dance, and both terms are easily interchangeable with all the terms of song and not wholly separable from ideas connoting drama, all of them implying each other as terms of experience. They all of them lie close to the processes by which experience is evoked and measured as life-accelerating movements. Not only is poetry, among Indians, understood as a life-provoking business, but there is the beginning of an understanding of the mechanisms by which this is achieved. Rhythm is realized as an explicit aid to clearly desired ends, and there is the beginning of stanzaic form and a gradual emergence of literary procedure designed to achieve the end in view.

Here in New Mexico the body of poetic composition covers all the forms from the individual lyric to the priestly epic. Rhyme has not yet emerged, but there is a disposition toward it in the vocal patterning, which distributes similar sounds throughout the song in something like a design. Narrative verse is not found among any American tribe, but there is something like narrative achievement in the arrangement of songs along a story not sung, but understood to signalize successive phases of activity. The great dance-dramas of the tribal rituals consist largely of such sequences, arranged along a story in lyric progressions, which are always present in the tribal recollection while the song is being danced. As a matter of fact, the great musical rituals of the aboriginal tribes resemble our form called Opera much more than they do anything modernly called Drama.

So it turns out that no one with a natural love of poetry and an intellectual curiosity about it can grow up in the Southwest without being taken informatively over the evolutionary ground of poetic form. He will, with ordinary interest, come out of it not only with a renewed freshness of association between poetic utterance and body gesture, but with new approaches to stanzaic form and the constructive shapes of poetic expression. He will have an appreciation of poetry as an allusive art, not possible to those brought up wholly in schools where poetry is a matter of the printed page. I am not sure, myself, that the immense advantage of knowing Indian poetry early is not in the primary realization of it as annotation upon processes going on within the poetizer, processes immensely more complicated and profound than get mentioned in the verse; the realization, in short, of poetry as experience more importantly than as expression. What must happen to the young poet, exposed early to the aboriginal influence, is inevitably a release from the cramping influence of verse shaped by convention to the restraints of syllabic measure, and a new realization of the use of stanza and line as provocative rather than final; a realization of poetry shaped from within, like a growing tree, and not from without, like a stone monument.

But it will not be only in the modifications of form that the growing poet will be influenced by the aboriginal poetry, with which the Southwest brings him in contact. Throughout, the aboriginal poet is concerned with the wholeness of experience and the reactions, one upon the other, of a multitude of things, and the meaning involved in those reactions. He makes verse as a means of making all things work together with Wocondah, the living principle, which he perceives as invading all things and all operations of nature. Aboriginal verse is much less intensely personal than the more sophisticated sorts, although one does not always appreciate that in the translations which tend often to reach back to later, more personal forms. The poetic mood of the aboriginal is almost invariably a high one, but having to do with realizations of beauty, impersonally achieved, rather than with personal intensities. Almost never is there intensity of passion, but an intensity of cooperation to achieve beauty of being and behavior. I recall in this connection a dance sequence at Jemez, which is all of light and moving tenderness, but which can neither be translated nor described in English, because, as the Jemez say, the English words "mean bad" but the ideas behind them do not "mean bad" to the Jemez. The dance refers, with great dignity and complete propriety, to the utmost tender intimacy of the sexual relation, though you would never guess that, either from looking at it or hearing it, unless its symbols had been explained in prose. That is what it means for an idea to be poetized by Indians, to be realized, as the Navajo say in most of their ceremonial verse, "in beauty":

In beauty it is finished.

Beauty for the aboriginal is a dimension, into which you rise to achieving, always an ascending dimension. Apparently the aboriginal never suffers our own need for occasional disorganizing and devitalizing reactions. It is not until we get into the Spanish zone of influence that we have any appreciation of that.

What most people do not know is that for the region described, including most of Texas, Arizona, California, and the lower part of Colorado and all of New Mexico, the written literature for between two and three hundred years was wholly Spanish, and came by direct descent from the golden century—*Siglo de Oro*—the high mark of creative literature in Spain. It was a period in which the literary impulse so completely flowered on the Spanish peninsula that there was practically no distinction between the literature called *folk* and that which became known as the distinguishing *classic* period of Spain. What it brought to the New World besides drama, which was more dialogue than dancing, and what was distinctly an innovation, was narrative poetry. At that time every important tribe in the Southwest was possessed of at least one, in some cases a group of them—long, poetic, esoteric origin myth narratives which had to do with the creation of man, of ordered society, and of the founding of the leading rituals. But for the first time Amerindian society came in contact with the poetic tale, drawn in this case almost wholly from the old Spanish *Cantares de Gesta* which were sung to the Spanish people of that time by the *jonglueres* and *trovadores*, and linger on in whatever corners of the world to which the Spanish settlers carried them. These, in the main, were in ballad form with four-line sixteen-syllable verses, and attained a higher quality of poetic value than the ballad in most countries. There were other forms of poetry at the time—songs, decimas (ten-lined, eight-syllabled verses), various sorts of hymns; but the ballad, because of its newness, its simplicity and its story interest, took sharp hold on the Indian populations of the New World.

Up to this time there had been practically no explicit story form in Amerindian verse, but under Spanish influence one rapidly developed, under the common name of *corrido* from *corer*, that which runs about, prevails, flourishes, that which is talked about. Being adopted by the Amerind, the *corrido* became immensely popular in Spanish America, and underwent changes in form. It retained the four-line structure, always sung or recited, kept a melancholy tone and was made to carry any sort of news event of wide contingence, such as the death of Pancho Villa:

Sad the end of that great man,
Whose fame mounted so high
That no one was his equal,
Though today in the camposanto he lies.

> Here goes the leave-taking
> With great pain and sorrow
> For the end so disastrous
> Of a man of such valor.

That man has failed of his adventure indeed who does not have two or three *corridos* to lament him, or at least one to describe what he did and where he got with his adventure. There is no form of poetic effusion in the Southwest which has such wide acceptance and popular use as the *corrido*. It is the one form of Spanish verse which made a place for itself in the Indian world, and gave the tone to valedictory poetry produced by the cowboy who usurped the place of the *cantador* in the short and simple annals of his own kind. It is, with *copla*, the still popular type of Spanish verse, produced by way of social entertainment in New Mexico. The *copla* is epigrammatic in form, usually of four to six lines, light in texture, and dealing, much oftener than not, with the relations of the sexes. To sing or recite popular *coplas* or verses is still a favorite social pastime in Spanish New Mexico, including as it does an expression of the sentiments and personal conclusions of the Spanish people in which local American poets are occasionally invited to join. There is in this exercise more rhythm, more grace and simplicity than in any other poetic expression.

> If I had the power
> I would put the stars below thee,
> The moon at thy feet I would place
> And with the sun would crown thee—

is the sort of thing that gets said in them, or

> If you wish that I forget thee
> Ask of God that He destroy me,
> For in life it is not possible
> To forget the one I love.

At any rate one would be quite certain that so long as so engaging a custom prevailed, there would be no loss of the intensity of common speech.

These two types of Spanish poetry, the *corrido* and the *copla*, not only held on in colonial society but notably influenced the sort of poetic composition which is still going on, and influenced, as has already been suggested, the kind of folk verse in English which has since been written here. There is half a page of titles of *corridos* in that notable anthology of folk-lore made by Ruben Campo of Old Mexico, half a hundred in the collection made by the writer and A. L. Campo for New Mexico, and the narratives of cowboy poetry made in America are practically all of the *corrido* model. The New Mexican type of cowboy ballad is, in fact, much more explicitly founded on the Spanish tradition of the ballad than on the English. It is closer to the singing form, carries the plaintive note of old Spain. And this relationship is more evident in the earlier forms of both Spanish and American types of narrative verse. All of which may be more readily discovered from the anthology, *El Folklore literario de Mexico* of Senor Campo, than in any collection available for New Mexico.

It is probable that such an anthology for New Mexico, when published, will show a higher quality of verse than any which has yet come from below the border, where the substitution of Spanish for native Indian poetry was more definitely forced. The anthologies of cowboy verse, however, markedly fall off from standards of native-American Spanish poetry, partly by reversion to standards of English balladry less sedulously cherished, and by being more narrowly restrained in their rhythm to the movements of cowboy activity, all of which are conditioned by the necessity of horseback employment, which are in nearly every case the lope and the trot and the slow "surround" of the sleeping herd.

Of the features of cowboy poetry which are expressive rather than structural, there are many which are derived from middle-class reminiscence; The Dying Cowboy has been traced to a sea chanty, The Cowboy's Lament to an Irish military melody of the eighteenth century, and many of the popular melodies are mindful of the Gospel hymns of the nineteenth century. But the Spanish ballads, even the recent ones, revert often to the older rhythms of infinitely greater variety—sword play, the military stride of Roman roads, the pontifical measure, gestures of persuasion and command, lute-playing, axe-stroke, paddle-stroke and the pioneer tread on unleveled earth. What the Indian brings in are still older measures derived from more primitive modes of progression—the swinging stride of the plains trail, pound and scour of the mealing-stone, sharp ascending and descending motion of mountain-climbing, heart-beat and breath. The monotonous unaccented rhythm of the primitive utensil brings Indian rhythms into identity with the beat and pound of modern machinery, as I have elsewhere described in reference to the ease with which the Indian singer fits himself to the movement of the automobile. That all our modern verse should begin to be underlaid by the accentless beat of machinery, as all primitive verse is shaped and sustained by the beat of the drum, is a coincidence that creates a fundamental alikeness in the two modes, which is more than incidental.

How much of other alterations in the poetic modes of the period are owed to recognition of alikenesses between aboriginal and sophisticated verse, and how much to an instinctive verging of such modes out of their common rhythmic schemes, can scarcely be guessed. There is in Indian verse no false passion, no eroticism whatever, nor the dragging weight of sugary phrases, none of the "mumbled moralities" which George Moore proscribed when he elucidated his theory of pure poetry; and except for the epic origin myth, which is found in most tribes, there is never a poem which exceeds, and seldom one that arrives at, the hundred lines which Poe allowed to the perfect poem. Nor does it ever arrive at that "keepsake air" of which Moore complains, nor contrive to be "blighted here and there by the subjective taint." What it does manage to do, and this is true of all the various sorts of verse which have served the poetic mood in our Southwest, is to conform in its structure to the various movements by which it has been structurally accompanied.

That these movements have been, in the main, the measures by which man has accommodated himself to the contours of the earth, may be due to the salience of such contours over every other feature of what in the main takes place on them. It is difficult, of course, to show in translations how this is really the case with the speech rhythms, the shapes and chimes of sentences; and on the other hand difficult even with the various languages in which the poetic impulse has been expressed, wholly to escape, even in translation, intricacies of form and expressiveness which the land gives rise to. What we have to deal with here is the certainty that although the country has been successively lived in by three groups of people long enough to put its imprint on their types of verse, it has in no case failed to do so, and that in every case it has been the contour of the land and the gesture by which it has been overcome that have been recorded.

How far the land will compel the character of the thing said in poetry thus produced, it is too early yet to guess. So far the one identifying trait of all its native verse has been its singing quality. Even its narratives are still sung rather than recited, and its epics vary lyrically from movement to movement. They have the quality that its landscape lines have of presenting themselves with the effect of movement, upspringing, rearing, swelling, falling away in sheer precipices, jutting forward. What one feels is the possibility, if the Southwest is not completely submerged in the flood of alikenesses that beset the majority of American life, of producing a variety of verse that even more than anything yet produced in America will have the quality of expressing the tremendous variety of the life lived here, its immensely aspiring, structural, and yet completely singing and sensuous rhythms.

32

John G. Neihardt's Expression of the West

1928

All at once, without quite knowing why, we are confronted with a revival of literary interest in the old West. It takes the form of multiplying biographies of the people, all the way from Billy the Kid to the latest Lady Wild Cat, who made the old West notable, if for nothing more than their outrageous parade of themselves in opposition to everything the West of today prides itself on being. Herein is raised a question of sharper pertinence to the young writer of the West than anywhere seems to be realized. For what stands out in these recent life stories of old Western hero-villains is that they are for the most part written by people more or less alien to the conditions that produced them, and acquainted only by research with their material. Such writers have in fact but seized upon the individual adventures of that period as fresh and fascinating material for the literary instinct to work upon, reworking it for story interest, with especial emphasis upon what is unique and entertaining from the point of view of the sophisticated intelligence. Meanwhile the young literary talent of the West is chiefly occupied in yearning toward that same sophistication and lamenting the lack of "literary atmosphere" in its immediate environment, while the sophisticates are scooping up dollars and kudos by turning this neglected material to account.

This is not the first time this has happened in the United States—that a region rich in human tradition has had to content itself with having the seal of interpretation put upon its most significant traditions by strangers to its intimate reality. It may be, indeed, that a tang of strangeness in the material is the indispensable fillip to the creative impulse.

This would seem to be the case in the field of biography and social history, for these are seldom satisfactorily written by the generation to whom the events occurred. But in the field of poetic narrative it is exactly the opposite, good story verse requiring first of all, the sense of the material as near and enriched by intimacy rather than by uniqueness. Racy and entertaining as the recent Western lives are discovered to be, what comes out definitely in all of them is the folk element, so that it is not nearly so important to know what happened as what was felt, what in the way of folk feeling can still be evoked by stories of Wild Bill Hickok and Calamity Jane. And for this sort of material the immortalizing medium is verse.

The question that concerns the would-be immortal recorder of the folk romances of the old West, is what form of verse, what rhythmic medium, what stanzaic construction? Several interesting experiments are already being tried, only one of which shows itself as generic to the soil from which the material sprung and flourished. This is not to say that some of the older, Europeanly devised forms may not prove equally satisfactory. These things depend more upon the gift of the versifier than upon literary dogma. Stanley Vestal stands well to the fore with his ballads of Kit Carson and other Western notables, in the semi-literate style which is native to the ballad and perhaps, all the world over, to the type of tale it records. Mr. Vestal uses the ballad narrative, omitting the refrain, which, in fact, is not used in the modern ballad anywhere except by flagrant imitation. Vestal is a natural story teller, and evidently feels that "almost physical gusto for the native flavor of his subject-matter" which he himself insists upon as a necessary factor in successful balladry. But technically excellent as his ballads are, to my mind they fail wholly in recreating a single element of the natural environment against which the events narrated took place, the long mesa lines, the sharp sky-lines, the threatening *cumbres*. The Kit Carson stories might, for all Mr. Vestal reveals, as well have taken place in New Jersey, except that we know that there is an inalienable affinity between places and behavior, which would make it impossible for New Jersey to have produced them. Nor do they record in their poetic movement anything of the body swings, the characteristic gesture of their native background. Edwin Ford Piper in *Paintrock* does better with the native gesture, but fails of the lyric spring. His verse seldom "lets itself out" as was the amiable and reprehensible practice of the men it celebrates. And that again seems to me the final insufficiency of any European model of poetic narrative that has come down to us. The mood of the Western hero-villain was often sportive. The sense of a justified revolt against repressive conditions which makes Robin Hood an immortal folk-tale never seriously and sincerely animated the Wild Bills and Jesse James' of the far West. Their revolt was too often play and their exhibitionism more than likely a response to the expanding Western scene.

For reasons like this, the literary experiment of John G. Neihardt's Indian Wars and his Epics of the West remains the most promising, because it is the deepest-reaching attempt to fit the story of the West to a native poetic medium. Much might be said of the skill and authenticity with which Mr. Neihardt has assembled his material. As a prose writer of distinction and an experienced story-teller, he has at once the advantage over the poet who draws only upon poetic resources, and a certain disadvantage of a superior subtlety of approach which takes something from the clash and clang which we instinctively look for in narrative verse. It is not however in these things that we are primarily interested but in the form of Mr. Neihardt's verse as an authentically Western medium. It is based upon the classic form called heroic, and if one had a fault to find in that basic choice it would be that Neihardt's verse remains throughout too faithful to the ancient mold. For long narratives so unvarying a stride is likely to grow monotonous. There is, however, no monotony in Mr. Neihardt's handling of it. Its cadences are fluent, the rhymes easy and invariably true tonal consonances; to an extent that almost takes off the curse of rhyme and reduces it to an element of structural finish rather than ornamentation. With this no one could quarrel unless, like the writer, he felt convinced that the West does not always rhyme perfectly; that there is more than a suggestion in the movement of Western life patterned dissonance, of chromatic rhymes, a tendency at intervals to complete the whole scale of the ablaut as a variant of the perfect concordance of vowel color. Mr. Neihardt, however, manages skillfully—or perhaps—and this is the greater compliment—unconsciously, to give the full effect of the landscape line. Years ago the writer discovered, after long study of Indian song and poems, that she could always tell whether a new song in an unknown language originated in the plains, the desert, the mountains or at the seashore. The marks of this distinction are too subtle to define or describe, but they do not fail. In the same way I can always tell where, in respect to the Western scene, Mr. Neihardt's heroes are. This is the thing the proponents of the ballad can not manage. The ballad is too well established; it imposes itself upon the landscape, gives rather than takes the cadence.

Another item of Mr. Neihardt's method that the young poet might study with profit, is the way in which he keeps his vocabulary and all his figures of speech within the scene. I do not mean that in any sense they are narrowly "Western," but they succeed in never leading the mind astray from the matter in hand: like a well-handled graver's tool they deepen the line without spreading it, as in these lines:

> *blown to smoke*
> *Before the blizzards of their people's ire.*
> *The Four Winds held their breath*
> *Before a vast serenity of death....*

I think myself that a closer correspondence between narrative rhythms and rhythms of the land can be attained; something at the literary level, which will nevertheless attain the correspondence between our native cowboy lyrics and the lope, trot and walk of the cow-pony which Newton Gaines has pointed out. But to this date Mr. Neihardt has come nearer to providing an authentic medium for Western narrative at a high literary level than any other poet who has tried it.

33

The Body, from
The American Rhythm

1923

The passing of the perception of rhythmic forms arising fortuitously in our environment—as the roll of thunder or the run of wind in tall grass—through the sensorium into the subconscious, is experiential in nature. It leaves a track, a mold, by which our every mode of expression is shaped.... Rhythmic forms are constantly presenting themselves to our experience, but before they can be reckoned with they must initiate the factor of movement. Such movement rises subconsciously in us in response to recurrent series of homogeneous stimuli. But the mere intellectual appreciation of such sequences is not enough. There must be a series of motor impulses started somewhere, before the experience is appreciated as rhythmic....

The suggestibility of the human organism in the direction of rhythmic response is so generous that the rhythmic forms to which the environment gives rise, seem to pass through the autonomic system, into and out of the subconscious without our having once become intellectually aware of them. Rhythm, then, in so far as it affects our poetic mode, has nothing to do with our intellectual life....

The major rhythms of the human organism are given by the blood and the breath. What is the familiar iambus but the *lub*-dub, *lub*-dub of the heart, what is the hurrying of syllables in the trochae but the inhibition of the blood by the smaller vessels? Within the organism many minor organs have each their distinctive rhythmic tempo, both nervous and functional. Very probably rhythm is a factor in thought formation. There are at any rate recognizable alternations of attack and relaxation of the cognitive process.... Every ordinary introspective individual is aware of these rhythmic adjustments going on in himself, varying with the character of the stimuli. Given a suitable arrangement of the stimuli, as in orchestrated music or poetic drama properly recited, or the consciousness of reciprocated passion, and the whole energetic plane of the organism is raised.

Here we have a basis for the poetic quest, and for the establishment of a traditional poetic mode, provocative of the maximum of well-being. The rhythms which give pleasure are those into which the organism has naturally fallen in the satisfaction of the social urge, the ego urge, the mating urge. Where the path to such satisfactions is deeply graven, the poet falling into it will find the whole sum of sensory material enriched by association. Where by changed motor habits the initial association is obliterated, and only the swing remains, the old rhythm will arise, at the recurrence of a given stimulus, with sourceless connotations of authority to which we give the name of instinct when we observe them in others, and inspiration in ourselves....

It makes very little difference whether you treat the increment of potentiality as inheritance or as instinct. For what is instinct in this connection but the memory of motor-emotional experience reduplicated often enough to set up a habit of response, the habit persisting after the memory of the associated fatigues have faded?... An instinctive rhythm is a habit of response of which the initiative is lost. Being lost is one of the conditions of our making poetry of it, for much of the pleasure of versification is in the discovery in ourselves of inestimable treasures of swinging thought, swinging with the momentum that exceeds the expenditure of consciousness as the swing of a skipping rope exceeds the effort of the wrist that turns it....

The physical basis of poetry appears, then, as the orchestration of organic rhythms under the influence of associated motor and emotional impulses, recapitulated from generation to generation. Of these influences two are outstanding and of measurable variability: the motor habit by which man wrests his living from the earth, and the social habit by which he relates himself to his kind. What experience is older or comes closer to the life of man than his Two-handedness? Taker and Holder: the play of them, one into the other; strike with the right, cover with the left; thus he conceived his Universe, two-handed.... And are not Taker and Holder the protagonists of the first drama, even as the

Amerind conceived them, Ahayuta, Matsalema, the eternal Twin Brethren, right and left hands of the Sun Power? One of them pulls the life-force up through the dust to corn, and the other pulls the corn back to dust.... So is all art form shaped on a system of oppositions, balance without parity. What we mean by composition in art is simply right and left handedness, one hand and a pot hook....

When I speak of rhythm here, I am referring to the basic motor impulses which underlie the English gesture. These are of the simplest; the *lub*-dub, *lub*-dub of the heavy footed Nordics, lightened occasionally by the use of two shorts to balance the long movement. In this measure all their great poems of action are written; an exceedingly ancient measure beyond which there is but one more ancient, the pyrrhic, sounding so faintly at the far end of our Greek vista that many scholars have supposed it a purely theoretic measure of the Grammarians. But to the thousands of Americans who have listened to the swift patter of its unaccented dub dub, dub dub, dub dub in the plazas of Zuni and Oraibi it is the very pulse of emerging American consciousness.

This we shall come back to. The English, who are not a dancing people, did no better by themselves, unless you count the slight clipping of one of the shorts of their heroic measures and the equal lengthening of the other, a hint which I suspect they accepted from their horseback habits, as they made half a league, half a league onward. For all their moods of high sensibility, for the languors and raptures of beauty and sensuously perceived, as well as to display the Gothic intricacy of their speech, they had recourse to the dance measures of the Classics, which by the era of American settlement had been transferred from the centers of self-realization and run off at the tips of waving swords or twinkling, lute-playing fingers.

Poetry is a man's game. Women are only good at it by a special dispensation as men are occasionally good at millinery. If you look for the determinant of poetic form in a given period, look for the gesture by which maleness is in that age expressed. In Europe for a thousand years before American settlement began, the sword had been the extended flourish of man's personality, as the cloistral pace was the measure of his profoundest meditation. In Elizabethan verse there was pomp, which folk never use, lute notes, which they could not if they would. America, though it carried too long like the dried shell of a locust, the shape of the derived culture of England on her back, proved no place for flourishes, nor this the time to go horsed on the poetic inventions of an earlier age. It was back to the foot pace on the new earth, ax stroke and paddle stroke. So it is that new rhythms are born of new motor impulses....

One winter at Tesuque I saw the Eagle dancers on a windy day catch up the rhythm of the wind through the tips of their wing-spread plumes and weave it into the pattern of their ancient dance, to the great appreciation of the native audience. After twenty years' observation, it remained for Ovington Colbert, a Chickasaw, to point out to me that the subtle wavering of the movement of the Squaw Dance, which I had supposed to be due to the alternate relaxation and tension of interest, was really responsively attuned to the wind along the sagebrush.... Perception of rhythmic form in nature is driven so deeply into his sub-conscious, that in those dances where pure appreciation of his fortunate relation to Allness takes precedence of the ritualistic element, he can seize upon and coordinate with his dance the rhythm of sun, wind, or falling water, making himself part of the inextricable pattern of the hour....

At the same time that the Amerind is using his body as an instru-ment of rhythm, he is using it as an instrument of realization of the result he desires to affect. He paints his body, decorates it with mimetic symbols, moves it through the phases of mimetic gesture, culminating in specific acts which are always mimetic even when most realized....

I have naturally a mimetic temperament which drives me toward the understanding of life by living it. If I wished to know what went into the patterns of the basket makers, I gathered willows in the moon of white butterflies and fern stems when these were ripest. I soaked the fibers in running water, turning them as the light turned, and did my ineffectual best to sit on the ground scraping them flat with an obsid-ian blade, holding the extra fibers between my toes. I made singing medicine as I was taught, and surprised the Friend-of-the-Soul-of-Man between the rattles and the drums. Now and then in the midst of these processes I felt myself caught up in the collective mind, carried with it toward states of super-consciousness that escape the exactitude of the ethnologist as the life of the flower escapes between the presses of the herbalist. So that when I say that I am not, have never been, nor offered myself, as an authority on things Amerindian, I do not wish to have it understood that I may not, at times, have succeeded in being an Indian....

All Amerind poetry, even the most personal, presents itself as three-plied movement and melody and words. When the expression is communal, the movement and instrumented rhythm may be of a complexity rivaling the harmonic intricacies of a modern orchestra. Witnessing the Corn Dance of the Rio Grande Pueblos, one realizes how it was that Aristotle came to treat of Poetry as comprising several arts which we now think of as distinct from it. The Corn Dance is an affective fertility rite, designed to bring rain and good growing weather to the sprouting crops. The dancers will number among the hundreds, according to the population of the community. The natural rhythm of their timing feet will run from the pound of the men's thick soles, through the softer shuffle of the women to the patter of children tailing and overlapping like a musical round, bound together but not necessarily synchronized by the beat of the tombes, steady and quick like the heart of the sun beating. In and out of these primary rhythms play the body accents, knee rattle and arm rattle of deer's hoofs or tortoise case, and the lovely silver clash of the wreaths of conus shells about the glistening torsos of the men. From point to point, like the rush of summer rain, runs the roll of prisoned pebbles in the hand-held gourds.

34

The Song-Makers

1911

The talk had been going on for nearly an hour without affording me an occasion for saying anything, which was exceedingly tiresome.

"The fact is," said the Professor, and the rest of the company agreed with him, "that the only place you can hear Wagner as he should be, is at Beyreuth." The pines outside quivered at this announcement, and a blear old sea fog came and peered through the panes at us. Suddenly the fire-log snapped asunder.

The red glow leaped into a three-inch point of flame. Instantly the fog caught it by reflection a rod outside and made of it a desert campfire spiraling upward from the crossed ends of the back log. Dark against it by some superior sort of refraction from my mind I could see the dreaming face of my friend Tinnemaha, the Medicine-man.

What I thought the Professor had said was that the only place nowadays where you could see any genuine song-dancing is in Shoshone Land, and, out of the velvet desert dark beyond, Kern River Jim answered him.

"But in the old days," said he, "right here in Sagharanite there was a Chisera who could sing the wind up out of the west with the rains behind it; and she could sing the rain away, too, when she had done with it; and you could no more be still when you heard her than the wind could, but you must get upon your feet and dance what she sang."

"In Shoshone Land," said Tinnemaha, "I remember a man who could dance the heart out of your bosom. He made a rattle of ram's horn stopped with a round of mescal stem and would keep time with it. He taught me to dance some of his songs for a bag of taboose, but

I could never match with him, for the best of his singing was that he made it new for every occasion."

What the Professor was actually saying at that moment was that Wagner's intellectuality made it improbable that the French should ever be able to interpret him, but I went on listening to Tinnemaha, for, besides being much the same sort of talk, it was vastly more interesting.

"Nowadays in the schools," said he, "they teach our children white man's songs, but they do not lay hold on your insides as the old songs do. White man's songs, they talk too much." He dropped out of his native speech into the clipped English in which he courteously held any criticism of white men's ways should be couched. "White man sings too much with his mouth," said he, "but Shoshone sings here"—he extended his hand across his body, palm inward, with that most expressive gesture of the Indian to include the whole region of the solar plexus, the seat of the Inside Man who sings and is sung to—"here." The hand moved outward, slightly clutching at the strings of sympathy.

"Sometimes," he went on, "you see Indian man singin' an' dancin'; he cryin' while he singin.' 'Tain't the words that make him cry. I'ss what he thinkin' 'bout when he sing."

"Last night," said Kern River Jim, "I dreamed that I sang, and when I awoke I was crying, but my song had gone from me."

"It was the wolf-song," said Tinnehama; and we were quiet while the flames lapped and flickered, musing on what I have told you in another place, how there was a man who, when the people met together, had no song and greatly desired one and was unhappy over it. Then one day he bought a song from the wolf for a basket of tule roots and sang it amid the tribe that night until the earth under him was beaten to a fine dust and he fell into the deep trance which waits beyond the last ecstasy of song.

So the wolf came in the night and stole his song away. It reminded me of an equally old tale of a Saxon singer, and I thought, Beast-god or Man-god, the myth told quite as much as I had been able to fathom for myself of the source of all songs, dropping into the mind spread to receive them, quietly as the shed of ashes of the fire.

"But all your songs," I wished to know, "do they come so from inside you?"

"Every man's own song," they averred, "the one he makes for himself, and no one dares sing without his permission. But sometimes when it is a very good song he bequeaths it to his friend, and the tribe uses it; other times a man's song is so precious that no one gets to know very well what it is about, and it dies with him."

"And when does a man make a song?"

"How can I tell?" questioned Tinnemaha. "It is when his Inside Man is raised up within him. Perhaps when he has killed his first buck or made a woman know that he is a man. When his son is born or his enemy is slain. Who knows his great moment?"

"There was one I knew," said Kern River Jim, "who made a song when he was drunk. Three days he had herded the Bar-N cattle up Tunawai in a sand-storm, scarcely eating or sleeping while the storm lasted, and when it was done, the foreman gave him as much whiskey as he liked, and when he was well drunken he made a song." Jim's eyes twinkled. "It was a good song."

I remembered to have heard that air, the most lugubrious Indian melody I had known, and I thought I should have felt just that way if I had been thoroughly intoxicated, but Jim esteemed it humorous.

We fell a-talking then of the songs that are not personal, but come down to the people from old times: cradle-songs, love-songs, songs for the beginning and the end of journeys.

Tinnemaha stood up and began to sing one of Victory:

"Ha...ah-a,
Ha...ah-a!"

A sharp, throaty noise, as if the Inside Man had waked and fed on what he relished:

"Ha...ah-a!"

while the Medicine-man stamped and swayed:

"Come, O ye buzzards,
The feast is prepared!
Ha...ah!"

Until I could fairly hear the sweep of their wide wings between the naked dead and naked heaven.

"My father saw that song made when he was a young man and we fought the Mojaves. We had killed the best of their fighting men and taken away their weapons, for they had long arrows that entangled in the brush so that they could not shoot so fast as our men with the shorter shafts. The dead were beginning to swell, and one of our men danced among them and made a song.

"Then one and another of ours took it from him, and all the way home they danced it until the women heard them returning on the trails. So the song came to the Shoshones."

"And do you always dance when you sing?"

"How else should it be?" said Tinnemaha, with mild amazement.

"First," said he, "the song *is*, then there are three things—the dance and the music—

"Ha...ah-a!"

The muscles of his chest rippled under the thin cotton shirt, the throaty syllables gurgled out of him as though jarred by the rhythm of his dancing. "And then," he finished, "there are the words. Sometimes the words are very old and are forgotten, and the people make new words, but it is not a new song because of that. The song is behind them."

It flashed upon me inwardly as accounting for the accompaniment of meaningless syllables that ran along with much of their tribal ceremonial, swelling with the movement of the ritual into even billows of song with just a sentence or two like a riffle of foam on the crest of each: the song behind the song singing itself out of all their memories and knowledges.

"Give me that song which you danced for me at the beginning of wild almond bloom," I begged, beating with my hands a sketch of the body rhythm that accompanied it.

"The grass is on the mountain."

crooned Kern River Jim. "It is a very old song of the Paiutes."

"And the song behind it?" I urged.

"Oh, a long time
The snow is over all the mountain.
The deer have come down and the big-horn,
They have passed over Waban.
A long time now we have eaten seeds

And dried flesh of the summer's killing,
We are wearied of our huts.
The mists have come down like a tent,
They have hid the mountain.
And on a day suddenly comes the sun.
The mists are withered away,
The grass is seen on the mountain!"

"Therefore," said Jim, "we make a dance and go to the meadow to look for taboose and the young shoots of the tule.

"Also," said he, "I remember a song a woman made to me on Kern River. I had come to it late in the evening and found it big with rains. The woman had a wickiup on the other side and went about her fire to tend the cakes; I called across to her, but I did not attempt the river because of the flood, and I saw that the woman was alone and no man came to her. By and by when it was dark she piled pitchy boughs on the fire till it leaped up and showed the straight high pines and the river between us like a thick, hurrying snake. Then she made a song and I heard it above the water. So I went into the river as I was, and the woman pulled me out half dead on the other side. But I did not mind it because of the song."

"And the song was?"

"The fire burns," quoted Jim. "It leaps up and nobody is warmed by it. Though it was a very long time ago, I have never forgotten it." I did not ask him for the song behind that....

Once when I had tried to persuade Poco Bill to render a love-song he had refused on the ground that "white men don't like those kind of words. Thass all right song for Paiute, but with white man those words mean bad." Later when one of the women translated the song for me I felt how immeasurably we had dropped behind the Indian in having no words with which to communicate the issues of life except such as "mean bad."

"But still," I insisted, "I do not understand why you must dance. We also have many songs, but we do not dance to them."

Something drifted down to me just then from the talk going on over my head to remind me that when the white man sings best and most expansively he comes as near dancing as is compatible with the utmost breath: feet of innumerable choruses twinkled across my memory, but

I didn't exactly see my way to explain that to the Medicine-man. I had heard a great deal that evening of how a certain cantatrice had waved her arms and swung her magnificent torso in the part of Lucia; there was not a whisper of why. I had seen the bucks in the beginning of October pawing up the earth in deep ravines, pawing and tossing their branched foreheads with a slow, majestic rhythm, and once at Buena Vista, where the slough fell over the ruined drop into the vast reedy lagoon, long since drained away to profitable fields, there in the middle of the hot morning mist I had seen the dipping of the pelicans to their mates, the strange wing-bowing, the retreats and advances of tall water-birds, with the white expanse of wing feather against the fawn-colored land, most like the extended arms and floating draperies that flee forever about the red ground of an Etruscan vase. I had seen these and diverse wonders that, with due respect to Mr. Darwin, I didn't altogether accept as the procreant urge of the world.

That was a good theory as far as it went, but it failed to explain the dance of the Grass on the Mountain, nor why the tenor felt obliged to declare his undying opposition to the basso with both arms at length in the direction of his chest expansion.

At any rate, it would be interesting to know what the Medicine-man said of it. He said it very much to the point.

"We dance always," said he. "It is the shortest road to the Friend of the Soul of Man."

I had heard more or less of this Friend among all the Indians I had known or known about, under various names: Great Spirit, The Mystery, The Power, The Trues, God or Holy Ghost. It has nothing to do with their ordinary spirits or supernaturals, has no appearance and no history. It is the supreme intelligence, perhaps, that plane of consciousness touched in great crises along which runs from mind to mind communicating fire. Through it cures are affected and messages transmitted from the dead.

"By dancing," said the Medicine-man, "the Inside Man erects itself, it is lifted up, it lays hold on the Friend; then singing comes, and many things are possible that were not."

"What things?"

Tinnemaha considered. "Do you know Mahala Joe?"

"Who was condemned to wear a woman's dress because he once ran away from battle?"

"He was scarcely grown and it was his first fight," said the Medicine-man, excusingly. "But it is not an easy thing to appear as a woman in the face of men, and Joe has told me often that unless he had danced greatly, until the Friend knew him for a very man, he could not have continued in it."

"It was he," continued Jim, "who danced the fear out of our minds during the great sickness."

This was an epidemic of pneumonia which decimated the campodies a few years back, and Tinnemaha nearly lost his life in it, according to the Paiute law, because his own dancing failed to check the progress of this disorder.

"That," he acknowledged, "was because there was no fear in the mind of Mahala Joe. But it is true that by dancing much for one's self the power grows. There was Carson Charlie. His father had been shot by a Washoe in a very old quarrel, and Charlie should have killed the killer, but he had been to Carson to school where they showed him the Jesus road and he was soft-hearted. Then I took him apart in the hills, for his father was my friend and it is not right that the son should grow fat while the killer of his father is abroad. Three days we danced and sang together, and it was not easy for Charlie, he had been to school so long; but I taught him our ancient dances. Three days I strove with him, fasting, and in the end he found the Friend."

"And—?" I queried.

The flicker of a smile played on the face of Tinnemaha, "And he was also not so soft-hearted."

He took up my thought and carried it on beyond the personal instance. "It is so," he said; "by dancing power comes to medicine the souls of men."

"And the bodies?" But, in fact, he had no phrases to signify the partition of man into physical and spiritual which is the graft of theology on an unscientific observation of life.

What he really believed was that if the Inside Man was invulnerable, as he might be made by Good Medicine, to assault of weapon or disease, so would his outside be. I had seen a Shoshone Medicine-dancer cure an abscess on the lungs by this method, and a Methodist

Evangelist brings souls to healing by singing of hymns and pounding on the pulpit, and found the processes not entirely dissimilar, but it hadn't occurred to me until now to attempt the valuation of literature and art on the same basis. O Dante! O Bach! The shortest road to the Friend of the Soul of Man!

I explained to Tinnemaha that we had songs and other matters of our own with which merely to be confronted was to be shot upward into the plane of power, but we hadn't been able, except in rare instances, to manage it with our dances.

"That," said the Medicine-man, "is because you do not dance to yourselves." He went on to say that once when he had been to Reno, in the matter of the Washoe Boundary Dispute, he had seen some dancing-women at a theater, and was quite explicit as to the effect upon his outside. But when a man danced to himself and the Friend, it was otherwise. He thought it was reasonable, the Inside Man being so entangled with the body that when it began to move itself aright the body would respond first, and when, by free motion the spirit ascended, then the song came and visions and healing.

"It is so," he explained, "that it is more fortunate to die in battle. For if a man dies before disease has eaten him, he can the better make his song.". . . It had taken, of course, much more explanation than this, on diverse occasions, for me to understand that death to an Indian is no such catastrophe as we modernly conceive it; rather an incident which even their gods and Great Ones are liable to suffer, but it needed no further touch just then to have me see in all manner of dying rites, death songs, battle cries, extreme unction, a vine of the spirit climbing till it laid hold on the Friend and sustained itself in the swelling of Jordan. I knew without a doubt where I should go if I died immediately upon reading:

"I was with Hercules and Cadmus once
When in the woods of Crete they bayed the bear."

Good Medicine! There I had the whole business of songmakers; painted songs, printed songs, or whatever; not to preach, not to please merely, but to make a short road to the mood of power, to touch the Friend. But you had by Tinnemaha's account to touch him yourself first, to swing up by the skirts of the Great Moment and to let down a hand to stumbling men.

The fire snapped and went out; the two ends of the back log burned so far asunder that unless you had seen the live flame at work on them you couldn't have told that they belonged together any more than the two ends of the conversations—mine with the Medicine-man, and the talk within the room, which had by this time fallen off into that reminiscent exchange of dates and places, as to when you last heard Melba or where you saw the portrait of Whistler's mother, which many estimable folk pursue determinedly under the fond imagination that they are talking Art.

As the company rose for breaking up I stood up with them, and it occurred to somebody to inquire why I hadn't said anything for quite an hour.

"I was thinking," I said by way of reply, "that I should like to write a song like this."

I swung my arms out, palms upward, the chest raised, the body slightly swaying forward, saluting the six Quarters, as I had seen the Medicine-man in the business of the cure of souls, and the company, especially the younger portion of it, looked at me commiseratingly. They understood that it was not my fault that I hadn't at that time had the advantage of the Metropolitan Museum and Covent Garden, and they meant, of course, to be kind. I could see the Professor, visibly in the interest of hospitality, hold back a disposition to lecture me. But they do not know even yet why I didn't particularly mind it.

Annotated Bibliography of Austin's Articles on Southwest Literature

Indicates Articles Included in this Collection

1911   "How I Learned to Read and Write." In *My First Publication*, by James David Hart, 61–65. San Francisco: Book Club of California, 1911.

In this short autobiographical sketch/memoir, Austin describes how she learned to read and write. She recalls learning to read before she started school and, because she was advanced, feeling isolated from her peers. This isolation prompted her to write. She discusses the progression of her writing and notes that her "style" resulted from writing in a way she thought cultivated people would relate to. She notes that she has become known for this distinct style.

*1911   "The Song-Makers." *North American Review* 194 (August 1911): 239–47.

Austin recollects a discussion with Tinnemaha, a Medicine Man, about Native American song and dance. Sitting around a fire, Austin questions the Medicine Man about the song and dance tradition. Tinnemaha distinguishes between native and white man's songs, saying that the white man "talks too much." In answer to Austin's question, he explains that by singing and dancing "power comes to medicine the souls of men." Austin reveals that it was at this moment that it occurred to her to "attempt the valuation of literature and art on the same basis." By the end of the story, Austin realizes that the main focus of song-makers is to "make a short road to the mood of power, to touch the Friend [Higher Spirit]."

1911 "The Reorganization of the New Theatre." *American Magazine* (November 1911): 101–4.

This is Austin's account of what the New Theatre should and should not be. According to Austin, a subsidized theatre should be free from pressure of commercialized interests, be audience appropriate, and reflect national scope and culture. At this time, she thought the New Theatre was falling short of that goal as it was too heavily influenced by outside tastes.

*1914 "Community Make-Believe." *Good Housekeeping* (August 1914): 213–19.

Austin offers an informative "how to" article on community theaters. She addresses the logistics of such performances including setting, audience seating, finances, costuming, and choosing actors.

1914 "Medicine Songs." *Everybody's Magazine* (September 1914): 413–15.

Austin explains that the complexity of American Indian poetry is that the full meaning of their poem, or Inside Song, is never expressed in just words. Music, dance, and phrase are integral to expressing Indian poetry. Austin says it takes someone with knowledge and familiarity of their artistic form to adequately transcribe their poetry as she has attempted to do with "The Heart's Friend" (a Shoshone love song) and "A Song in Time of Depression" (from the Paiute), which are included in this article.

1914 Foreword. "Fire." *The Play-Book* (October 1914): 3–6.

In this foreword to her drama "Fire" Austin regards Indian poetic and dramatic forms as a "medium of [the] mind affected by a natural environment." She explains that aboriginals do not specifically distinguish verse from dancing; they have no name for drama. For the aboriginal, drama occurs when word, tone, and movement come together. Therefore, the manner in which an Indian tells a story is naturally poetic and dramatic in form. Austin illustrates the Indian tradition of poetic speech by translating Paiute phrases. For example, "the moon of tender leaves" refers to the first week in April. Their primitive speech, she says, is "immensely more poetic and sophisticated [than ours]." Austin concludes by explaining that "Fire," her interpretation of an Indian legend, is a "suggestive imitation of the sort of material that lies, sprung from our own soil."

*1915   "Art Influence in the West." *Century Magazine* 89 (November 1914–April 1915): 829–33.

Austin begins this article by comparing the beautiful landscape of California to that of Greece and Italy, where beauty in art is thought to originate. Western art, she says, is reflective of and affected by color, simple form, and great detail of landscape. In her opinion, great art-producing peoples are often agriculturists who dramatize their relationship between man and nature. Likewise, poets are more naturally bred from people intimate with land than from people at a university. Austin also purports that Western art is reflective of religious form. She notes that many outdoor theaters in California are home to rich poetic dramas religious in theme, and she credits Indians with capturing the spirit of the land itself in forms of verse and drama.

1915   "Mexico for Mexicans." *World Outlook* (December 1915): 6–7.

Austin tries to show Americans that although Mexico wants to settle her economic and industrial difficulties, Mexicans do not necessarily want to settle them "after the fashion of the USA." She believes our failure to understand their temperament and capacity leads to a mistaken attitude toward the Mexican situation. She discusses the wage system and reminds us that Mexicans are a hand-working, artistic, simple people and, therefore, a wage system reflecting our long-driving day would not suit them. She says we have a hard enough time making our own wage system practical and credits Mexico for avoiding that problem. Our role, she says, should be in helping Mexico produce the best kind of Mexican and not a poor American imitation.

1915   *What the Mexican Conference Really Means.* Booklet. New York: Latin American News Association, 1915.

Austin says Americans are generally ignorant about many things, especially other cultures like that of our very own neighbor, Mexico. She believes the root of Mexico's problem is that they are a "dislocated people." She explains that Spain disrupted Mexico's established development of native religion, relation to the land, and adopted government. Austin says the idea of private land is foreign to Mexicans. She compares their idea to animal instinct in that they use as much or as little land as they need and stick to the environment (habitat, plants, climate) in which they are bred. In addition, they thrive on communal activity, whereas Americans focus more on individual effort. She urges us to keep these things in mind when considering Mexico's position. She accuses American investors of wanting reform in Mexico that quickly benefits their investment rather than taking the time to do what is in Mexico's best interest.

*1917   "A New Medium for Poetic Drama." *Theatre Arts Magazine*
1.2 (February 1917): 62–66.

Austin explains how the poetic forms of the Amerind reflect the feel of the land in which he lives. This expression, she says, is unique in its roots and inevitably influential on future forms of literary art in America. According to Austin, Amerind drama has not attained a conventional form, yet, as with the Greeks, it is thematically centered on man's relation to a higher power. The religious significance makes it important to study as a literary medium. She points out that one very important characteristic of aboriginal drama is that it is easily remembered and apprehended. This is the reason rhythm and sound sequences are vital to the life of aboriginal drama. Beyond creative expression they serve as a memory aid so that dramas can be passed on from generation to generation.

The rest of the article is devoted to Austin's experience of trying to develop and utilize aboriginal form in her work and the difficulty of its acceptance in literary circles. She notes, however, that aboriginal influence upon modern American arts is undeniable.

1918   "Where We Get Tammany Hall and Carnegie Libraries."
World Outlook (January 1918): 5–6.

At a time when the United States is entering into war with Europe, Austin finds the "awakened interest" in the American Indian amusing yet natural. She takes advantage of the occasion to expand on the concept of nationality and illustrates how aboriginals established our native nationality. She gives numerous examples of how modern America has unknowingly adopted originally indigenous practices—including "lodge night," the position of women, experimental social solutions, property distribution, and a peace league—and she ponders the idea that perhaps the land is dictating our living standards.

*1918 Introduction. In *The Path on the Rainbow*, ed. George W. Cronyn, xv–xxxii. New York: Boni and Liveright, 1918.

Austin calls this compilation of aboriginal work the "first authoritative volume of aboriginal American verse." In discussing Amerind poetry, she credits the natives with the original use of Imagism as a poetic device. Their poetry, she says, is a reflection of their relationship with the environment. She explains how song is very much a part of aboriginal poetry: "By singing, the soul of the singer is put in harmony with the essential Essence of Things." The melody of the poetry also assists memory, in that its movement makes a poem distinctive. If adequate records were available, Austin believes evidence would show primitive verse to be of epic quality. Moreover, Austin notes that although we may not hear specific form in aboriginal verse, she feels confident that Indians "recognize a certain correspondence between form and meaning." Aboriginals, she explains, are more interested in the reaction their poetry produces within the poet over how it affects others. They create songs from important moments in their lives. As poetry is so personal, Austin says, "it is in the very nature of primitive verse that it should require interpretation, even among the audiences for whom it is originally intended." Austin believes that delving deep into any Indian poem would produce the "profound and palpitant humanism without which no literary art can endure."

1918 Letter to Henry James Forman on the Art of Writing. The Rare Books Collection at the Huntington Library # 350967. 1–6.

Austin says there is a difference between best writers and best sellers. She accepts herself as the former. With that said, she explains that creative writing comes from the subconscious. Various planes of the mind allow her to work on completely different topics at the same time. To accomplish this, one must dip into the deepest levels of the mind in order to improve and write quality work. She advises using conscious intelligence only

— to acquaint one's self with the quality of the mind which has in the past produced the kind of thing one wishes to do;

— to collect the best material possible out of which the work is to be constructed;

— to trim and finish the final product.

She finds dancing to be the best exercise while writing because it keeps the body responsive to emotional impulses. She says that getting a story to write depends on the art of experiencing it.

*1919 Letter to the Editor. *Dial* 66 (May 1919): 569–70.

In this letter to the editor, Austin comments on Louis Untermeyer's review of *The Path on the Rainbow*, an anthology of American Indian verse. She calls his literary judgment "New Yorkish," not American. She explains that Imagism in Indian verse is not only the words but also the "beat of a drum or pounding of feet." In other words, the complete package comprises the image. She allows that something is often lost in the translation of Indian verse. Like other poets, Austin says that Indian poets are occasionally "banal and commonplace" and that Untermeyer should take this into account when using such labels.

1919   Letter to the Editor. *Dial* 67 (August 1919): 163.

This is more commentary on Untermeyer's review. According to Austin, he failed to see the Imagism in Indian verse in its complete form. Indians use varied methods to produce an image. Again, Austin chides Untermeyer for his New York view of things.

*1919 "Non English Writings II—Aboriginal." In *The Cambridge History of Literature*, eds. William Peterfield Trent, John Erskine, Stuart P. Sherman, and Carl Van Doren, vol. 3, chap. 32, 610–34. New York: The Macmillan Company, 1945.

Austin begins the article by discussing the conditions associated with aboriginal literature. For one, always present is a "complete democracy of thinking and speaking" in its form. Because there were no "intellectuals," no class advantages, and no scholastic sources, aboriginals used language common to all members, allowing literature to be available to and understood by all. This, Austin believes, is the very thing America is and should be striving for, that "literature be the possession of all the people." Another requirement of aboriginal literature is that its form be "rememberable." Aboriginal literature was transmitted mostly orally, and, according to Austin, aboriginals often used rhythm as a memory aid for the story. The use of rhythm, she says, is distinguishable according to the type of literature it is applied to. Austin further explains this by saying, "The thing that came out of the Amerind heart was poetry, but if it came out of his head it was prose." She finds it unfortunate that most of the preservation of aboriginal literature was done by ethnologists rather than by literary specialists, for their focus has been on elements like mythology and language and not literary form.

Austin moves on to discuss evidence of Indian orators composing speeches in units, the arrangement specifically formulated for a particular audience. This, she asserts, would relate the art of oratory to drama. She then focuses on poetry of the aboriginal, citing this medium as the choice for intimate expression and, as such, its typically religious theme. By religion, Austin explains the aboriginal's tradition of putting himself in touch with a Higher Spirit. This form of literature included rhythm in order for the Amerind to heighten the spiritual and emotional experience. Thus, song sequences were formed. Austin finds long poetry of the Amerind common to epics of the "old world." The difference, she says, is that aboriginals focused on their relationship with the land and agriculture and not to old-world warrior themes.

Finally, Austin delves into aboriginal literature as drama, citing early evidence of stagecraft and dramatic instinct among aboriginals. In conclusion, she stresses the importance of realizing the literary quality and influence of aboriginal literature.

1920   "The Situation in Sonora." *Nation* 110 (1920): 680–81.

Austin describes the political uprising in Sonora, Mexico, where citizens are holding out against federalization. Although there is corruption in the Mexican government, Austin is against imposing a ballot system like that of the United States. She says it will result in similar downfalls in that suppressed classes will not have fair representation and access in the system. She claims that the candidate with the most powerful backing wins anyway.

*1920 "Supernaturals in Fiction." *The Unpartizan Review* 13 (March-April 1920): 236–45.

Austin discusses the long history of supernaturals in fiction and states that "among the stories most enjoyed by human kind" are those that include supernatural characters or supernormal incidents. In fact, she asserts that for a story to survive over time, some element of it must be supernatural. She explores the early use of supernaturals in Greek literary tradition. Like our native storytellers, she says, the Greeks "had a hankering to have the Universe explained." The rise of Greek and Christian literature shows how supernaturals were used to link people to the Infinite and to each other. Austin explains that the appetite for supernatural fiction stems from our desire to question truth and our place in the universe.

1921 "Zuni Folk Tales." *Dial* 71 (1921): 113–17.

This is Austin's exploration into Frank Hamilton Cushing's book *Zuni Folk Tales*. She considers him a reliable source, as he was adopted into the Ashwini tribe, completely immersing himself in their lifestyle. Austin explains that the main difference between Zuni folk tales and European folk tales is that the Zuni tales flourish on their native soil while the European tales revolve around removal from their homeland. Zuni tales, however, resemble patterns of the human experience similar to those of Greece and Rome. Although Cushing reproduced the tales to the best of his ability, Austin feels he was not able to capture the dance measure that "accompanied and controlled them." The sacred legends of the Amerind are mingled with melody and dance. Austin asserts that this mix represents a unique form of literary development that must be considered poetic drama.

1921 "Songs of the American Indian." *Harper's Magazine* 143 (1921): 77–80.

Austin reviews and translates various songs of the American Indian, including "Woman's Song," "San Juan Love Song," Rain Songs from the Rio Grande Pueblos, "Lament of a Man for His Son," "Songs of the Friend," and "Song for the Newborn."

She points out that Indian songs are not wordy but to the point of what they are trying to express. Much of the meaning of the song is derived from a particular occasion or story. She stresses the fact that aboriginal verse is sung, chanted, or danced to, and that all of this allows expression of a complicated idea in one word or limited words. Austin considers everything when translating a song: the emotional content, the story, and what it accomplishes for the singer. Like poetry, she says, the song is expected to accomplish something for the person's soul.

1921 "Book Service to Main Street." *Bookman* 53 (April 1921):
      97–101.

Austin explicates the need for better distribution of books to small towns because reading is a part of culture. She is concerned that music and movies be made accessible and fill the need for reading. Austin urges New York publishers to think about readers beyond their immediate region and publish books that appeal to people in other parts of the country. She says American readers will take the time to read if they feel they can relate to some aspect of the story or feel they can learn something.

1921 "The Writer Who Never Grew Up." *The Ladies Home Journal* (December 1921): 7ff.

Austin discusses the life and work of Sir James Barrie.

1922 "English Books and American Reviewers." *Bookman* (January 1922): 183–84.

Austin points out that just because English books are receiving critical attention in New York does not mean the rest of America is interested in buying or reading them. She says, "What goes on in New York is by no means all that is going on in the mind of young America." She explains that Americans distinguish between literature (more formidable) and "reading matter," but that it is not that they lack the intelligence or desire for the former. According to her it is simply that they don't like being told which books are significant and well-written, that they "resent the literary dictatorship of New York."

*1922 "The American Form of the Novel." *The New Republic* Spring Literary Supplement (April 12, 1922): 3–4.

According to Austin, the most influential factor on the form of the American novel is the idea of conforming to the "state of collective consciousness rather than to its direction." A writer must be a participant in the American consciousness to really be inside the novel.

1922 "Native Rhythms." *Literary Review of New York Evening Post* (July 1, 1922): 769–70.

Austin begins by stating that there are three influences in English verse that are recognized in America: Greek, which is foot music; Roman, which adds the singing note of personal passion; and Hebrew, which belies the movement and rhythm of the sort that "goes on inside a man's head." Because they are not indigenous to the English but "selected" by them, Austin calls them the rhythms of privilege (different from folk songs and poetry). She says that "folk thought" is more direct and better reflects life lived rather than life observed. Because rhythm is a form of experience, she believes the folk better capture this authentic experience. She considers Stephen Crane the only new poet to arrive instinctively at the perfect form of experiential rhythm. Austin calls movement of rhythm kinetic energy and explains that because it cannot be confined to regular meters, it eventually bursts and produces what is known as free verse or, as she calls it, the landscape line. She finds that the verse of the Victorians does not have this explosive energy about it. She goes on to explain that the reason young poets take to free verse because it is "easier" is actually because it is native. It's always easier, she says, to do the native thing than to do the imitative thing.

1922 "Amerindian Folk Lore." *Bookman* 56 (November 1922): 343–45.

Austin believes Amerindian folklore is wrongly "forced into the mold of Greek mythology...[or] of Grimm Brothers and Hans Christian Andersen." She finds that critics fail to consider Amerindian folklore as an original genre. This article reviews Elizabeth DeHuff's "Taytay's Tales," of which Austin approves as an attempt to present the American Indian folk tale in its aboriginal form. However, she feels DeHuff misrepresents the universal folk-tale motif of misadventure and death, representing it as savage when it is typically used to present a lesson through humor.

1923   "How I Would Sell My Book, 'Rhythm.'" *The Bookseller and Stationer* (May 1, 1923): 7.

Austin describes how she would market *The American Rhythm* to specific audiences. For women's clubs who work for Indian welfare she would assume their interest in the influence of Indian poetry and offer a comprehensive explanation. To young people, who she says love controversy, she would address the idea that free verse comes from the American experience on the subconscious and not from the French. To total strangers she would ask them what they think of her ideas on the rhythm of the Gettysburg address. Moreover, she would explain that when she was a poor, young girl living in the desert without books or access to a library, the Indian songs and stories were her only literature. Finally she says she thinks this book was worth writing [regardless of its reception] because it "deals with phases of American life that are so rapidly passing away that in ten years it would hardly be possible for such a book to be written."

1923   "The Politeness of Questa la Plata." *Century Magazine* 106 (May-October 1923): 65–68.

In Austin's opinion, Questa la Plata is a town especially notable for its polite disposition and pride in its town product—goat cheese. She tells the story of the government's ridiculous attempts to teach the people of Questa la Plata food conservation when the government was totally unfamiliar with their habits. For instance, the government urged the townspeople to eat meat only once a day when in actuality they were unaccustomed to eating it at all. Moreover, a government expert was sent in to teach them how to make goat cheese when that had been their specialty for two decades. The people of Questa la Plata acted as if they had no idea of this process and graciously "learned" how to make goat cheese. The government representative never discovered the mistake and left the small town thinking of the remarkable contribution he had made to it.

1923   "Arizona: The Land of the Joyous Adventure." *Nation* 116
        (1923): 385–88.

Austin calls Arizona the newest state with the oldest civilization, distinct
from other states. She discusses its political development and explains
how the history and topography of Arizona influence the population.
She says Indian culture in Arizona is a "formative influence in the art
and literature of the state." On the surface, she says, cities in Arizona
may appear as any other U.S. city with recent advancements (except for
the Spanish flavor kept for tourists) but the Arizona attitude is different, more open-minded than Eastern (New York) cities. She uses the
Bisbee mining labor incident as an example, showing how Arizona han-
dled it in its own quiet, old-school manner whereas Eastern liberals
made a big fuss over it.

*1924   "Cactus Country." *Century Magazine* 108 (May-October
        1924): 384–91.

Austin lyrically and informatively describes native plants of the Southwestern desert. She calls the saguaro the king cactus and the home to
many woodpeckers and pygmy owls. It can thrive, she says, even when
uprooted. It is popular with Pima and Papago women, who harvest its
fruits. She says the bisnaga is often mistaken for the saguaro. Austin
denies that the ocotillo is a true cactus and calls it part of the mesquite
family. She offers rich descriptions of prickly pear and chollas. Throughout the article, Austin speculates on the evolution of desert plants.

1924   "The Colorado River." *Century Magazine* 108 (May-
        October 1924): 462–70.

Austin explores all aspects of the Colorado River front, including
mountains, water, wildlife, treacherous passes, discoveries made by
original explorers, Indian grounds, and plant life. She believes that all
of these things enrich human history and form culture.

1924   "The Days of Our Ancients." *Survey* 53 (October-March
        1924): 33–38, 59.

Austin explores primitive village life using the architectural evolution of
the Native Americans as a framework. She provides detailed description

of the relationship of the "ancients" to the land, tracing it by architecturally formative periods: the Pit House Period, the Small House Period, the Tower House Period, and the Great House Era. Each period was born out of necessity and aimed toward the goal of community development. According to Austin, "invasive modern America" has caused a decline in this community spirit and resulted in breaking up and decentralizing cooperative efforts in the Native American world.

*1924 "The Trail of the Blood." *Century Magazine* 108 (May-
     October 1924): 35–44.

This is Austin's detailed account of the Los Hermanos Penitentes and their annual dramatic reenactment of Jesus' crucifixion. According to Austin, the reenactment often ended in a "realistic and sometimes fatal crucifixion" of one of the members.

   Austin believes that their observance of this tradition is more sacred than the formal observances of the church. She pities the typical American disposition that causes people to harshly judge such a tradition rather than try to understand it. Austin attributes environment and landscape with shaping this art and the community. She had occasion to witness and participate in this dramatic interpretation and calls it legitimate dramatic art because of the release of an emotional complex.

1925 "Cults of the Pueblos." *Century Magazine* 109 (November
      1924–April 1925): 28–35.

The subtitle and subject of this article is "An Interpretation of Some Native American Ceremonies." Austin begins by describing the general Native American attitude toward death and specifically the significance of an incineration burial (releasing the dead from the bonds of flesh) and the intramural burial (burying the body into structure). In the next section, Austin explains the important Native American idea of attaining magical powers through the spirits of past members, called *wakonda*. She discusses certain symbols and their significance in Indian ceremonies. She concludes that early cultures are introspective because they had no records to rely on. They placed importance on dreams for guidance. To them, ceremonies are a faith-based concept. They believe that a desire articulated in a symbolic act has a better chance of being realized. Austin calls the Indian group effort of ceremony a total "one-mindedness" that works with the earth in order to survive. This, their culture, is their existence.

1925   "The Creative Process." *Southwest Review* (April 1925):
       70–76.

Austin discusses the creative process at length, beginning with the two processes that should occur in a creative undertaking. First is free streaming association, or reverie, which is the constant flow of the psyche. Austin believes the educational system should encourage more free association and less selected "ideal patterns." The other important element is ideation, or the forming of an idea. She says it is better to translate emotion into an idea than an idea into emotion. From there, putting the work together—pattern, detail, form, content, etc.—is a process Austin calls polarization. She recommends prayer and mental discipline to sustain the capacity for polarization. She ends the article by discussing the role of true evocation, which she claims stems from her definition of genius (which she says she does not have the space to elaborate on here).

1925   "Artist Life in the United States." *Nation* 120 (1925):
       151–52. (First of a series of articles by American writers to
       answer the question: Can an artist exist and function freely in
       the United States?)

Austin believes that artists get much inspiration from the beauty of the United States but have a difficult life due to the absence of dependable work criteria. She points out that it is all up to the critics, who are often unfit to judge the work. One disadvantage of democracy is that there is no blanket standard to which writers are upheld. She explains that this results in a lack of dependable help and constructive criticism from the public for writers.

1925   "The Future of the Southwest." Letter. *New Republic* 42
       (February 25–May 20, 1925): 186.

In her letter to the editor Austin refutes an article concerning the Colorado River. According to Austin, the author's suggestion violates the United States' treaty obligation with Mexico. It is her opinion that the United States failed to have the moral and intellectual insight to acquire the rights from a willing Mexico in which all parties would have bene-fited. Austin believes the Boulder Dam Project would fail Americans and threaten the future of the Southwest based on unequal water dis-tribution and rights.

1925   "American Marriage." *American Mercury* 6 (1925): 1–6.

This article contains three stories of Indian marriages, all of which have American twists or conflicts.

The Way of a Woman: A fickle daughter fights her father about the husband he has chosen for her. After much anguish, the father gives in and grants her her freedom. The daughter then decides she wants the man her father chose for her.

Papago Wedding: A white man refuses to grant an Indian woman, the mother of his children, a legal marriage, but the woman outwits the man in court.

The Man Who Lied about a Woman: A pompous Indian man lies about the chastity of a young woman in a vengeful act and is made a fool of when she births a white baby.

1925   Foreword. In *American Indian Love Lyrics*, ed. Nellie
        Barnes, 7–11. New York: Macmillan, 1925.

Austin gives a favorable review of Barnes's ability to convey authentic expression of Native American poetry in her book. She praises Barnes for realizing the richness in Native American poetry and seeing the importance of discovering the "source and mould of poetic form" on our native soil.

1926   "The Indivisible Utility." *Survey* 55 (October 1925–March
        1926): 301–6, 327.

Austin contrasts the European community pattern to the aboriginal community pattern. According to Austin, European society has existed on the possibility of escape from the community into economic inde-pendence. She points out that this pattern is not viable in the South-west, where land conditions force dwellers to cooperate and work in tandem. In this setting, economic success is dependent on a coordi-nated group effort. Austin uses the term "indivisible utility" to describe the inescapable bond by which a country cannot be free of a town nor a family free from a community. Undoubtedly there is a relationship between the natural environment and social patterns. She uses the example of a farmer in the Southwest who must concern himself with water and power issues of the community if he plans to farm success-fully. Likemindedness, she says, plays a key role in communal activity, but the downside of this is intolerance of change.

1926 "Buck and Wing and Bill Robinson." *Nation* 122 (1926): 476.

Austin refers to Bill Robinson's "buck and wing" dance as a throwback to primal rhythms. She says it is unlikely that Robinson knows to relate his talent to his ancestry in Africa, where the buck and wing dance was performed to increase spiritual power. In Austin's opinion, Robinson offers audiences art and culture and restores their appreciation for pri-mal rhythms.

*1926 "The Road to the Spring." *Nation* 123 (1926): 360–61.

Indian song—with its body movement, drum, rattles, rises and falls—is the original rhythm of poetry, according to Austin. Aboriginal expres-sion is poetry of the land and environment. She explains it as a totally pure expression, working from the inside out. In her opinion it should be considered an admirable medium, and the movement should be studied as poetic.

1926 "Three Tales of Love." *American Mercury* 7 (1926): 346–52.

The Man Who Was Loved by a Woman: One young, egotistical Indian man is outsmarted and made a fool of by a respected female Indian.

Hosteen Hatsanai Recants: An Indian couple questions the Chris-tian religion (which has been imposed on them by missionaries) when the husband is required to take on another wife to care for his first wife, who has become blind. The first wife is thrilled with the arrangement but the missionaries call them sinners and imply the couple's previous good works have been canceled out.

Approaching Day: The story of two men who fall in love with the same beautiful woman but fear her for her beauty.

1927   "Primitive Man: Anarchist or Communist?" *Forum* 78 (July-
        December 1927): 744–52.

Austin discusses the misunderstood notions of primitive life. She views
primitive man as living to the best of his abilities under the conditions
of nature before he became self-conscious of what he *ought* to be doing.
What one *ought* to be doing, she says, is a modern concept. Austin
explains that greed and thrift were undeveloped in the primitive consciousness. Excess possessions, linked with greed, were typically disposed of or dispersed in primitive society. Primitive people took pride
in the ability to give away more than they received by contributing
excess possessions to the group. Moreover, she says, the concept of
thrift was a natural instinct in primitive people; they did not take more
than they needed. The "caveman myth" (mating habits) is in Austin's
opinion a European product. She has found lifelong, monogamous
mating habits to be frequent in primitive communities. In addition, the
institution of marriage was found in various forms in early human
species.

Austin also explores religion in primitive life. She credits modern
religion with the origins of fear. Primitive religion, on the other hand,
was based on confidence. Theirs, she says, is an "unselfconscious religion," looking for guidance to natural religious impulses rather than to
overrationalized tradition. Austin calls it unintelligent to perceive practices of primitive man as irrational just because they are primitive.

*1927   "Native Drama in Our Southwest." *Nation* 124 (1927):
        437–38, 440.

Austin explains that in native cultures, celebrations (of land discoveries, of religion, etc.) are expressed through drama (pageants and plays).
It is her opinion that these dramas are of literary quality. She calls the
passion in native drama the root of art. She finds it unfortunate that the
"Passion Play" is now an American (touristy) version, the realistic features of the original drama having disappeared. The Penitente play links
Spanish Colonial theatre with pueblo Indian dance drama. Indian
dance drama reveals gestures as speech; Spanish Colonial plays reveal
the relation between manners and art. According to Austin, native
dance drama tradition is a mine of information for modern theatre. She

believes that these aboriginal dramas are more honest, true, and interesting than modern American drama.

*1927   "Gesture in Primitive Drama." *Theatre Arts Monthly* 11 (July
       1927): 594–605.

Austin begins by describing the "evolutionary curve" of drama, explaining that it began merely as gesture (body movement) and became more sophisticated from there. She calls primitive gesture the oldest, most universal form of language. This "sign language" is the foundation on which gesture of all primitive drama is based and from which our modern gesture is derived. Austin finds three uses of gesture in primitive art, including gesture speech, gesture pantomime, and dramatic recitative. She distinguishes between the first two by explaining that gesture speech evolves into literature and gesture pantomime evolves into illustration. In dramatic recitative, a solo speaker orchestrates movements to accompany rhythmic patterns of a chorus. Austin offers evidence that the canon of gesture was present in Greek tradition. Like Amerindians, Greeks often explored the relationship between mankind and "Immaterial Reality." She notes, however, that when expressing this idea using gesture in drama, Native Americans do not submit to the gods but work toward a psychic capacity in order to work *with* the gods. Therefore, gesture reflects the urgency toward this relationship but does so without implying submission. Austin also explores gesture in Native American comedy and explains that many gestures used in such drama would be unrecognizable to white observers. This is especially true in fertility dance drama, as whites would consider any fertility gesture indecent. Austin concludes by saying that the evolution of gesture toward sophistication began when gesture became expressive rather than communicative.

1927   "American Literature Moves On." *The World Tomorrow*
       (December 1927): 502–6.

In this article, Austin discusses the progression and changes in modern literature. Most notably, she finds that because modern audiences are interested in intellectual authenticity, American writers are freer to focus and devote expression toward the explanation of subjects.

Because of this, writers do not necessarily have to hide intellectual opinions in fiction. In addition, poets are less bound by molds and patterns and can express themselves in a number of ways in order to get to their true meaning. Austin says that ideas in modern poetry are arranged in a more primitive form so that they work together to generate a meaning as opposed to conveying separate ideas.

1927   "A Poet in Outland." *Overland Monthly* 85 (1927): 331, 351.

Austin explains that the inspiration for her book *Outland* came from acting out imaginary "lost treasure" scenes with George Sterling and friends.

1927–28   "The Colorado River Project and the Culture of the Southwest." *Southwest Review* 13 (1927–28): 110–15.

The implementation of the Colorado River Project is at a standstill due to the disagreement between California and Arizona. California feels that because they are more developed they are entitled to more water. Austin compares this situation to that of two brothers: just because one is young and the other is older and established does not mean that the younger brother should be cut from the inheritance. According to Austin, it is characteristically American to side with the least reasonable party, which in this case is California. She makes the connection between people and environment and adds that manipulating the environment, as in the Colorado River Project case, threatens culture because of the inevitable separation of people from their environment. She concludes that Arizona's culture will suffer because of California's greedy position.

*1928   "John G. Neihardt's Expression of the West." *Southwest Review* (January 1928): 256–58.

This is Austin's review of Neihardt's book *Indian Wars*. Unlike other writers of Westerns who fail to capture the true essence of the West, Neihardt accomplishes a native poetic medium evident in the way he describes the landscape and uses authentic vocabulary and speech patterns.

*1928 "Primitive Stage Setting." Theatre Arts Monthly (January 1928): 49–59.

Austin begins by explaining that primitive drama was used for "getting things done" and had nothing to do with storytelling. Primitives used drama to communicate with universal powers in order to work toward the good of mankind and the community. She says that actors and spectators worked together in the performance and used rhythm as a way to increase the feeling of the desire. According to Austin, this "raising the voltage" was what connected people to the higher power and it is still present in the good drama of modern times. Before modern dramatic elements such as dialogue and architecture became a part of the performance, man was the sole dramatic vehicle of primitive drama. He, in fact, was the stage. Austin explains that although aboriginal drama is not concerned with telling a story, there is always a story concerned with the play. She then makes the argument that Amerind drama can be connected with the origins of classic drama in Greece. The connection is recognizable in the most primitive forms of the dramas where the performance of ritual acts prevailed over an actual story. She also suggests that aboriginals introduced the idea of the stage by performing the rituals around their sacred locales. By this means altar and wall decorations became a part of the stage setting, such as those of a temple or a kiva. The common factor of all primitive stage setting, Austin says, is that they were "*suggestive* rather than *representative*."

1928 "Indian Arts for Indians." *Survey* 60 (April-September 1928): 381–88.

This informative article discusses Indian art, specifically focusing on the Pueblenõs pottery. According to Austin, the Pueblenõs worked in many mediums but could use "the colored earth freely" for expression on utensils of daily use, like pots. Her studies find that Pueblenõs were superior potters over other tribes and primitive potters of the world. Austin breaks down the elements of pueblo design into four general groups: sky signs, earth signs, air signs, and geometric signs. It is her feeling that Indian art comes from an inner creative impulse. She also discusses the establishment of an Indian museum committed to catering to the needs of the Indian artist rather than to those of a half-interested tourist. Austin dedicates part of the article to the appropriateness of

Santa Fe and its uniqueness among American towns for having "the absolute background for creative life." Austin fears the imposing effects of Americanism will suppress everything natively American. She says that it is important to keep the arts alive and let Indians express themselves creatively through native and natural instincts.

*1928 "Folk Literature." *The Saturday Review of Literature* 5 (August 11, 1928): 33–35.

In Austin's opinion, Americans do not consider themselves candidates for folk literature because their dubious mixture of cultures makes it hard to recognize local roots. Austin defines folk as "people whose culture is wholly derived from their reactions to the scene that encloses them." She believes folk literature is becoming more apparent along borders, using Creoles of the South, cowboys of the West, and lumberjacks of the North as examples. Austin goes on to focus on the Spanish and Indian influence along settlements of the Rio Grande. The folk product of the Spanish is mostly lyrical and dramatic. She describes how Spanish pioneers amused themselves by performing plays on horseback. She also explains that *corridos* and *coplas* can be characterized as folk songs. Building upon her earlier definition, Austin asserts that folk attitude and expression are a result of a group reaction to aspects of common life. She raises the question that often plagues scholars: whether folk literature is always actually produced by the folk. She gives numerous examples of successful folk literature produced by writers and not actual folk. What makes them successful is the fact that they do not only identify with the folk, but, more importantly, capture activity that usually occurs only among the folk. Austin calls this "shared limitation" and remarks that once the realization of an audience is present, the authenticity of the folk expression is threatened. In conclusion, Austin describes folk literature as "regional mastery" and says it provides a sort of natural escape back to the earth for a very diffuse American culture.

*1928 "A Drama Played on Horseback." *The Mentor* (September 1928): 38–39.

This is an article about an old Spanish play called "The Moors," presented three and a half centuries ago in what is now New Mexico. According to Austin, the Spanish celebrated their *entrada* into what is now the United States with this pageant play. Native American onlookers watched as the Spanish actors performed the play entirely on horseback. Austin believes that the original manuscript was brought from Spain, but that existing manuscripts were recorded from memory only. The rhythm of the dialogue in the play suggests that it was written in poetic form, likely, Austin says, in the conventional blank verse of the period.

1928   "Poetry That Children Choose." *The Saturday Review of Literature* 5 (October 13, 1928): 246.

According to Austin, children coordinate their own rhythm into the experience of poetry as naturally as aboriginals. She explains that at young ages, poetry is not about sentiment or learning morals, but about attention to detail of an object. In addition, most children, even those raised in the city, take an avid interest in nature poetry. The lack of Southwestern poetry prompted Austin to work with students of this region to publish their own collection of Southwestern poems called "The Children Sing in the Far West." During this project, Austin discovered that children between the ages of five and seven "voluntarily abandon body rhythms of Mother Goose" and tend to prefer what she calls "rhythms of attention." In rhythms of attention the leading statement is repeated but slightly changed, such as: "I'd like to be an antelope / A prong horn antelope / A bounding, bouncing antelope." This, she says, is a progress of perception to interior levels. From ages seven to ten, Austin noticed a growth in the appreciation of rhythm. She recommends not choosing poetry based on sentiment for grade-school children as it retards their objective perception. She does, however, advise presenting children with intellectually advanced poetry for exposure to its poetic quality, which will later enhance their capacity for literature.

*1928   "Poetry in the Education of Children." *Bookman* 68 (November 1928): 270–75.

When Austin began teaching in the Southwest she realized that there was little written linking the common people to their environment. She points out that plenty has been written about Eastern landscapes and as far as poetry goes, the most pertinent examples available to Southwestern children include Wordsworth's *Daffodil* and Bryant's *Water-*

fowl. Therefore, she desired to introduce students to poetry about their own environment. This is important, she says, because the feeling one gets from the land serves as the root of culture. In her experience she finds that young children demand verse, not poetry. It must be rhythmic, with singable vowel tunes and repetitive and incremental consonance. One popular form she finds close to poetizing as opposed to versifying is "I'd rather's," also known as "D'rathers." The more advanced the student, the more appreciation there is for poetry over just verse. Included in the article are poems written by Austin and her students: "Children's Songs of the Far West" (an "I'd rather"), "Thanksgiving," "A Feller I Know," and "Texas Trains and Trails."

1928   "A College with Roots." *The New Student* (November 1928): 13.

Austin warns that if universities are to be anything more than a "nine months' Chautauqua" they must become a "dynamic reservoir...of information that the inhabitant can use in converting his region into a rich and responsive background for his national capacity." Austin feels universities are guilty of importing culture rather than fostering their regional roots to enhance education.

*1928–29   "Regional Culture in the Southwest." *Southwest Review* 14 (1928/29): 474–77.

This article is Austin's response to the question posed by *Southwest Review* to its advisory board: Do you think Southwestern landscape and common traditions can/should develop a culture recognizable as unique, and more satisfying and profound than our present imported culture and art?

According to Austin, the culture of the Southwest depends upon the people who contribute to it. People must adapt to the land's conditions because the land always prevails. She explains how early Spanish and Indian inhabitants lived agreeably and in harmony with the land by utilizing what it offered them and producing from it. She refers to the "white element" in that people are more interested in "being cultured than creating culture." She concludes by saying that people of the Southwest need to work with the environment to produce culture and stop importing it.

*1928–29 "The Meter of Aztec Verse." *Southwest Review* 14 (1928–29): 153–57.

Austin discusses evidence of similarity between Finnish and Aztec verse. The incremental thought rhythms are a fundament of all Amerind poetics. She allows that there is greater latitude of poetic license in Amerind verse than in English. Fragments of Aztec verse are included as examples in the article.

1929 "Why Americanize the Indian?" *Forum* 82 (1929): 167–73.

According to Austin, Indians should not be treated as "broken down whites" but as Indians. She makes the point that Indians mean more to the country as Indians (with their arts, traditions, etc.) than they do as imitation whites. The "Americanizing" has caused the downfall of Indian communities (i.e., tuberculosis and trachoma, terrible conditions in boarding schools for Indian children). Moreover, Austin argues that Native Americans have no use for the things being taught to them by an intrusive American government.

1929 "Indian Detour." *Bookman* 68 (February 1929): 653–58.

Austin uses the physical Indian detour, places in New Mexico and Arizona where tourists visit to experience rich Native American history, as a metaphor for describing the independent, creative, and artistic way of life. She says there is much inspiration in landscape and ceremony; therefore, artists move to Santa Fe for these benefits and not for inexpensive living. Austin surmises that Santa Fe artists feel a kinship with New Mexican Indians because both are dedicated to their craft regardless of outside judgmental and economic pressures to live the typical "good life." She goes on to compare primitive Native American verse to that of early Greek and Aristotle tradition. She implies that Americans do not have to claim their creative history from Europe, because all that went on there was occurring here and still is. Austin laments the American approach to art as being for "show" and prefers art such as Indian dance drama, which she finds true and meaningful. She explains that most primitive art can be analyzed back into rhythmic structure. She says Europe has lost much of the rhythmic structure of primitive art, but it is still evident in Indian art. Finally, she discourages the continued attempts to change Indians into modern Americans at the risk of losing an important culture.

*1929 "The Delight Makers: A Study of Primitive Comedy among the American Indians." *Theatre Guild Magazine* (March 1929): 23–25.

According to Austin, most clown figures have resemblances to one another in appearance: black and white garments, wide mouths, and shapeless, tattered clothing, to name a few. This is certainly true and found in the Zuni of New Mexico, for whom this appearance is significant and symbolic. Austin believes the function of clowns in European history is not unlike that of the Koshare (Delight Makers or comedic figures) of New Mexico. The Koshare aid social corrective behavior by poking fun at unacceptable actions in a way that minimizes personal criticism and the singling out of offenders. Audiences both enjoy the performance and develop a sense of socially acceptable behavior. The Koshare is an integral part of ceremonial occasions, illuminating prayers and dances with cries and gestures. Austin insists we must view the originality and authenticity of the Koshare as primitive comedy and consider it influential on American folk theater. Koshare performances are secretly and specifically enacted to meet with unacceptable tribal behavior. The plays are short and simple and include dialogue. Austin finds that observing the Delight Makers reveals the roots of drama, that theater is "man's natural way of realizing society." Just like us, she says, the Delight Makers use traditional plots and devices to show humor. Important among native tribes is the idea that comedy directly aids fertility and, thus, the Delight Makers assume a major responsibility in assisting this cause. Austin concludes with the idea that studying the technique of the Koshare will renew our understanding of the sacred social use of comedy.

1929 "Sekala Ka'ajama: An Interpretive Dance-Drama of the Southwest." *Theatre Arts Monthly* (April 1929): 267–78.

Austin attempts to "reinterpret" a dramatic myth for the stage. Her introduction to the short drama, which discusses much dancing and stagecraft, explains the origins of the story of the rape of the flowers

(maidens) by the Hot Wind and their consequent rescue by The Death-
less One through gambling.

*1929 Letter in *Theatre Arts Monthly* (August 1929): 561–67.

In letter format, Austin explains why she is trying to restore Spanish
drama in New Mexico, calling it "the only genuine folk drama still productive in the U.S." She feels compelled to help the Spanish continue
this long tradition of plays, which she considers of literary quality,
because she says Americans "stupidly destroyed" this native art.

1929 "Aboriginal Fiction." *The Saturday Review of Literature* 6
      (December 28, 1929): 597–99.

Austin begins by pointing out that every literary culture draws vocabulary and characteristic expression from its own authentic base/roots.
This is true of the United States, which has its own richly characteristic language of myth, legend, fable, and human experience. Because it
is not very well known, however, it is difficult for writers to utilize.
Thus, Austin credits Stith Thompson's *Tales of North American Indians* with making aboriginal literature more accessible to the public but
faults his method of classifying the stories. It is Austin's opinion that
Thompson and his colleagues failed to recognize the complexity of literary form in aboriginal fiction. She uses the example that one would
not lump together Shakespeare and Jane Austen merely because both
have written about "young love in opposition to parental prejudice."
    Austin defines two ways of classifying tribal stories: (1) stories that
satisfy and illustrate common experience, and (2) stories that rational-
ize the universal mysteriousness of nature. Stories in the first group are
informally related, and those in the second are a more formal and "hier-
atic version of esoteric narrative." Austin calls the ability to distinguish
between the two "literary intelligence." She says it is important to realize that aboriginal literature is born out of a man's relationship with his
environment. For the aboriginal storyteller, fiction was not created for
entertaining audiences, but for understanding his place in the universe.
In primitive society, the story was used to illustrate tribal wisdom.
Austin compares this idea to the purpose of writing the biography of a
successful man. Because aboriginal fiction is not chiefly for entertain-

ment purposes, it lacks the highly dramatic climaxes typical of fictional stories. Without knowledge of the relation of tribal thought forms to literary styles, Austin says it is difficult for Americans to appreciate aboriginal literature.

*1929–30 "American Indian Dance Drama." *Yale Review* 19 (1929/30): 732–45.

Austin begins by dismissing the perception that all modern forms of dance drama derive from the Greeks. She says that Amerind dance drama is comparable to that of the Greeks and shares all of the same cultural stages of primitive Greek drama. She feels that Indian dance drama is unfortunately often mistakenly perceived as strictly a tourist attraction. The origins of aboriginal dance drama, however, are based upon man's genuine expression of his relationship with his environment. Austin explains that the Amerind dramatizes his desires toward the invisible forces of the environment through "rhythmic motion, descriptive gesture, and auto-suggestive words." Later, color, form, and design were added to this performance.

In appreciating Southwestern primitive drama, Austin recommends considering the tribal-mindedness as the production of the play. Moreover, to understand it, the nature of the wish being dramatized must also be considered. She explains that obvious wishes are easier to dramatize; for instance, a wish for increase of wild game is dramatized through pantomime. More subtle desires are less easily transcribed in acts, such as those for health. Austin points out three elements indispensable to intelligently approaching Amerind drama:

1. knowledge of Greek procedure;
2. sensitivity to dramatic mediums either of gesture, rhythm, color, or design;
3. sympathy for the tribal mind.

Another element important to understand is that no two tribes perform exactly the same ceremony. Austin proceeds to explore examples of Indian drama. Finally, she concludes that if America does not do more toward preservation of aboriginal drama and arts it will inevitably realize its irreplaceable loss.

1930   "Beyond the Hudson." Letter to the Editor. *The Saturday Review of Literature* 7 (December 6, 1930): 432, 444.

In this Letter to the Editor, Austin responds to an article called "The Promise of American Life." She says we must look "beyond the Hudson" to realize the promise of American life. She uses her own writings to illustrate how, though she was repeatedly snubbed by East Coast critics, many important figures, including Theodore Roosevelt and H. G. Wells, recognized her work as valuable. She contrasts her regional writing to that of Thoreau by explaining that Thoreau wrote about places that people had lived in for a while; it was familiar to writers, critics, and the general public. But any writing by Austin or John Muir about the Southwest, for example, would include terms specific to the landscape with which New York critics are wholly unfamiliar. Austin is optimistic, however, about the future acceptance of such writing and uses her success as an example of the promise of American life. Although the battle to introduce regional literature has been a slow and difficult one, Austin credits the country with finding its own authentically poetic mode relatively early for such a modern nation.

*1930–31   "*Rimas Infantiles* of New Mexico." *Southwest Review* 16 (1930/31): 60–64.

Rimas infantiles are lullabies/cradle songs or folk rhymes. Austin explains that although many came from Spain, some are wholly New and Old Mexican. *Rimas infantiles* are usually a four- or six-line verse with strongly assonated terminal syllables, often an exact rhyme, and are fairly easy to translate into English. She finds all of them to be "singsongy," which she claims is the genius of the Spanish language. Many of the New Mexican nursery songs are religious in subject. Austin wants to make *rimas infantiles* available for American children. In translating them, she leaves the original Spanish word where appropriate, where it is easily understood and better suited to the poetry.

*1931   *Indian Poetry*. Pamphlet/booklet. New York: The Exposition of Indian Tribal Arts, Inc, 1931, 3–5.

Austin explains that poetry to the Indian is the "formal expressiveness into which a man puts the whole of himself...to explode into something which signalizes his experience of the moment." She discusses the use of animals in their work and says Indian poetry seldom rhymes but instead "chimes." She connects primitive art with Chinese art in that they share a subtle network of the association of ideas, which is often hard to translate. Words and phrases in addition to being literal also refer to myths, religion, or tribal incidents unfamiliar to outside audiences. Important to the Indian, she says, is using the art of poetry to invoke *wakonda* and spiritual communion with the Powers.

1931   "A Selected List of Books on the Southwest." *New York Herald Tribune*, Sunday, December 13, 1931.

Austin offers a comprehensive list of her recommended literary picks of the Southwest.

1931   "Mexicans and New Mexico." *Survey* 66 (April 1931– September 1931): 141–44.

Austin explains the history of immigration from Mexico into New Mexico and the subsequent blending of cultures. She tells us that Spanish and Indian elements are a part of America's history and, therefore, its future. Most notably, she urges the consideration of the practice of communism throughout this early civilization. She explains that Mexican and Indian people tend to work "flock-mindedly," a method Americans consider "corrupt." Austin describes Americans as fervently practicing individualism instead of thinking of benefiting the community as a whole. Because Americans are obsessed with possession and owning things, she fears that they are imposing this idea on the once group-minded culture and causing a "lessened capacity for making things." She says that Americans are always pining for cheap labor but have caused these once "wantless" craftsmen to want things and, therefore, labor prices are rising.

1931   "New Mexican Spanish." Letter to the Editor. *The Saturday Review of Literature* 7 (June 27, 1931): 930.

Austin responds to criticism of her grammatical use of New Mexican Spanish in *Starry Adventure*, saying she employed a young woman born and raised speaking New Mexican Spanish to check her use of the language. She also responds to the criticism that she used too many Spanish words in general. She argues that America is practically a bilingual country and that Spanish words are so deeply embedded into English already that most take it for granted (e.g., canyon, adobe, and arroyo). English, she points out, absorbs words from many other languages. She finds it amusing that she is often rejected for incorporating Southwestern dialects, such as Indian, into her works, but publishers accept work with dialects from all other parts of the country. Austin makes it clear that she does not adhere to Spanish stresses and accents in *Starry Adventure* but allows the rhythms to represent the New Mexican Spanish that she believes will make the most significant contribution to American speech.

1931   Introduction. In *Zuni Folk Tales*, by Frank Hamilton Cushing, xix–xxix. Knopf, 1931.

Austin calls Cushing's collection of Zuni folk tales the "best-sustained translation of aboriginal American literature." She says that although the value of aboriginal literature is still underappreciated, the reprinting of a book such as this is encouraging. Austin finds that many people mistakenly believe that Indian tales are a source of Indian beliefs and that the aboriginal is not any more likely to believe his own tales than we would ones that are familiar to us. Austin offers a brief biological sketch of Cushing's childhood that leads to his extraordinary life among the Zuni, where he spent six years and was adopted by the Macaw clan. Because he mastered the language and lived so intimately among them, Austin finds his work "more nearly to that of an Indian than has been possible to any other recorder of Amerind myths and tales." Austin advises reading this collection along with Cushing's *Creation Myth,* as many of the tales are popular, fictionalized versions of this sacred story but not necessarily themselves sacred. She says reading this collection without the Creation Myth is like trying to understand English literature without the King James Bible. In the end, Austin laments Cushing's untimely death and all of his uncommunicated rare knowledge and unfinished projects.

1931   "Recent Indian Tales." *Herald Tribune* (December 13, 1931): 8.

Austin briefly reviews a number of children's books with Indians as the subject. She observes that as the reading public becomes more discriminating there is less room and excuse for writers to "filch effective bits from one tribal practice to use in the story of another." In other words, Austin says that each Indian tribe is distinct and their details cannot be used interchangeably.

1932   "Social and Economic Organization of the New Mexico Pueblo." *Progressive Education* (February 1932): 117–21.

By giving a detailed description of the social and economic organization of the New Mexico Pueblo, Austin is able to illustrate how harmful she feels it is to impose American practices on Indian society. She describes the social basis of the pueblo as matriarchal, not meaning mother ruled but rather that kinship is counted on the mother's side. Children belong to the mother's clan, a man takes his religious affiliations from his mother, mothers choose wives for their sons, and husbands move into their wife's house. This considered, disrespecting one's mother is the worst social act committed by a man. Another disreputable act in the pueblo is neglecting one's duty to perform ceremonies to the Higher Powers with caution and respect. The fundamental religious core of the pueblo is that the Powers are well disposed toward man, and that ceremony, as an act of worship, helps protect and provide for the pueblo. These concepts are among many that Austin discusses in the article. She comes to make the point that missionaries and government officials are doing a huge disservice to the Indian community by forcing unnatural ideas into their lives. Austin feels that the thwarting of Native Americans' right to preserve their tradition and fundamental ideals will cause the entire people to feel dislocated and, therefore, regress instead of progress.

*1932 "Regionalism in American Fiction." *The English Journal* 21 (February 1932): 97–107.

Austin believes that regional environment is constantly and subtly shaping man; it forces behavior patterns upon him and influences his way of life. She says America should celebrate these different patterns, recognize them as regional, and not try to mold everyone into one form. By insisting that fiction be common to all regions, Austin considers the level of literary fiction "pulled down." People want to recognize themselves in fiction and this can happen only if all regions are represented.

The test, she says, for measuring a book as regional is that its events could not have occurred anywhere else. In addition, the region should act as an instigator of the plot, much like a character, and not simply provide background. Austin outlines the four great causatives shaped by region: climate, housing, transportation, and employment.

1932   "Frank Applegate." *New Mexico Quarterly* (August 1932): 213–17, 345.

Austin uses this article to recall fond memories of her recently deceased friend and colleague Frank Applegate and to praise his contribution to the preservation of Indian and Spanish Colonial arts. She describes their relationship and endeavors in this joint venture and specifically laments the incompletion of their collaborative work effort on a book of Spanish Colonial arts.

1932   "Why I Live in Santa Fe." *Golden Book* (October 1932): 306–7.

Austin cites the following as her main reasons for living in Santa Fe: the dramatically beautiful mountain country, the appealing mystery of the desert, and the element of aboriginal society, which she has a passion to study. Most importantly, Austin feels as if she is a vital part of the community because not only does she take from it, she can give something back.

1932   "Historical Memorial." *Commonweal* 26 (October 5, 1932): 533.

Austin describes a historical chapel called Castrense located in Santa Fe.

1932–33   "One Smoke Stories." *Yale Review* 22 (1932/33): 525–32.

Austin offers a rich descriptive account of the one-smoke-story ritual. A group of Indian elders sit around a fire and methodically and meditatively exchange stories. Each story or tale offers some wisdom or guidance and takes place in the time it takes to smoke one cornhusk cigarette. Austin translates four stories in this article.

"The Medicine of Bow Returning": A man adheres to the practice of separating himself from his tribe for a certain period of time in order to obtain his "medicine" (his life's meaning) from the Allness. His medicine turns out to be that man can hurt nothing without hurting himself and, thus, he is assigned the name Bow Returning. Eventually he becomes too involved in teaching others his medicine and ignores his family. As a result, he loses his family because he lost true sight of his medicine.

"The Spirit-of-the-Bear-Walking": A man named Hotandanai is overly consumed with the legend of the Spirit-of-the-Bear-Walking, for seeing him without first being seen determines the greatness of a hunter. Throughout his marriage and the birth of his son, he is still preoccupied with being the greatest hunter. Only when his son dies and he is overwrought with grief and unselfish feeling for his son does he finally see the Spirit-of-the-Bear-Walking.

"Wolf People": This story explains the relationship between wolves and people. Wolves are their own people but work together with Indian people in hunting practices so that both parties benefit. Eventually wolves left their own kind and came to live with man of their own free will. Children began naming the wolves, and, thus, the wolves turned into dogs.

"The Shade of the Arrows": When one man is banished by his older brother for pulling pranks, he is allowed to take with him only his bow, arrows, and medicine pouch. Arrows are important because they are considered the purpose of a man. The older brother expected the banished brother to die in the harsh land but found that he had resourcefully used the shade of his arrows, arranged in a half circle, to protect him. The lesson learned from this story is that a man should live by his purpose.

1933   "Character and Personality Among American Indians." *An International Quarterly for Psychodiagnostics and Allied Studies* 1.3 (March 1933): 234–37.

Austin delves into the mental processes and attitudes of Native Americans that she believes form their character. To begin, she discusses what she terms a "subtending mentality," which includes all aspects and varieties of intuition (including hunches, premonitions, dreams, clairvoyance, etc.). She explains that Indians rely on this subtending mentality to guide them more than what we might call an intellectual process.

Austin considers Indians a more creative people, using their abilities for creations of high artistic merit. Moreover, she finds that Amerinds have an extraordinary interior discipline that manifests itself in the activity and tradition of tribal life. Finally, Austin shows that their character is highly influenced by their complete acceptance of and propensity toward group life.

*1933   "Story of the Guadalupe Play, Matachines Dance." Saturday, January 28, 1933. Unattributed newspaper clipping, Center for Southwest Research MSS 31, Box 2, Folder 4.

Austin explains the connection between the Guadalupe play and the Matachines dance, each an expression of a story in Mexican history pertaining to a miracle wrought at the Chapel of Our Lady. Austin offers a brief history of the story and discusses the original manuscript concerning the incident, written by Don Jose de la Pena, and its subsequent variations.

1933   "American Indian Murals." *The American Magazine of Art* (August 1933): 380–84.

Austin begins by pointing out the differences between Indian and "white man's" painting methods. She finds significant similarities, however, in the styles of the Indians and the Chinese. Both, she says, have the "talent for occupying space without filling it." Austin describes the initial opportunity that brought recognition and future work for Indian mural painters. She makes the argument that the symbol and design elements that the Indians use in their painting are a better American symbol than a conventional Greek figure. Finally, she warns audiences not to approach Indian arts as curios, as their art uses "ancestral material to express the profoundest present insight." Pictures accompany this article.

1933   "Folk Plays of the Southwest." *Theatre Arts Monthly* (August 1933): 599–606.

According to Austin, Spain's *entrada* into the United States marked a significant time for Spanish drama. The interest in writing drama transcended class, as both the "king" and "common man" participated in it. Austin discusses this as the period of the "teatro de corrales" with street sections roped off, crude scenic effects, and citizens standing about to enjoy performances. She explains that *autos* are dramas in celebration of Christian sacrament and goes on to summarize several early religious plays, including *Los Moros y Los Cristianos*, *Los Pastores o La Estrella*, *Los Reyes Magos*, and *El Niño Perdido*. Austin also discusses the Matachina—a dance that displays a story, a ballad dance—and from there considers the influence of Spanish drama on the Indian. She doesn't believe it has affected original Indian dance drama, but it may have found its way into the "less important, lighter" performances. Austin compares the Spanish *entremeses* and the Indian Koshare, both adding comedic aspects to drama. Finally, Austin describes a drama "of serious mutual participation" reflecting a military alliance between the Spanish and Indians against the Comanches called *Los Comanches*.

*1933 "Geographical Terms from the Spanish." Center for Southwest Research MS 31, Box 2, Folder 5, 8–9.

Austin explains why Spanish terms have become commonplace in describing Southwestern geography. No English terms, she says, could match the suitability and dramatic explanation found in the Spanish vocabulary for describing the land. She offers in-depth description and background information for much of this terminology and includes a vocabulary list of Spanish words and their translations.

1933 "Sayings." *The Virginia Quarterly Review* 9 (October 1933): 574–77.

Austin says a wise saying is "probably the earliest form of a popular story." She attributes its universality to keeping it in the form of a saying rather than a tale. She offers examples of sayings from three groups: the Ancient Man, sons of Conquistadors, and Spanish New Mexico.

*1933 "Sources of Poetic Influence in the Southwest." *Poetry* 43 (December 1933): 152–63.

Austin says that for any given region there are two sources of poetic influence: (1) the shape and rhythm of the land, and (2) the dwellers' relationship with the land. She says poetry among Indians is understood as "life-provoking business," and the rhythm of poetry helps them to achieve their desires. For those who are interested in poetry,

Austin recommends learning the Indians' appreciation for poetry as an "allusive art." This includes the recognition of the relationship between "poetic utterance and body gesture" and "new approaches to stanzaic form and the constructive shapes of poetic expression."

Most importantly, she believes one should view poetry as an experience more than as an expression. A poet must let his art grow from the inside out, and not the outside in, as many do when trying to adhere to particular measures and patterns. By studying aboriginal poetry of the Southwest, one can learn to appreciate the wholeness of the experience. Austin continues by exploring the Spanish influence on poetry, particularly in narrative form. She discusses in some detail the *corrido* and the *copla* and illustrates the fact that cowboy poetry is influenced by the *corrido*. Finally, Austin concludes by projecting that all poetry of the Southwest reflects the sounds and rhythms of those interacting with the environment. The one identifying trait of all native verse is a singing quality, which is a direct effect of the movement of the land (the slopes, peaks, falls, etc.).

1933–34   "Spanish Manuscripts in the Southwest." *Southwest Review* 19 (1933–34): 402–9.

Austin describes her collaboration with A. L. Campa to put a collection of Spanish manuscripts in the Laboratory Museum of Santa Fe. She explains how for years nothing was written down but was rather transferred by word of mouth or through participation in plays. She differentiates between New Mexican Spanish literature and Old Mexican literature, calling New Mexican Spanish literature its own genre and discussing the discovery of "a new versification particular to the region." She claims that the verse forms of New Mexico are more sentimental and older than those of Old Mexico. Old Mexico's verse form is more fresh and vital than New Mexico's. A discussion of different types of verse ensues, including the following definitions of the *copla*, *corrido*, and *décima*:

Copla: Occasional verse used for social gatherings and entertainment, sentimental and having to do with relationship of the sexes (more prevalent in New Mexico).

Corrido: Quasi-ballad form dealing with current events. A four-line stanza of irregular verse, the *corrido* is the most "alive" of Spanish poetry. (In New Mexico, a favorite *corrido* subject is the life and death of Pancho Villa.)

Décima: A long poem dealing with religious and philosophic thought (prevails in New Mexico).

Austin attributes many of the Spanish ballads to New Mexico origin.

*1934 "The Folk Story in America." *South Atlantic Quarterly* 33 (January 1934): 10–19.

Austin begins by differentiating between her idea of local color and an editor's. Editors, she says, wanted "reading matter next to which" advertisements could be placed and, therefore, looked for highly colored stories. She, on the other hand, considered color "something you ought to find already on the reader's hands," a "background completely existent." From there, Austin offers her thoughts on storytelling and explores patterns of stories by using examples of hunting and sheep dogs able to recognize/understand themselves in stories of their own adventures. She describes tale telling as a rehearsal of life. In studying story telling, she learned that there should be no more than four active elements/characters in a story, but does allow that characters can be grouped together under a general title to count as one (such as the wicked stepsisters of Cinderella). This leads her into a discussion of the patterns of Native American tales. There is no "exhibitionism" in Native American stories, meaning that the teller purposefully leaves his attitudes and feelings toward the story out of it so the audience can focus solely on the story itself. In addition, Austin calls the short, short story the "true Indian genre." She describes exchanges and influences of storytelling patterns among Southwest dwellers including Native Americans, the Spanish, and cowboys. Austin concludes by announcing "we are the folk" and, therefore, should recognize our own authentic inheritance of "folkness."

*1934 Introduction. In *One Smoke Stories*, xi–xv. Boston and New York: Houghton Mifflin Company (The Riverside Press Cambridge), 1934.

Austin describes the ceremonial manner in which Native American stories are told. Indian elders sit around a fire and tell stories in the time it takes to smoke one cornhusk cigarette. The story is either a tale or an experience that usually ends by implying some moral idea or wise saying.

*1934 "Speaking of Bears." *One Smoke Stories.* Boston and New York: Houghton Mifflin Company (The Riverside Press Cambridge), 1934.

Austin reveals the abuses of one bear trapper's stories. The article revolves around a work called "The Bears of Quamash," which was based on the "true" life and capture of a young grizzly bear now named Muckamuck. The author, Seaforth, relied on the trapper's (Al Kellerman's) account of capturing the bear to write his story. Seaforth, seeking Kellerman's general approval, asked the trapper to read the completed manuscript and inquired as to how he might acknowledge Kellerman for his contribution. Kellerman declined acknowledgment, saying he didn't want to take away from Seaforth's achievement when, really, he intended to present Seaforth's story as his own. Kellerman was able to publish the story under his authorship before Seaforth's work was published.

As if the question of story ownership did not create enough murky waters, Austin obtained additional behind-the-scenes knowledge that adds to the mess. Austin spoke with a ranch hand who worked at the same place Kellerman and his guide were stationed while seeking a bear. It turns out the bear Kellerman "trapped" had been a pet to a few Mexican men who let Kellerman "capture" it after working out a financial deal with Kellerman's guide. Kellermen used a book called *Adventures of Samuel Adams, Bear Trapper* to find fantastical trapper stories to use as his own tale of capturing Muckamuck. Ironically, the original Samuel Adams book enjoyed a resurgence of popularity due to the situation. Austin raises interesting points in the article regarding story ownership and nature faking.

1934 "The Copla." Unpublished essay in The Mary (Hunter) Austin Collection at the Huntington Library AU 84. 20 pages.

In this unpublished essay preserved by the Huntington Library, Austin offers an in-depth discussion of the *copla,* one of the most popular forms of Spanish poetry found in the Southwest. The *copla*, or *verso popular*, expresses a complete judgment or idea in four short verses. She says composing, singing, and reciting *coplas* was a popular social pastime in eighteenth- and nineteenth-century New Mexico. She describes the *copla* as the "poetry of the people" for its ability to translate all classes of sentiment. Austin offers examples and explanation of the varied topics poeticized in *coplas,* including *coplas* of love (most numerous), satire, philosophy, religion, old age, education, ballroom, and humor.

1934   "The Magazine West." Unpublished essay in The Mary
        (Hunter) Austin Collection at the Huntington Library AU
        331. 8 pages.

Austin colorfully distinguishes between the "Magazine West" and the real West. She offers humorous examples and evidence of Eastern and other misguided authors writing about the West as it is mistakenly perceived or as it is desired to be perceived—"Bad Men," "Señoritas," "Tenderfeet," and gunslingers. She discusses a number of writers who are guilty of this misrepresentation and a few who actually capture the Western state of mind.

1934   "Modern Lore of the Pueblos." Unpublished essay in The
        Mary (Hunter) Austin Collection at the Huntington Library
        AU 364. 4 pages.

Austin explains that pueblo lore is founded on fundamental aboriginal beliefs. The powers and personalities of their beliefs are represented in masked dances, called Katchinas, masked to indicate that no man really knows spiritual reality, with masks and costumes symbolic of the powers and their functions. To communicate with the powers, Austin says that Pueblenos use "sympathetic magic," suggestive and dramatic acts designed to make plain what they want. They use symbols such as smoke and feathers to further their ceremony. She describes the Koshare as sacred clowns who "cheer the tribe with amusing antics so that they may grow fat with laughter." Austin says it is the Indian's beliefs and spiritual vitality that give him a reverent and happy attitude.

1934   "Traditional Ballads in the Southwest." Unpublished essay in The Mary (Hunter) Austin Collection at the Huntington Library AU 597. 16 pages.

Austin discusses the songs of the Indian, the Anglo, and the Spanish. Of the Indian song she says that much of its meaning is derived from a particular occasion or story of its origin, which is always present in the mind of the singer but not necessarily that of the hearer. The emotional content is carried by the melody and rhythm of dancing feet. According to Austin, the best music of the Indian is found in his religious and ceremonial songs, and the melodies that he plays on his only musical instrument, the flute.

Anglo songs, she says, are based upon the historical and social background of the day. She discusses cowboy ballads in particular, saying there are two types: those of the oral tradition, and those clipped from print, fitted to a situation, and handed down as genuine folk song. In the process of passing ballads, reshaping of words or verses is common. Austin explains that a lot of cowboy songs are used for practical ends—sharp rhythmic yells to stir up slow cattle or softer lullabies to quiet and soothe them.

Spanish ballads, she says, are believed to be derived from old epic poems. Songs of New Mexico are born of emotion and characterized by "wit, quaintness, charm of phrase and peculiarity of construction." Love is the favorite motive of New Mexican folk songs, many of them sad and only rarely comic. She adds that most all are sung in a minor key. Another type of song she describes is the "*alabados,*" which are religious compositions customarily about the life of a saint. At the end of the article Austin provides a list of ballads classified by the following categories: historical, novelesque, humorous, religious, and tragic.

N.D.   "Life at Santa Fe." Center for Southwest Research MSS 611, Box 2, Folder 37. 10 pages.

Austin approaches all aspects of life in Santa Fe in a very descriptive and lyrical manner. She covers diverse areas—from landscape and business practices to Native American tradition and architecture—and gives a very clear picture of the uniqueness of the city. She explains that artists are drawn to Santa Fe because the town itself is a force of creative expression. According to Austin, art is simply the result of living in this quaint little place. She describes living in Santa Fe as the "good life" because art is such a natural and accepted part of the environment.

N.D.   Introduction. *Native Tales of New Mexico.* Center for South-
        west Research MSS 97, "Frank Applegate Papers,
        1886–2000," Box 5, Folder 52. 4 pages.

Austin introduces and praises the work of Frank Applegate, saying he masterfully compiled and genuinely relates tales of Native Americans in his book.

N.D.   "Indian Pottery of the Rio Grande." Booklet III B, Enjoy
        Your Museum Series, ed. Carl Thurston (Pasadena: Esto
        Publishing Company, n.d.): 1–14.

Austin prefaces her informative description of Rio Grande pottery by giving a short historical explanation of the need for pottery and ideas behind its decorative design. She explains that the best finished pots are found in purely agricultural villages where corn is the prevailing staple food. Meat-eating tribes primarily relied on the grilling method, and thus did not require pots for cooking corn. Another major function of pots called for the handling and preserving of water. According to Austin, the water jar, or *tineja*, is the one type of pottery that univer- sally prevails among pueblos. Following that is the cooking bowl and then the storage jar. As for the decorative design of pottery, Austin explains that always there is "something more implied than mere dec- oration." To Indians, design is an expressive language of nature and its processes. She says that decoration is less about adornment and beauty and more about promoting the pots' successful use in nature. Not to recognize nature's process in design is disrespectful and can therefore lead to those processes not working. After offering this base of knowl- edge, Austin proceeds to discuss specific designs of various Indian pueblos, including Taos and Picuris, San Juan, Santa Clara and Ilde- fonso, Tesque, Cochiti, Santo Domingo, San Felipe, Isleta and Laguna, Jemez, and, together, Acoma, Laguna, and Zuni. Each pueblo has its own unique design technique mostly due to what elements of the land there is available for each to work.

Introduction. In *Room and Time Enough*, by Augusta Fink, 55–59. Flagstaff: Northland, 1979.

Austin ponders beautiful landscapes that make her feel connected to the universe and a higher being—much like what Indians refer to as *wakona*. She describes a favorite cactus garden, the seasonal colors of the Rio Grande Cañon, and the beauty and fear created by mountains.

N.D. *An Open Letter to Club Women and Business Men of the South-west*. The Rare Books Collection at the Huntington Library #285680. 4 pages.

Austin expresses her concern that the people of the Southwest will be unable to evaluate the elements of a regional culture and be uninformed about their own intellectual and artistic assets. She says there are two types of important American cultural activity. The first type is that of a group whose business it is to discover, create, and distribute works of art (as evident in Santa Fe). The type two group gathers not to produce art, but to learn, study, and discuss it (as evident in the Chautauqua Circle). Austin says these two groups cannot exist together in the same town because ultimately the creative type is driven away. The fact that the Federated Women's Club desires to establish a type two group in Santa Fe greatly alarms Austin and other Santa Fe residents. She explains that they cannot coexist because they want exactly opposite things. The creative colony wants a quiet, uninterrupted environment to work and the "summer colony" wants social events. Austin says she realizes her view deprives the Chamber of Commerce funds anticipated from the Club but that it would be worse to remove these women from their own towns where native energy and acculturation reside. The arts, like charity, she says, must begin at home.